D0754597

Critical *i*nventions

General Editor: John Schad
University of Lancaster

"a creative intellectual enterprise as rare as it is necessary in an
academy which is now over-institutionalised and deadened by bureaucracy."
Jonathan Dollimore

To Doctor King,
that crrritic of crrritics,
wherever he is.

Royalties

Should we ever find Dr King the royalties from this book will go
to keep him in tobacco, roll-ups and *Kit-Kat* wrappers;
in the meantime they will go to Oxfam.

Crrritic!

Sighs, Cries, Lies, Insults,
Outbursts, Hoaxes,
Disasters, Letters of
Resignation, and
Various Other Noises
Off in These the First
and Last Days of
Literary Criticism,

Not to Mention the
University

Edited by
John Schad and Oliver Tearle

sussex
ACADEMIC
PRESS
Brighton • Portland • Toronto

Foreword, Afterword, and editorial organization of this volume, copyright © John Schad and
Oliver Tearle; Jonathan Dollimore and Geoffrey Hartman hereby
retain copyright © of their respective chapters; all other chapters copyright
© Sussex Academic Press, 2011.The right of John Schad and Oliver
Tearle to be identified as Editors of this work has been asserted in
accordance with the Copyright, Designs and Patents Act 1988.

2 4 6 8 10 9 7 5 3 1

First published in 2011 in Great Britain by
SUSSEX ACADEMIC PRESS
PO Box 139
Eastbourne BN24 9BP

and in the United States of America by
SUSSEX ACADEMIC PRESS
920 NE 58th Ave   Suite 300
Portland, Oregon 97213-3786

and in Canada by
SUSSEX ACADEMIC PRESS (CANADA)
90 Arnold Avenue, Thornhill, Ontario L4J 1B5

British Library Cataloguing in Publication Data
A CIP catalogue record for this book is available from the British Library.

Library of Congress Cataloging-in-Publication Data
Crrritic! : sighs, cries, lies, insults, outbursts, hoaxes, disasters, letters of
  resignation, and various other noises off in these the first and last days of literary
  criticism . . . not to mention the university / edited by John Schad and Oliver Tearle.
  p. cm. — (Critical inventions)
Includes bibliographical references and index.
ISBN 978-1-84519-342-3 (hbk. : alk. paper) —
ISBN 978-1-84519-382-9 (pbk. : alk. paper)
  1. Criticism. 2. Critics. I. Schad, John, 1960– II. Tearle, Oliver.
PN85.C77 2011
801'.95—dc22

                                                                    2011004530

Typeset and designed by Sussex Academic Press, Brighton & Eastbourne.
Printed by TJ International, Padstow, Cornwall.
This book is printed on acid-free paper.

Contents

HISTORIES

OFF THE WALL

IDEAS

OVER THE WALL

LIVES

INVENTIONS

Acknowledgments

John Schad and Oliver Tearle are grateful to Robert Kory of RK Management for permission to quote from Leonard Cohen's song 'Hallelujah', and to Faber and Faber for allowing us to include three poems which first appeared in Mark Ford's *Six Children* (2011) as well as the 'crritic!' passage from *Waiting for Godot* as part of the prefatory material to this book.

The Critical Inventions Series

> Do I dare / Disturb the universe?
> (T.S. Eliot, 'The Love Song of J. Alfred Prufrock,' 1917)

In 1961 C.S. Lewis published *An Experiment in Criticism*; over forty years later, at the beginning of a new century, there is pressing need for a renewed sense of experiment, or invention in criticism. The energies unleashed by the theoretical movements of the 1970s and 1980s have been largely exhausted – many now say we are experiencing life *after* theory; some, indeed, say we are experiencing life after *criticism*. Criticism, we might say, is in crisis. But that is where it should be; the word 'criticism' comes, as we know, from the word 'crisis.'

Talk of crisis does not, though, fit easily within the well-managed contemporary academy; with its confident talk of 'scholarly excellence,' there is a presumption that we all know, and are agreed upon, what scholarship and criticism is. However, to echo Paul de Man, 'we don't even know what *reading* is'; and what is, potentially, exciting about our present crisis is that now we *really* know that we don't know what reading is. It is, then, in a spirit of learned ignorance that we propose *critical inventions,* a series which will feature books that, in one way or another, push the generic conventions of literary criticism to breaking point. In so doing the very figure of the critic will shift and change. We shall, no doubt, glimpse something of what Oscar Wilde famously called 'the critic as artist,' or what Terry Eagleton called 'the critic as clown'; we may even glimpse still more unfamiliar figures – the critic as, for example, autobiographer, novelist, mourner, poet, parodist, detective, dreamer, diarist, flaneûr, surrealist, priest, montagist, gambler, traveller, beggar, anarchist . . .or even amateur. In short, this series seeks the truly critical critic – or, to be paradoxical, the critic as *critic*; the critic who is a critic of criticism as conventionally understood, or *mis*understood. He or she is the critic who will dare to disturb the universe, or at least the university – in particular, the institutionalisation of criticism that is professional, university English.

Establishment English is, though, a strange institution that is capable of *dis*establishing itself, if only because it houses the still stranger institution of literature – which, as Jacques Derrida once wrote, 'in principle allows us to say everything/ anything [*tout dire*].' We, therefore, do not or cannot yet know of what criticism may yet be capable – capable of being, capable of doing. *critical inventions* will be a series that seeks to find out.

> ***Read the text right and emancipate the world.***
> (ROBERT BROWNING, 'Bishop Bloughram's Apology,' 1855)

The Truly Critical Critic

J. Hillis Miller

Wow! What can one say more? After this book, academic "discourse" (note the "scared quotes") in all its genres, not to speak of poetry, and not to speak of the distinction between creator and crritic, will never be the same again. This book fulfills, and then some, the project of John Schad's series, "Critical Inventions": ". . . this series seeks the truly critical critic – or, to be paradoxical, the critic as *critic*; the critic who is a critic of criticism as conventionally understood, or *mis*understood. He or she is the critic who will dare to disturb the universe, or at least the university – in particular, the institutionalisation of criticism that is professional, university English." The twenty-four critical creations gathered here are almost all by Britishers, two by European-born immigrants to the United States, one by an Australian. These include poems that are critical essays; autobiographies that are really critiques of the British institutionalization of literary study; critical essays that flaunt the established conventions of such essays, et cetera. The law of genre is shamelessly defied. Allusions overt and covert abound, as if to indicate that the flotsam and jetsam of the Western literary tradition is floating around the minds of these writers in strange juxtapositions, testifying, it may be, to the not entirely predictable result of much academic literary study. Perhaps the most devastating effect of this collection is to make the reader, this reader at least, feel that everything he has ever written has been unconscious parody. Read, but read at your peril. Caveat lector.

Crrritic!

VLADIMIR:
Ceremonious ape!
ESTRAGON:
Punctilious pig!
VLADIMIR:
Finish your phrase, I tell you!
ESTRAGON:
Finish your own!
Silence. They draw closer, halt.
VLADIMIR:
Moron!
ESTRAGON:
That's the idea, let's abuse each other.
They turn, move apart, turn again and face each other.
VLADIMIR:
Moron!
ESTRAGON:
Vermin!
VLADIMIR:
Abortion!
ESTRAGON:
Morpion!
VLADIMIR:
Sewer-rat!
ESTRAGON:
Curate!
VLADIMIR:
Cretin!
ESTRAGON:
(*with finality*). Crritic!

Samuel Beckett, *Waiting for Godot* [1955] (London: Faber and Faber, 1956).

Crrr___ (by way of a foreword)

John Schad

Well this is it: the end, last gasp, final straw; in short, the concluding dark volume in a series of books some idiot called 'critical inventions'. Let us be like wry Oscar Wilde, said the idiot, and dream of the critic *as artist*, or at least as someone else, as someone other than who we had thought he was, or been taught he was. Let us, continued the idiot, set the critical dogs off the leash and see what they come back with; and back they came with eight noisome books, eight monographs – eight single voices, one-man shows. Time now, we thought, for a variety performance, an out-cast of thousands, or at least as many as could be squeezed into one crowded house. And here they are: no less than twenty-four press-ganged souls all huddled together for warmth; some are critics, some are poets, and some are critic-poets, and then there is Dr King, that dear mystery and vagabond, Dr King of the University of Life, School of Hard Knocks. Of the Doctor, more anon.

So, twenty-four voices, twenty-four shots in the dark, or maybe shots *at* the dark, or possibly the head, or even the foot. But whatever, each is a shot at pushing the perambulator of dear old criticism so far and so fast that someone somewhere – whether in anger, derision, or pain – might just cry 'Crritic!', that curse of all curses, the best of all possible anathema, the winning insult in that great game of insults which is played forever on a road next to a tree by two tramps on an empty stage. (You know who they are.) But maybe, just maybe, the exclamation 'Crrritic!' will double as a *cri de coeur*, or howl of self-loathing, or scream of delight, or laugh in the night, or just a smashed-up and battered old prayer. We shall see.

Yes, we shall see, but at first, in the beginning, in our opening volley of pieces, a cluster we call **Manifestos,** we have, it seems, a call to arms, a thumping of the tub, a striking at the board. (I will away.) And first on is Oliver Tearle who is, by his own admission, off his head and a danger to himself with his 'Lexicon of Punk Criticism', a high-wire performance with nothing but the alphabet to save him. This same shabby old safety-net is again pressed into service by Tony Sharpe in the very next piece, 'Our never-to-be-slighted "fun"'; here, though, we hurtle backwards, as if from Z to A, or least L to H: namely, from *Larkin* to *Kafka* to *James* to *Hancock* – Tony

Hancock that is (the critic as suicidal comedian). Cue *G* for *Goodby*, John Goodby, he who offers our next essay, an essay in couplets, a work of criticism as poetry, or perhaps poetry as criticism, criticism of itself, above all criticism of its own safe self. Yes, there is, by now, an air of anger in our exclamatory book. Cue Steven Connor who is angry even with anger itself in 'Rage, Rage Against the Dying of Delight' – and so he does, for he sees, you see, that the writing is on the wall.

And **On the Wall,** it just so happens, is the alias we have given to the gang of three poems that follows – poems from, respectively, Helen Farish, Mark Ford and Michael Symmons Roberts, this last being upon that very first writing on the wall, the divine graffiti that condemns poor King Belshazzar. (The letter so killeth.) This poem, you will have already spotted, is about reading; and all the poems that slip and sideways sidle into our house are either acts *of* reading or *about* the act of reading – or maybe, just maybe, both at once. In short, in brief, in sum, and in anything but haste, here we have poets who can't quite escape the insult 'Crrritic!' Heaven help them.

And perhaps it may if God should over-hear the very next piece, Kevin Mills's 'Broken Hallelujah', the stuttering half-a-prayer that doubles as a scholarly reading of the Welsh Revival. It is also, by the ways, the opening scribble in a triadic cluster called **Histories**, three night-raids on the past. In Mills's case it is a swoop on 1904, but in the case of Graham Holderness, next along, it is a raid on old Shakespeare, a sortie in which criticism turns into the glorious rack-and-ruin that is poetry. 'Things go from bard to verse', whispers someone; though not of Dr King, the drink-edged hero of 'The Critic as Fiction; or Dr King on Sheds', where things just go to the pub, to the backstreet boozer in which the currently unemployed Dr King, fag in hand, shares his opinions on Thomas Carlyle's ignoble creation of 1838, Herr Teufoldsröckh – Mr. Devil's-Shit, I am told.

This way lies madness, I know: the critic as learned lunatic. Time, then, we felt, to interpose three poems which we oh-so-cunningly denominate not 'On the Wall' but **Off the Wall** – for these are poems possessed by a fine madness, the madness of reading. The text that maddens Helen Farish is *The Alexandria Quartet*; for Mark Ford it is the work of Walt Whitman; whilst for Geoffrey Hartman it is that play about one who is himself the craziest reader of all, bonkers Prince Hamlet – as his quick-footed mother cries, 'But look where sadly the poor wretch comes reading'.

Here, though, you can see the poor wretch come *thinking*, for next up, next down, next across, we proudly present four acts of reading that are pushed to the very edge of reason by, well, reason, or thinking, or dear philosophy – and these four readings we astutely call **Ideas**. The ideas in question, or in trouble, come from here and there, then and now, round and about. First off, the ideas are those of G.W.F. Hegel who provokes Drew Milne into 'The Bruise that Heidegger Built', a prose-poem which takes a hammer to what he calls 'the house of ideas' and ends in 'ruins'. And ruins or rubble are all over the place in our very next offering, Esther Leslie's 'Critical Criticism's Critique: 13 Theses, or, It is All Rubbish', a critique of the critique of critique, and all in the name of, the letter of, the spirit of, that poor and great ruinist, Herr Walter Benjamin. Ideas, it seems, are dangerous, a suspicion confirmed by the ensuing piece, Harold Schweizer's 'Of the Falling of Stones' – a reading of the philosopher Henri Bergson which flickers, or falls, between analysis and poetry, dissection and distraction, angles and angels. It is, some might say, an experiment in reading philosophy that is housed within the shabby laboratory of the imagination – if so, it prepares the way for Peter Middleton's 'Do We Live in an Age of Science and of Poetry? An Interview with Charles Olson and a Time Traveller', a strange tale of the pale evening in which Professor Middleton met both a man from the future who thinks primarily of science and a man, a poet as it happens, who is primarily dead.

Talking of the dead, or rather talking of talking *to* the dead, takes us to our final triptych of poems, each of which has to do with how the act of reading is shadowed by the act (if act it is) of dying. Not, then, 'On the Wall' or 'Off the Wall' but **Over the Wall** – over the wall and over the page, over the wall and far away. Here come Jonathan Taylor, Kevin Hart and Mark Ford, whose poems are followed by one who did himself famously leap a wall, the university wall, and has not stopped running since. I speak of that runaway and prodigal, Jonathan Dollimore, whose memoir 'On Leaving' is the first of three texts called **Lives** in which the critic finally turns on himself and becomes a critic not just of Life but of his *own* life, whether that be a life spent within the university – see Willy Maley's 'The Uni and Me' – or a life borrowed from the killing jungles of Vietnam: cue Susan Bradley Smith's 'How to Kill a Labrador'.

How indeed. But you will see, or read. And once you have, and learnt how to kill, you will turn to our final house of scribbles which goes by the name of **Inventions** as here, at the very bitter end, we try to map or see or glimpse or maybe just squint at the point when the critic most literally and vividly turns artist. Witness Duraid Jalili's 'Lamenting Maud's Worth Becoming Maud' where something is going wonderfully wrong with a postmodern interrogation of Tennyson's *Maud*. Hot on its hobbling heels limps my own sorrowful work, 'GodotOnSea', in which quite everything is going terribly wrong with a week in Blackpool. And, finally, if you dare, witness the beginning of a novel called *Dunsinane* by Ewan Fernie and Simon Palfrey where the wide *world itself* has gone wrong in the wild wake of the death of Macbeth. It is time, to quote the very end of that play, for 'the grace of Grace'. Amen.

MANIFESTOS

MANIFESTOS

The Lexicon of Punk Criticism

Oliver Tearle

> Pressed between yellow leaves of a book that has never been opened.
> (T. S. Eliot, *Four Quartets*)[1]

I'm punked, I'm done, I'm in a lexical nightmare, caught in a web of words, a worldwide and wordwilde web, I'm the critic as artist, the artist as critic, the critic as lexicographer, I'm Doctor Johnson, I'm off the page, I'm off my head, I've left 'aardvark' out, I'm worn out from my task. I'm doing the whole gamut of criticism from A–Z, not so much a dictionary as a contra-dictionary, an anti-dictionary, designed to be torn up and disagreed with, grappled with, altered, reinterpreted. Running against or *contra* to what the dictionary is designed for, what follows is not an attempt to define words that already exist but to invent new words which have yet to have any meaning or application in the world. Each word or term is followed by suggestions, not definitions. Oh my, I'm speaking in tongues, mindful of the *glottis* or 'tongue' that hides in glossary, here is my gluttery . . .

I've gone back to Gilbert, to the patron saint of creative critics, he who speaks in Oscar Wilde's 1890 essay-dialogue 'The Critic as Artist' about criticism as 'the only civilised form of autobiography'.[2] But what if criticism were not so much autobiography as antibiography, an erasing or erosion of oneself from the piece, an attempt at misdirection, an anonymous or pseudonymous joke? What if criticism were collaborative and communal, the domain of the outcast, or at least presented itself as such?

But criticism has always carried within itself the potential for revolution. Wilde's reaction against Arnold in 'The Critic as Artist' is a good example, or the entire volume of *Intentions*, which might as well be the bible for the creative-critical movement, obsessed with adopting a persona, a mask, telling a lie to get to the truth. That is, it *would* be the bible, if it weren't for the simple fact that punk criticism resists all bibles, all holy and sacred texts and all figures. It worships no one, not Johnson, not De Quincey, not Arnold, not Wilde, not Empson, not Derrida. No names needed: it is words in which we are interested now. And we thrive on division, just as politics thrives on division: no division, no politics, no debate, no criticism. *Through anonymity not unanimity*: that could be our motto (were it not that we shun mottoes as well).[3]

The following indefinitions, descriptions, manifestoes, explanations, and apologies have been gathered together from a number of dirty corners, dark places, and undesirable areas. These include (but are not limited to): fluorescent yellow adhesive notes found tacked to random landmarks and shop doorways in town centres; inscriptions on toilet walls in numerous public conveniences (and inconveniences); and scrawlings in blood-red ink (indeed, the ink may *be* blood) in old library books. These mini-ideas and micro-responses are the dark sphinx of the world, posing as many riddles as they answer, if they answer any. These contributions are a collection, garnered from anonymous sources across society, and yet somehow all written by the same man, our author (who is also the editor, critic, judge, jury, and executioner of what follows), O. T., the Old Testament, the Oscar Tribute, the Only Theorist.

They may be considered utterly unnecessary supplements to the *OED*, unpleasant swellings or dangerous OEDemas, diseased and already putrefying.

Each definition may be viewed not so much as an 'entry' as an entrée, a mini-idea, a re-entry, a shameful exit, an emergency exit, or else a simple act of micro-criticism, a beautiful but imperfect fragment, a nano-essay.

All definitions and attempts at explanation are quite useless.

                                                                                                    O. T.

anti-reading, *n.* [from *anti-*, prefix denoting 'against', and READING]

A wilful misreading of a text which not only misses the 'point' or authorial intention of the text (if such a thing can even be detected on the reader's radar), but which decides what the authorial intention of the text probably was and then argues that the text achieves the exact opposite of what was supposedly intended. Thus in *Paradise Lost*, as Blake saw so well, Milton was 'of the Devil's party without knowing it', rather than actually seeking to 'justifie the Wayes of God to men.'[3]

Thus, also, we might read Wordsworth as being in favour of industrialisation, Larkin as a cheery sod (he does write of happiness, occasionally), that Hamlet knows exactly what he's doing, that Sherlock Holmes hated his work, that Astrophil thought Stella a fat cow, how now, wow.

What would be the point of such wilful misreadings?

One only finds out by experimenting. One particularly interesting way of exploring these opposites or polar readings would be to rewrite the text in question but with the opposite point of view: Sherlock skives off work, Hamlet gets on with it and dispatches Claudius shortly after he's made that paltry punning son/sun remark, Astrophil rewrites his sonnets as essays of disgust against Stella (he did, after all, dislike her at first sight: what about his second sight?). Perhaps through such a wilful anti-reading we'd glimpse the dangers of the death or dearth of the author: once Barthes has buried him, he won't get up, goddammit, keep kicking him, he might get up, but if he's gone, then that's it, we're done for, we've given carte blanche to all manner of misreadings, and that way lies danger. That way lies death. Yes, dear me, yes, the death of the author reveals the way to death: for if *my* reading is as valid or important as any other, then what's to stop me from taking action when I start to believe my reading is *more* valid, more important?

Such criticism might, though, end up bringing out the central theme of the text through inverting its intention. As Wilde has it in 'The Critic as Artist': 'the primary aim of the critic is to see the object as in itself it really is not'.[4] *Really?* Or not . . .

antitextuality, *n.* [from anti- and TEXTUALITY, whence **antitextual,** *adj.*]

Like intertextuality, Julia Kristeva's term for the phenomenon whereby a text interprets and responds to earlier texts, antitextuality is the not-name given to the phenomenon whereby one text rejects previous texts through not only revising but, in effect, *negating* them: thus Wilde's 'The Critic as Artist' issues a contrarian and fully successful rebuttal to, and rejection of, Arnold's 'The Function of Criticism at the Present Time'. No more be said, no more need be said: criticism is at its best when it is antitextual, as are texts.

I begin to hear voices and can't concentrate

asthmatic criticism *n.* [from ASTHMATIC and CRITICISM (perh. surprisingly)]

Wait, I've got to get started, how do I start, I've started. A simultaneous application of, and reaction against, T. S. Eliot's (internally contradictory) thesis that criticism is 'as inevitable as breathing' and yet only obtained 'by great labour.'[5] To quote from the Doctor (before he became 'the Doctor'), Doctor King, and his unpublished words on T. S. Eliot:

> **2005** S. KING *Mosaic and Mandala* 'Tradition . . . cannot be inherited,' Eliot writes, 'and if you want it you must obtain it by great labour.' Labour, though, has an ambiguous role in Eliot's essay; the 'work of the critic', for example, is elsewhere described as being 'as inevitable as breathing' – hardly a deliberate act of labour.[6]

Therefore 'asthmatic criticism' would take the form of something both natural (a creative act performed upon the text, for instance) and laborious (close, one might say exhaustive, lexical readings of the language of the text, for example).

As an asthmatic myself (whoever 'myself' might care to be at this moment), the advantages to a form of Eliotic asthma are apparent from the outset, from before its outset. Asthmatic criticism would employ a sort of breathless stream-of-consciousness akin to that found in the great modernist writing of Joyce and Woolf, thus aiming to tease out the writer-critic's unconscious or unrecognised thoughts on, and reactions to, the text. A kind of automatic or asth-o-matic writing, letting the hand be guided by the sunken mind, asthmatic crit is inspirational and expirational, it's a wheeze, a hoot, a breeze, a breath of fresh air. Or – not –

creative criticism, *n*. [from CREATIVE and CRITICISM]

I've got to catch my breath. Creative criticism: this would be, then, the broad umbrella term which encompasses all acts of criticism which are creative in terms of their literary style, whether poetic or novelistic in tone, structure, etc. and thus distinct from more conventional criticism written in formal style. Here there are, broadly speaking, two forms of creative criticism which should be distinguished:

1. Perhaps the most sustained work to address the potential crossovers between creative and critical acts since Wilde's 'The Critic as Artist' (and before the present volume) is an academic textbook. Rob Pope's 1994 book *Textual Intervention: Critical and Creative Strategies for Literary Studies* is out to provide a template for combining creative impulses with critical responses to famous literary texts. It's a textbook. It really is. As Pope writes: 'The best way to understand how a text works is to change it: to play around with it, to intervene in it in some way (large or small), and then to try to

account for the exact effort of what you have done.'[7] The 'analytical tools' which can be used, he goes on, range from 'the "micro-linguistic" (to do with localised choices and combinations of sounds, meanings and grammatical structures) through to the "macro-linguistic" (to do with the larger-scale organisations of choice and combination we know as narrative, argument and exposition).'[8] It is notable that many of the most famous acts of creative 'intervention' (to borrow and intervene with Pope's phrase) that have been undertaken have been done by writers themselves (witness George Bernard Shaw rewriting the final scenes of Shakespeare's play as *Cymbeline Refinished*, or Wendy Cope's 'Waste Land Limericks'). Moving closer to literary criticism, there is Nicolas Abraham's 'sixth act' to *Hamlet*. Such interventionist tactics are not only novel and interesting, but are potentially what criticism has long needed: a way to be faithful to the text while performing an act of interpretation upon it. And yet, and yet. . . . One wants to do damage to the text, one doesn't want to be faithful, one wishes to tear it apart and mould it anew, in order the better to understand the beautiful vision of the author, which is really just the beautiful revision of the reader. Of course, it may be possible to be faithful and perform a more traditional act of interpretation or criticism upon a text; but what Pope proposes as a method of undergraduate teaching has broader implications in the fields of academic research. For a creative act of criticism that takes the form of the text which it critiques – a poem if a critique of Wordsworth, a fragment of a play if a critique of Shakespeare, etc. – also addresses one of the key issues which literary criticism has essentially ignored for over a hundred years: namely, while literary criticism may continually if sporadically move on in terms of philosophical and political influences, drives, etc., in terms of its *style* lit. crit. has advanced or altered very little since English became a common subject for study at universities. While fashions change and poststructuralism may have encouraged a freer and less stuffy style or register in literary criticism, most essays remain, essentially, boring to read, unless a critic happens to be a very gifted wordsmith capable of making timely allusions to literary texts, or playing with meaning, or being such a consummate stylist that, even though he may speak in the conventional register of lit. crit., we find ourselves won over by his exuberant gift with language. But such critics are few and far between. Creative responses to literary texts may be one method of freeing up lit-crit from its musty and stale-smelling old modes.

As Barthes has it, 'Let the commentary be itself a text.'[9]

Creative interventions, or responses to literature, also encourage literary critics to put themselves in the shoes of the writer whose work they should be handling with care by doing a number on it. Just as anyone who has sat at a pottery wheel and attempted to mould clay into a fine jug or bowl has a new-found respect for the potter who can fashion such wonderful items, so the critic can find a new-found respect for the writer who chose his words carefully, and who slaved over every individual comma in a piece of work. As Nick Everett has it in an illuminating article from 2005 called 'Creative Writing and English': 'Creative exercises form a bridge between the students' experience and concerns and the academic topic in hand; and they are especially satisfying when they bring students to the subject who, without them, would almost certainly have not engaged with it at all. But they don't just stimulate interest. As [Rob] Pope's subtitle reminds us, they are critical as well as creative. Striving to do the best creative job they can, students are inevitably at the same time elaborating critical responses to the literature they're studying.'[10] So it should be for students; so it should be for all academics.

2. The second form of creative criticism may not necessarily adopt the form of the 'host text', but nevertheless be marked out as creative in style: thus an 'essay' on modernist fiction may well adopt a stream-of-consciousness motif, but equally a creative-critical response to Dryden or Thackeray or Chaucer may adopt a SOC-style, in order to enact a kind of 'asthmatic criticism' upon the text, so to attempt to bring out the reader-critic's primal responses to the text. As Gilbert puts it in 'The Critic as Artist' (hear, hear): 'To the critic the work of art is simply a suggestion for a new work of his own, that need not necessarily bear any obvious resemblance to the thing it criticises.'[11] Indeed, we can have graffiti criticising *Hamlet*, a novel criticising a sonnet by Keats, a post-it note offering a micro-critical response to *Clarissa*. More than this, it may emerge that the less resemblance there is between the thing criticised and the work of criticism itself, the better: that way, like a form of anti-reading, we can better bring out the ideas of the text, through looking at it from a completely different angle.

I may be wrong, I'm reaching for my inhaler, the text helps me to breathe, what if this is it, what if *this* is the future of criticism, then what?
The
malfunction
of
criticism
at
the
absent
time

DIY criticism, *n.* ['DIY', initialism representing 'do it yourself']

Criticism that adopts the 'DIY ethic' of much punk and post-punk music, and is self-produced and self-disseminated. Examples include, at the most basic level, graffiti and marginalia. Examples on a grander scale include whole monographs, tracts, pamphlets, leaflets, flyers, magazines, and journals which are privately printed (esp. at home on a home printer or in the creator's garage) and disseminated for the sake of it, not to satisfy any 'line' in a CV, but simply in order to publish criticism for criticism's sake, in its purest and most uncorrupted form.

DIY criticism exists for nobody and nothing but itself, seeking to further nobody's career and fill no research tables or frameworks. Instead, DIY criticism is non-referential, not quantifiable or qualitative, as bad as it likes, as marvellous as it wishes. Wilful and without agenda, DIY-crit simply doesn't care what you think of it.

Of course, the internet also provides a platform for the dissemination of DIY crit. Email, blogs, websites, Twitter, and so on, all provide platforms for the twenty-first-century critic, no? How to write an essay in 140 characters or less? As universities increasingly require students to submit electronic copies of their essays, albeit only alongside so-called 'hard' copies, what future for the act of micro-criticism? Could a student 'text' in their essay, in 160 characters or fewer? Could that be done? I think so, for the very important reason that *some text missing*

do-nothing criticism, *n.* [from other compounds containing 'do-nothing', such as 'do-nothing gardening', etc.]

This thesis for the future of criticism takes its name from the subtitle of the first part of Oscar Wilde's 'The Critic as Artist': 'with some remarks upon the importance of doing nothing'.[12] Criticism has 'done' Practical Criticism (the most do-ful form of criticism, as its very name implies), structuralism, New Criticism, poststructuralism, New Historicism, feminism, Marxism, post-colonialism, nuclear criticism, ecocriticism, and all the other isms and post-isms you can name; perhaps it is time for criticism, finally, to 'do nothing', to sit still and not attempt to implant a new political or philosophical agenda onto itself.

Of course, it is impossible to remove all political and philosophical concepts and theories from any act of writing, especially criticism, but that should perhaps be the *ideal*. Listen in, come on, gather round, said the chap in the station waiting-room. The train was late, and we all sat and listened.

His breath reeked of whisky, his coat smoked nicotine like steam from a kettle, but we all listened raptly. Research, he said, has become such a key part of academia that teaching has, for the most part, become lost under the pile of papers: bureaucracy has seen off pedagogy. We exchanged glances. Couldn't argue with that, we thought. He went on: By 'doing nothing' in criticism (and thus producing 'do-nothing criticism', which is not the same as doing *no* criticism), academics would free up more time to focus on what really matters in a university: teaching. Education in all the forms in which it comes: informing, inspiring, suggesting, entertaining, quizzing, encouraging.

Do-nothing criticism is not so much a manifesto as an anti-manifesto, encouraging as it does the acceptability of picking up a text, reading it, doing some background research, and writing down one's thoughts on said text, without seeking to lose the text under complex philosophical notions or heavy and largely unnecessary contextual material. Do-nothing criticism strips the art back to what really matters: the text, its (ancillary and secondary) context, and what the critic-as-reader makes of the text. That is all.

That is all? One of our party asked of him.

He looked at the speaker as if he had just been knocked down. Of course, was his reply, his teeth clicking in his mouth like a rattlesnake.

At this point the announcement came over the station that his train was arriving. He rose to his feet and stepped out into the cold, cloudless night, as the train doors opened.

And yet, and yet, our drink-sodden spokesman went on, continuing his speech as his fellow passengers pushed past him onto the train – and yet, do-nothing criticism is something whose worth can only be found out by *doing* it, by doing it ourselves, by DIYing it, by *praxis*. It is found out by doing. Do (or don't do) what you want.

And with that, the doors hissed closed behind him, and the train pulled out of the station; and we, who each had other platforms to find, went our several ways, as we already had somewhere else to be.

Did I dream all that? I have no recollection now. No way of knowing.
                                                                    Psalm 6: 6

Gilbertian dialogue, *n*. [Gilbert, one of two interlocutors in Oscar Wilde's 1890 essay-dialogue 'The Critic as Artist', after 'Socratic dialogue']

A dialogue between two or more persons, in written or in spoken form, which presents two or more arguments concerning a literary text and attempts to weigh up the merits and demerits of each point of view. Like a Socratic dialogue, the aim would be to work through ethical and philosophical problems and dilemmas, but especially those relating to the literary critic and the idea of 'literature' in relation to the world. Here, again, I wave my copy of *Intentions* above my head, for not only is 'The Critic as Artist' a prime example of the Gilbertian dialogue, but, to a lesser extent, so is 'The Decay of Lying'. Such a way of presenting an argument would seek to free literary criticism from the established confines of the essay form, and would therefore have obvious advantages.

 —Such as what? I fail to see any.

 —Shut up with that piano-playing, then, and listen.

 —I'm listening.

 —What was that noise?

 —Nothing again everything.

 —Criticism can be expressed in many forms. Wilde has shown that an essay-dialogue can be a fine and effective way of putting forward a point of view in a measured and balanced way. He also shows how this can be done with a great deal of *style*. In presenting the two opposing views of a text in the form of a dialogue, we enable both to speak fully, rather than stifling one, albeit unintentionally, under the weight of our own prejudices and preconceptions. It is in this very special quality that perhaps the greatest strength of the Gilbertian method is to be found.

 —I still fail to see it. There is something in what you say, but that's probably just waffle. Wouldn't an essay-dialogue just be a sort of essay, but with style dominating over substance? Isn't substance far more important?

 —That is what we must find out . . .

 (Curtains close on the scene.)

graffiticism, *n*. [from GRAFFITI and CRITICISM]

Acts of micro-criticism carved, inscribed, or daubed on the walls of public and private buildings, whether found or created. They are the property of nobody, and nobody has the privilege to claim authorship over them. The author is dead (so Barthes says) anyway, so that settles things. Examples include the message 'Back soon – Godot' found written on wall of a toilet in a London theatre.[13] This three-word act of graffiticism was unsigned, and unsought by any academic institution; indeed, its very existence would presumably be frowned upon by the owners of the establishment, the theatre, in which it appeared. This unnecessary supplement to Beckett's play may act as a starting-point for the new practice of graffiticism. Graffiticism is the daubings on the house of fiction, the scrawlings on the academic edifice, the writing on the wall . . .

Oh God, I'm back to T. S. Eliot. Something I saw scrawled in the toilets at Leicester University: 'T. S. Eliot is an anagram of toilets.' Where would be go with such a piece of graffiticism? Is there anywhere we can go, or is it for the flush? Gimme a moment, I'm thinking, goddammit. Beyond the sheer lexical delight of finding the rearrangement of the letters of Eliot's initials and surname form the English word for lavatorial amenities, is there any literary argument or impression that could be launched, in all, or at least in some, seriousness? I'm trying not to pun too much here, trying to expunge or flush thoughts of the 'empty cisterns' from *The Waste Land* ('waste' again!), or all thoughts of the scatological (just why are the 'dirty hands' quite so dirty on 'Margate Sands'?).[14] But there is the issue of the private and public, both key issues for this at once very public and deeply private poet, critic, bank clerk, and husband. 'Toilets' in the plural, after all, implies public amenities ('where are the toilets?'), does it not? I'm rambling, forgive me. In trying to elaborate on this perfect statement of graffiticism, in taking it literally off the wall, I have made it off-the-wall, untenable, ridiculous. Like Wilde's aphorisms there is no paraphrase for graffiticism: the meaning is there for those with eyes to see and a call of nature to answer.

But perhaps this needs more attention. That is the great thing about criticism, or at least should be. To take Wilde's cue once more, 'the contemplative life that has for its aim not *doing* but *being*, and not *being* merely, but *becoming* – that is what the critical spirit can give us.'[15] I'm full of critical spirits. Graffiti is an essential aspect of all advanced cultures. Therefore it is perhaps not our place to close the door on this matter, and it requires more research. As André Gide had it in his diary in 1917, 'No graffiti in the urinals. Switzerland is proud of this; but I believe this is just what she lacks: manure.'[16]

When I want to write a book, I read one

jekyll, *v.* [from *Strange Case of Dr Jekyll and Mr Hyde*, 1886 work by Robert Louis Stevenson]

1. (Of a critic) To perform an act of creative writing as it were by night, while keeping one's 'day job' as literary critic, tenured academic, etc.

2. (Of a novelist, poet, playwright, etc.) To perform an act of criticism by night, thus complementing (contradicting?) the act of creative writing done in the course of one's day. Thus to 'jekyll' is to reverse roles, and balance out one's more famous or 'respectable' career or job through undertaking surreptitious (and sometimes more public) acts on the other side of the camp (if there can be said to be any clear demarcation between camps).

And what I mean by this, by what I might call 'the jekyll effect', is that we are all jokers-and-hides: critics by day, artists by night, or vice versa. The jekyll-and-hyde effect is becoming more apparent than it previously was: less hydden, we might say. But it has always been there, throughout history, in some of the greatest critics: Dr Johnson, who was also poet and novelist; Coleridge, who when he wasn't taking opium or taking a hike, was writing poetry; and De Quincey, who spent most of *his* time taking opium, it would seem, at any rate. The critic as addict? But I wean myself off that, I'm going coldturkey, I'm off into the twentieth century moving closer to the present time, for there was William Empson, or W. H. Auden, or T. S. Eliot, or A. E. Housman . . .

land messages, *n.pl.* [from the practice of record companies and bands inscribing 'secret' messages on the 'land' or run-off groove around the centre label of vinyl LP records]

The practice of leaving notes, sentences, orders, final demands, declarations, calls-to-arms, inversions, subversions, conversions, aversions, and inflammatory statements in unusual places in a work of criticism, whether article, book chapter, yellow note, monograph, edited collection, etc. Examples include 'phantom' or unusual entries in the index, surprising mentions in the 'acknowledgments,' and marginal messages.

This inflammatory idea shares much with the concept of the Derridean 'trace', where 'language bears within itself the necessity of its own critique.'[17] Or, to borrow from E. M. Forster, we cannot know what we think till we see what we say. This is one of the shortest and most illustrative examples of 'micro-criticism,' the central ethic (insofar as it allows itself one) of the punk criticism (or punkism) movement.

pissoff.

lexstasy, *n.* [from *lexis*, 'word', and ECSTASY, lit. 'standing outside oneself']

Along with and aside from Wilde's *Intentions*, the other not-bible of the creative-critical movement would perhaps be (or not be) *Hieroglyphics*, Arthur Machen's 1902 book which outlines a theory of literature based upon the feeling of 'ecstasy'.[18] Machen, a Welsh author of novels such as *The Great God Pan* and *The Hill of Dreams*, writes that with 'ecstasy' we have 'the touchstone which will infallibly separate the higher from the lower in literature, which will range the innumerable multitude of books in two great divisions, which can be applied with equal justice to a Greek drama, an eighteenth-century novelist, and a modern poet, to an epic in twelve books, and to a lyric in twelve lines.'[19]

The best thing about Machen's theory of literature is that it is not really a theory at all, and that's why we like it. As with the smell of a newly creosoted fence or the fresh wind following a rainfall, we cannot say precisely *why* it is so wonderful, but we merely know that it is. Here I think of the grandfather again, T. S. Eliot, trying to put into words *why* the two words, *Ah, soldier*, make such a crucial difference to *Antony and Cleopatra*, but finally being unable to: 'I could not myself put into words the difference I feel between the passage if these two words *ah, soldier* were omitted and with them. But I know there is a difference, and that only Shakespeare could have made it.'[20]

Thus lexstasy would seek to analyse what it is about a particular writer's use of language and words that lends their work this vague and indefinable 'ecstatic' quality. From Shakespeare to Hopkins, Carroll to Joyce, the ways in which authors use words to create this feeling of euphoric grandeur and inspiration is perhaps impossible to analyse. That is precisely why the punk critic would seek to do so. It is deliberately vague, because it is based on deeply personal experience – and yet, somehow, strangely anonymous and distanced.

micro-criticism, *n.* [from *micro-*, Greek prefix denoting 'small', and CRITICISM]

Any act of criticism, however small, which can be deemed shorter than what is generally considered criticism in the measurable sense (journal articles, book chapters, monographs). Micro-criticism embraces any criticism which can be described as interpreting another text ('text' being itself interpreted in the loosest sense), no matter how short the piece of critical writing may be. It may be a piece of anonymous graffiticism, or a note left in a public place. One possibility lies in the books which people travelling the world read before leaving in a public place for another traveller to find and do a similar thing with; since the text is already being shared in this communal way, why not tack or append to said text an adhesive note conveying, in a few words, one's thoughts and theories about said text? Just imagine. A whole dialogue could thus be instigated through post-it notes . . .

neological, *adj.* [from *neo-*, denoting 'new', and LOGICAL, ult. from *logos*, 'word, speech, discourse, reason', after NEOLOGISM]

Adjective describing criticism which seeks to explain and explore new ways of discussing literature, culture, society, etc. through *neologisms*, new words and phrases, etc. esp. those which invert or subvert the idea of the *–ism* (structuralism, postcolonialism, Marxism, etc.) by being either very small in scope (graffiticism) or by being only semi-serious (asthmatic criticism, schizm). Neological criticism would harness the power of the neologism in order to highlight how language is constantly being remoulded and rein-vented by writers; why should critics be any different? (See also OEDipus complex.) Some writers, such as James Joyce, Lewis Carroll, George Orwell, Charles Dickens, and (of course) William Shakespeare, are famed for their invention of new words; but these writers also use language in a markedly different way from other writers, and we need to rewrite the lexicon to take account of what they are doing.

We have yet to see the true critical equivalent of 'Jabberwocky.' A work of criticism that needs notes just to explain *itself*, let alone another text.

OEDipus complex, *n.* [from *OED*, abbrev. of *Oxford English Dictionary*, and 'Oedipus complex', term coined by S. Freud]

The difficulty encountered by a literary critic when, in the course of her or his work, the critic finds the definition of a word or term offered by the *Oxford English Dictionary* to be insufficient, evasive, or incomplete; a state or instance of this.

This phenomenon is particularly common among those who favour what might be called 'lexicographical criticism', close reading that often zooms in on specific words in a text and has recourse to dictionaries in order to try to pinpoint their meaning, ambiguity, etc. in a given text.

In the course of such work, the lexicographical critic may have to grapple or wrestle with the 'father' or grand-daddy of all English dictionaries, the *OED*, and overcome it, in order to offer a sufficient reading of a given passage in a novel, poem, play, essay, etc. This can be equated to Freud's delineation of the Oedipus complex where the child wishes to kill the father and marry the mother; here the 'father' can be thought of as the traditional and established lexical definition found in the *OED* and the 'mother' is the text, which we wish to understand closely in order to interpret it.

Criticism is at bottom a poetry of life

> **post-it criticism,** *n.* [from 'post-it note,' a brand name for pieces of paper with adhesive strips on their reverse that enables them to be attached and re-attached to various surfaces; after post-criticism]

In our throwaway culture, the age of disposable pleasures, perhaps it would not be out of place to speak of the age of the post-it. Not only are we ushering in the genre of 'post-criticism', but we are heading for 'post-it criticism'. This is my post-it, which I tack onto the wall and leave for someone else to find: post-it criticism would be a sub-category of micro-criticism, and enable the literary, literary-critical, and so-called 'non-academic' world, to embrace the trivial, the small, the aphoristic, the concise and economical. For what can be more economical than the post-it note? The brighter the better. The wall should be littered with bright yellow leaves of paper, slips of observations to be slipped into the book we have never opened. A rip-off, a screw-up, a throwaway thesis. There to be torn apart or else stuck to, adherently and endearingly. Men and women and scraps of paper, blown about in the tidal wind of thought and idea, coming at us down the dark tunnel, bringing light and illumination like yellow autumn leaves to this cold underground station as we join and rejoin the trains of thought.

> **punkism,** *n.* [blend of PUNK and CRITICISM, from 'punk music', a style of music originating in the 1970s and characterised by a flouting of convention and (frequently) angry or disaffected youth. A conflation or portmanteau of 'punk' and 'criticism', so as to distinguish between this new movement and the older, established phrase denoting criticism of punk music (*'punk criticism'*)]

Punkism is a movement in criticism that draws on a number of different influences – indeed, there is no limit to the genres, styles, or areas of culture and the world on which punkism may draw. Chiefly, however, it may take its cue from:

1. Modernist literature and art, as set out by Gregory Ulmer in his 1983 essay 'The Object of Post-Criticism' where he writes:

> Criticism now is being transformed in the same way that literature and the arts were transformed by the avant-garde movements in the early decades of this century. The break with 'mimesis,' with the values and assumptions of 'realism,' which revolutionized the modern arts, is now underway (belatedly) in criticism, the chief consequence of which, of course, is a change in the relation of the critical text to its object – literature.[21]

Nearly thirty years on, we are still waiting for the revolution in criticism which Ulmer's words seem to gesture towards, but with the recent rise in 'creative writing' as a ubiquitous university course and the rise in interest in 'creative-critical' writing, we are, perhaps, finally ready for the revolution.

2. Punk music, with its interest in unsettling the spectator and the world at large and anyone who cares to listen. The break with conformity, the departure from the privileging of often abstruse philosophical and historical readings at the expense of reading *literary texts* themselves, that takes its cue from the punk explosion in music and culture in the late 1970s, is now almost underway (belatedly) in criticism, a big *fuck you* to those readings which have for so long obscured the literary text itself, and a return to the basics, to three chords and a crap singer, if you like.

3. Close reading, which (as Shawn Rosenheim has already noted), like cocaine addiction and American spiritualism, works on a cycle of thirty years.[22] Go back thirty years and you get the high point of theory, particularly poststructuralism, in universities; with this came an attention to the text and a preoccupation with picking apart (whether through an interpretation or misinterpretation of deconstruction) the language of texts. Go back another thirty years and you get the high moment of New Criticism with its obsession with 'the words on the page' – wisdom-tooth criticism, to adapt the words of Terry Eagleton.[23] Go back another thirty years and you have Practical Criticism with its attempts to emphasise the importance of the text. But each time close reading re-emerges as an important force in literary criticism it is used in a different way. This time it is through attention to the language of texts that we can bring about new creative readings of literary texts: following the lead of Nicolas Abraham in his important 1988 'essay', 'The Phantom of Hamlet', we can use close reading as a way of reinterpreting the meaning of literature, creating our own supplemen-

tary readings (and re-writings) of canonical (and not-so-canonical) literature.[24] *Or re-enter the* TEXT, *stage right* –

> Poetry, in life, is a criticism of bottoms

scared quotes, *n.pl.* [from phrase, 'scare quotes']

Scared quotes, or 'scared quotes' as they will hereafter always be known,
already placed within themselves, cocooned or cordoned off from the text
which surrounds them, are new punctuational markers to be used to denote
when a phrase, particularly in academia, is unknown, unsettling, uncertain.
Rather than seeking to scare others by placing 'scare quotes' around such
phrases as 'research excellence' or 'creative writing,' perhaps we should use
'scared quotes,' quotation marks which highlight the uncertain nature of
such phrases. In the case of the former, it is that 'research excellence' (placed
in 'scared quotes' now rather than 'scare quotes') is an unknown and
unknowable quantity, signifying something in the academic arena which
remains ultimately slippery, unquantifiable to you or me. In the case of the
latter, the phrase 'creative writing,' suggesting and denoting all research in
the university which cannot be labelled 'critical writing', thus brackets
itself off from critical writing and reinforces the idea that criticism cannot
in itself be creative, since it is 'non-creative,' it doesn't come under the
banner of 'creative writing.' Thus this phrase must be placed in 'scared
quotes' to highlight my own unsettled and unsteady attitude towards the
phrase as it has developed in the university.

> I'm creative, honest guv, gimme a chance

schizm, *n.* [SCHIZOPHRENIC and CRITICISM, after SCHISM]

An act of 'schizo-criticism', or 'schizophrenic' criticism, taking as its cue
the figurative, Eliotic sense of 'schizophrenia' meaning roughly 'split
personality', as originated by T. S. Eliot in 1933:

> 1933 T. ELIOT *Use of Poetry and Use of Criticism* For a poet to be also a
> philosopher he would have to be virtually two men; I cannot think of any
> example of this thorough schizophrenia, nor can I see anything to be gained
> by it.[25]

Thus Eliot's opening-out of 'schizophrenia' from the literal, clinical
meaning to the figurative, Jekyllian meaning points up one of the dangers

of schizm: if to be a poet and a philosopher would involve something undesirable and perhaps even unwholesome, then perhaps to be both a 'creative
writer' and a critic is to approach a similar state of Jekyllian meltdown.
What we need are new labels, as our 'scared quotes' are out to demonstrate.
For it may be possible and indeed passable to be both creative and critical;
it depends on how we view these terms and how distinctly and disparately
they are categorised.

Perhaps this would be the end and end-point of punk criticism: the
schism and schizm of the reader-critic's mind. No 'creative writing' no, no
more, only *writing*.

Notes

1 T. S. Eliot, *Four Quartets*, in *Collected Poems 1909–1962* (London: Faber and
Faber, 1974), p. 210.

2 Oscar Wilde, 'The Critic as Artist', in *The Artist as Critic: Critical Writings of
Oscar Wilde* (London: W. H. Allen, 1970), p. 365.

3 William Blake, *The Complete Poems*, ed. Alicia Ostriker (London: Penguin,
1977; repr. 2004), p. 182; and John Milton, *Paradise Lost*, in *The Complete Poems*,
ed. B. A. Wright with an Introduction and Notes by Gordon Campbell
(London: J. M. Dent & Sons, 1980), p. 160.

4 Wilde, 'The Critic as Artist', p. 369.

5 T. S. Eliot, 'Tradition and the Individual Talent', in *The Sacred Wood: Essays on
Poetry and Criticism* (London: Methuen, 1920; repr. 1972), pp. 48–9.

6 Simon King, 'Mosaic and Mandala: Contexts and Intertexts for Herbert Read's
Literary Prose' (unpublished doctoral thesis, Loughborough University, 2005).

7 Rob Pope, *Textual Intervention: Critical and Creative Strategies for Literary Studies*
(London: Routledge, 1995), p. 1.

8 Pope, *Textual Intervention*, p. 1.

9 Roland Barthes, 'Theory of the Text', trans. Ian McLeod, in *Untying the Text*,
ed. Robert Young (London: Routledge and Kegan Paul, 1981), p. 44.

10 Nick Everett, 'Creative Writing and English', *Cambridge Quarterly* (2005) 34
(3): 231–42 (pp. 235–6).

11 Wilde, 'The Critic as Artist', p. 369.

12 Wilde, 'The Critic as Artist', p. 340.

13 Cited in Pope, *Textual Intervention*, p. 137.

14 T. S. Eliot, *The Waste Land*, in *Collected Poems 1909–1962*, pp. 78, 74.

15 Wilde, 'The Critic as Artist', p. 384.

16 *The Journals of André Gide, Vol II: 1914–1927*, translated from the French and
annotated by Justin O'Brien (New York: Alfred A. Knopf, 1948), p. 208.

17 Jacques Derrida, 'Structure, Sign, and Play in the Discourse of the Human
Sciences', in *Writing and Difference* (London: Routledge, 2001), p. 358.

18 Arthur Machen, *Hieroglyphics: A Note upon Ecstasy in Literature* (New York:
Mitchell Kennerley, 1913).

19 Machen, *Hieroglyphics*, pp. 24–5.

20 Cited in Christopher Ricks, *T. S. Eliot and Prejudice* (London: Faber and Faber, 1988; paperback edn. 1994), p. 160.

21 Gregory L. Ulmer, 'The Object of Post-Criticism', in *Postmodern Culture*, edited and introduced by Hal Foster (London: Pluto Press, 1985), p. 83.

22 Shawn Rosenheim, *The Cryptographic Imagination: Secret Writing from Edgar Poe to the Internet* (Baltimore, MD: Johns Hopkins University Press, 1997), p. 119.

23 Terry Eagleton, *Literary Theory: An Introduction* (Oxford: Blackwell, 1983; anniversary edn. 2008), p. 77.

24 Nicolas Abraham, 'The Phantom of Hamlet or The Sixth Act, preceded by The Intermission of "Truth"', in Nicolas Abraham and Maria Torok, *The Shell and the Kernel*, vol. 1, edited, translated, and with an Introduction by Nicholas T. Rand (London: University of Chicago Press, 1994), pp. 187–205.

25 T. S. Eliot, *The Use of Poetry and the Use of Criticism: Studies in the Relation of Criticism to Poetry in England* (London: Faber and Faber, 1933; repr. 1955), pp. 98–9.

Our never-to-be-slighted 'fun'

Tony Sharpe

Thou wretched, rash, intruding fool, farewell!
I took thee for thy better.

Hands up, who likes literary critics? Not me, of course: such a derivative, parasitical class of being. Marianne Moore, in the same poem announcing her dislike for poetry, delights us – does she not? – with her provocative vignette of 'the immovable critic twitching his skin like a horse/ that feels a flea';[1] a dull-witted creature, then, whose infected judgment registers the stimulus of 'genuine' art merely as irritant to his vast mammalian complacency. It may also be remembered that in the latter stages of *Waiting for Godot* Vladimir and Estragon engage in an escalatingly offensive but inherently competitive bout of name-calling, whose comminatory crescendo moves alliteratively from 'sewer-rat!' through 'curate!' and 'cretin!' to the flourish of Estragon's last trump: 'Crrritic!'. 'There's no answer to that', as Eric Morecambe used to observe, and the stage direction indicates that Vladimir *'wilts, vanquished, and turns away'*;[2] for even in the semi-suspended animation of a world in which, as was once asserted (by a critic) 'nothing happens, twice,' there is a still lower order of yet more vacuous inauthenticity. And is it just me who catches, in Vladimir's defeated and diminished turning-away, a distant echo of that more sonorous Scriptural dismissal where the accursed servant Gehazi turns from his master Elishah, a dismissal reverberating through my compulsorily-chapeled boyhood: 'And he went out from his presence a leper, as white as snow' (2 Kings 5, 27)? Well, probably it *is* just me; for that's exactly the kind of self-advertisingly recondite connection the critical mind delights in making.

Why can't criticism be content with its appropriately lowly status? Gehazi was cursed for his vulgar materialism, for being on the make and tricking Naaman into giving *him* the gifts Elishah had disdained to take for curing Naaman's leprosy; it's a mistake to seek to get above yourself: was that what I was supposed to have learnt in the uncomfortable pew? 'Here endeth the lesson' was the formulaic phrase that followed Gehazi's appalling transformation, and yet no patly moral admonition retains for me any of the dreadful, unfathomably vivid immediacy of that scene where a man turns, disgraced in his newly-glistening skin. 'We shall all be changed, in a moment, in the twinkling of an eye': but not necessarily for the better. Aspiring to have wings like a dove you might become the butt, instead, of a nastier metempsychotic joke; you might awaken from a night of troubled dreams, for example, to find yourself transformed into 'a monstrous insect' ('*zu einem ungeheuren Ungeziefer verwandelt*'),[3] in which predicament you'd certainly have fulfilled the inverted aspiration of getting *below* yourself.

Enforcing the lessons rather than the pleasures derivable from texts has indeed been one of the functions of a criticism that derived its methods, along with a self-regard appropriate to the high seriousness of its cultural mission, from precedent traditions of Biblical commentary. 'I would endeavour to interpose myself' was Lytton Strachey's happy solution to the hypothetical attempt on the honour of his sister by a rampant *Boche*; and a certain kind of criticism less happily tried to interpose itself between any presumptuously under-instructed readership and the sanctities of secular scriptures. For, as John Gross has described the mid-Victorian scene, 'there was also a large public which, emerging from a dominantly religious culture, both believed in the importance of literature and felt uneasy with it, which venerated the printed word and at the same time hardly knew where to begin.'[4] Time was when the critic exercised a cultural authority that our (doubtless more discerning) age confers only upon the figure of the 'celebrity': that is, as a validator, a person though whom an experience must flow and to whose specialised existence it must be referred, in order to accrue significance for those un-exalted, deferential lives downstream. Nowadays, we value artists themselves according to their successful functioning as celebrities (sometimes, indeed, by their ostentatious repudiation of publicity), and any self-interpositioning critic merely becomes the person obstructing a stage-struck view. Sit down thy vanity, I say, sit down. Of one Victorian interposer, Gross recalls that 'there was a time when thousands of readers were happy to be swept along by his dogmatic, wildly emotional judgements and his strange billowing style' – yet O! he and his hobby-horses are forgot.

You may justly object that here I pillory a man of straw, dispersible by the back-draught from a modestly-powered vacuum cleaner. But is not criticism itself – when it exerts itself above dogmatics or wild emotion – concerned in the antithetical dispersal of 'magic' by the analysis and explanation of effect, rewriting *ars est celare artem* as *ars criticus est monstrare artem*?[5] Nowhere is this more visually enacted than on certain congested pages of the Arden Shakespeares, where, as in some Poe-like fantasy, a resentful *esprit de l'escalier* on the editor's part causes his *apparatus criticus* to compress

Shakespeare's text ever more airlessly against the page's ceiling, encroaching on it much like the 'vile and loathsome crust,' 'most lazar-like' that consumes the 'smooth body' of Hamlet *père*. This is Eliot's 'devil of the stairs' with an *apparatus* of unhappiness – a presumer, attempting to rise above his true station like the ghost of Peter Quint in *The Turn of the Screw*, memorably encountered on the staircase at Bly and forced to retrace his airy steps back down again by the plucky resolve of a Governess sufficiently determined to police the line dividing 'above-stairs' from 'below.' If poetry is 'a criticism of life,' as Arnold said, then the criticism of poetry becomes merely the criticism of a criticism, a tertiary epiphenomenon akin to the shadow cast by a reflection, not fit to trespass into the drawing-room of the mansion of Art:

> I definitely saw [Quint's figure] turn, as I might have seen the low wretch to which it had once belonged turn on receipt of an order, and pass, with my eyes on the villainous back that no hunch could have more disfigured, straight down the staircase and into the darkness in which the next bend was lost.[6]

And thence, we suppose, further downward, its truest destination, the cellar, rather even than the *salon des refusés*, where a doubtlessly dank coffin will await.

But just as Peter Quint keeps reappearing – It's That Man Again! – the critic's 'white face of damnation'[7] keeps peering in at the windows, irrepressibly returning like the indiscreet undead. I confess that, for this paper's irresponsible purposes, I have been imposing on you, alongside lepers and hunchbacks, two flagrant caricatures of the Critic: as a resentful, malevolent servant, and as a kind of mutton-chopped Victorian incapacitated by his ludicrous seriousness from taking the true measure of art's *serium ludere* – in either case, a figure embodying irreconcilable differences between creative and critical impulses. Such differences might not have seemed unbridgeable to Alexander Pope when writing a poem called 'An Essay on Criticism,' itself aware of classical models of verse treatises, such as Horace's *Ars Poetica*; nor to Matthew Arnold who, whilst conceding that 'The critical power is of lower rank than the creative,' still felt it might be considered as 'a free creative activity.'[8] The differences were, however, asserted by Eliot in 'The Function of Criticism' (1923; the title alludes to Arnold), where he insisted on an apparently hierarchical relationship in which the act of criticism must always be ancillary, whereas the creative act can be 'self-delighting' (in Yeats's phrase): 'I have assumed as axiomatic that a creation, a work of art, is autotelic; and that criticism, by definition, is *about* something other than itself.'[9]

The poet may know his 'fine frenzy,' then, but the critic, necessarily coming after that event, can at best register the 'intoxication of belatedness,' and is in fact more likely to bring to bear 'an age of prudence' on the 'awful daring of a moment's surrender' that originated the work of art: indeed, from Eliot's point of view it may be better thus, since in an earlier essay ('The Perfect Critic') he was especially hard on those whose criticism was 'the satisfaction of a suppressed creative wish.'[10] All that said, however, he recognised – as part of his disagreement with Arnold – the significance of the operation of the critical faculty in the act of creation:

> [H]e overlooks the capital importance of criticism in the work of creation itself. Probably, indeed, the larger part of the labour of an author in composing his work is critical labour; the labour of sifting, combining, constructing, expunging, correcting, testing: this frightful toil is as much critical as creative.[11]

An example of such critical acuity, embodied in an 'ear' of quite exceptional sensitivity, was seen when, in *The Waste Land* (V), Eliot wrote of 'The awful daring of a moment's surrender,/ Which an age of prudence can never retract': preferring that second line's colloquial inflection to its more shapely alternative, 'Which an age of prudence never can retract,' where the specious satisfactions of metrical sonority do not achieve the truth-telling disruptive force of the chosen version. Or was it? The earliest written version has 'cannot retract' with the 'not' struck through and replaced with 'never.'[12] So is it, then, a belated critical irrelevance to say what I just said about it? 'Teach me to heare Mermaides singing,' demands John Donne, evidently requiring the impossible, and simultaneously suggesting the gross difference between what it is to teach and what it would be to hear a mermaid's song. Yet, when Prufrock allusively confesses of his mermaids that 'I do not think that they will sing to me,' does the teacher perform a disservice in remarking that this line derives some of its exactly-judged plangency from the assonantal pararhyme of 'think' with 'sing,' and from its enactment of visionary diminution in progressing from the 'I' with which it opens to the 'me' with which it ends?

Such perceptions of a poem, whether or not they conform exactly to any of the 'frightful toil' involved in the actual composition, can be seen, not as an upstart's interference, but as a proper tribute to the finished work. If the unexamined life is not worth living then to deny examination to the poem we read is to fail to respect it enough. The argument against this, however, is that criticism can be too committed to a doctrine of intelligent design in explaining literary effects. The aspects of 'Prufrock' briefly commented on above may be attributable less to conscious artistry than to the more occult operation of what Eliot subsequently defined as 'the auditory imagination,' resonating below conscious formulation. Significantly, he offered this concept as part of a critique of Matthew Arnold's deficiencies: 'the feeling for syllable and rhythm, penetrating far below the conscious levels of thought and feeling, invigorating every word; sinking to the most primitive and forgotten, returning to the origin and bringing something back.'[13] Critical commentary inevitably falsifies such a process: condemned to a life of 'thoughts' rather than 'sensations,' the critical act cannot 'surprise' by 'fine excess,' to follow Keats further, because, not being 'autotelic,' it must, like a bad poem, always have a 'palpable design' in view.[14] This, in turn, prevents it from inhabiting the sphere of '*Zweckmä igkeit ohne Zweck*' (purposiveness without purpose) where, for Kant in the *Critique of Judgment*, beauty existed. There may be something protective, for Eliot, in insisting as he does in the final lecture of the series on 'the depths of feeling into which we cannot peer,' and in speculating whether 'the self-consciousness involved in aesthetics and in psychology does not risk violating the frontier of consciousness.'[15] Wallace Stevens seems to imply something similar when he declared in a letter that 'There is a kind of secrecy between a poet and his poem which, once violated, affects the integrity of the poet.'[16] This violation was in both cases to do with over-*explication de texte*, the professional vice of explicators who are keen to have the 'meaning' even at the cost of missing the 'experience'. As Philip Larkin declared in an interview: 'I'm not a teacher. I couldn't be. I should think that chewing over other people's work, writing I mean, must be terribly stultifying. Quite sickens you with the whole business of literature.'[17]

This is, however, somewhat to oversimplify a matter that is complicated – which, indeed, to a high degree flourishes in complications, of a kind that are made more apparent if we substitute the term 'interpreter' for 'explicator.' To examine these, and to tease out further implications of Larkin's phrase 'the whole business of literature,' I will step back a letter in the alphabet and refer to the work of three writers whose surname begins with 'K.' As well as the potential self-righteousness already noted, literary criticism inherited from precedent traditions of Scriptural commentary a particular concern with secrecy, according to Frank Kermode's analysis that also emphasises the corporate framework within which this activity habitually proceeds: 'Interpreters usually belong to an institution,' he asserts, 'and as members they enjoy certain privileges and suffer certain constraints. Perhaps the most important of these are the right to affirm, and the obligation to accept, the superiority of latent over manifest senses.'[18] This is a very ancient state of affairs, he acknowledges; but one that has been reinvigorated by Freudian theory and by the establishment within the modern university of legitimated interpretative expertise – 'We who *know* are the possessors of an institutional competence' – which extends an hierarchical exclusion zone beyond the sacred or occult texts that were formerly the preserve of the initiated, to engross secular literature as well. The unsanctioned reader is, naturally, not debarred from engaging with the canon, but will simply not be taken seriously when he does: 'The real difference between the outside and the inside is marked by the insistence of the outsider that he can say what he likes about Shakespeare and the tacit knowledge of the institution, which he therefore hates, that nothing he says is worth attending to.' He duly sinks like Icarus, in the negligent wake of the expensive, delicate ship of Higher Learning – on which, meanwhile, '(w)e wean candidates from the habit of literal reading. Like the masters who reserved secret senses in the second century, we are in the business of conducting readers out of the sphere of the manifest.'[19]

There are those, not merely common readers or Icarian flops, who regard this institutionalisation of literary response as a sorry business (with a particularly dead sound on that final noun). Milan Kundera coined the term 'misomusist' to define a person who doesn't like the arts: a dangerously virulent example of this condition is when it leads, not to logically-legitimated indifference, but to 'an intellectual, sophisticated misomusy' that actively engages with art in a spirit of spiteful revenge – 'Who could not win the Mistress, woo'd the Maid;/ Against the Poets *their own Arms* they turn'd,/ Sure to hate most the Men from whom they *learn'd.*'[20] Its cultural symptom is precisely that professorialisation of literature outlined by Kermode, licensing in Kundera's view those 'for whom a work of art is merely the pretext for deploying a method (psychoanalytic, semiological, sociological, etc.),'[21] reversing both natural hierarchy and historical sequence:

> I'm too fearful of the professors for whom art is only a derivative of philosophical and theoretical trends. The novel dealt with the unconscious before Freud, the class struggle before Marx, it practised phenomenology (the investigation of the essence of human situations) before the phenomenologists.

The novel, asserts Kundera, and by extension all literature, 'is born not of the theoretical spirit but of the spirit of humour'; its presiding genius is the digressive jocosity of Sterne rather than Leibniz's '*Nihil est sine ratione*' ('nothing is without its reason'). Starting as they do from false premises, professorial engagements destroy rather than enhance such texts: 'By insisting on decoding him, the Kafkologists killed Kafka.'[22]

This clacking Kafkophony duly ushers in my last alliterative example, the writer who most definingly outlined the significance of 'business' – its office mentality and bureaucratic appetites – in producing modernity. Kundera notes that Gregor Samsa's predominant concern, straight after his nightmarish awakening, is with how he'll manage to get to the office in good time. Whether, like Nabokov in his *Lectures on Literature*, you regard this tale of transmogrification as one of the pinnacles of twentieth-century fiction or, like Rebecca West, as 'an absurd *avant garde* story . . . [which] has no merits except its discovery of a striking symbol for an inferiority complex,'[23] it offers a productive arena of critical engagement. For, albeit separated by their differential valuations of its merits, each may be thought to diminish Kafka's story by 'decoding' it: West (who admires some of his other work) does so in cursorily dismissing it as modish and assigning a single symbolic function to Gregor's beetlehood; Nabokov, whilst much more sensitive to details of authorial artistry, rather sentimentalises Kafka's account as a fable of decent Gregor's betrayal by his heartless family. Both approaches can be viewed as recuperations of an essentially unaccommodating strangeness in the story, that evades their methodologies. When entomologist Nabokov briefly speculates that Kafka's description of Gregor's new shape suggests him to be a winged beetle, and that therefore he might address his predicament by taking flight from his room's open window, the question begged but overlooked would lead back to this tale's intransigence: for, even were he winged like a dove, whither in his present shape could he fly that would be any better?

'In theory they were sound on Expectation/ Had there been situations to be in;/ Unluckily they were their situation';[24] thus Auden, describing would-be pioneers, but neatly encapsulating what afflicts and defines Gregor Samsa, who *is* his situation; just as much as the critics who over-read or under-read his story *are* theirs, whatever theoretical expectations they bring along. *Il n'y a pas de hors-texte*, and it is not even a question of making the appropriate generic recognitions (what sort of beetle Gregor turns into rivals the question of how many children Lady Macbeth had). Anthony Easthope, paraphrasing Heidegger, expresses it thus: 'Realism and anti-realism mirror each other for both presuppose a point at which Knowing might stand outside Being. No such point exists.'[25] Picking up Derrida's notorious assertion, quoted above, he adds the rider that there isn't any 'inside-the-text,' either; for 'We are not in a position to decide fundamentally where the text ends and reality begins (. . .). If we discard the claim that reality provides knowledge of itself, more or less directly, then fiction and fact, what's inside and outside the text, arrive together, a package deal.'

Our inability to disintricate the contents of that package constitutes a large part of our experience of Kafka's tale, which proffers so irresistible yet ultimately unachievable an invitation to close its 'hermeneutic gap' (an aperture inspiring readerly aversion at least as acute as Mr Woodhouse's, in *Emma*, for a recklessly opened window). The useful things we say about it – such as Nabokov's suggestion that Gregor is a human disguised as an insect surrounded by insects masquerading as humans – seem compromised by their very utility. This clicks us back another alphabetical notch, to revisit James and his haunted house of fiction. Kermode uses the phrase 'hermeneutic gap,'[26] to describe the deliberated irresolubility of such a work as *The Turn of the Screw,* 'a piece of cold artistic calculation,' as James described it, 'to catch those not easily caught'[27] – phraseology in which the *auteur* seems to exhibit a considerable *hauteur*, for all the 'fun' he derives from such a catch. For who is to be 'caught' and how? Why, we ourselves, Gentle Readers, trapped in its web of words like flies, or *Ungeziefers*. If, thus, we have been changed ('Just like that!'), such change might necessitate self-recognition, less as Gentle Readers, than as *hypocrites lecteurs*, who have preferred what's behind the arras to what's *en clair*, and have Poloniastically discovered that 'to be too busy is some danger.' Indeed, we did make love to this employment, as Hamlet also puts it, for '(o)ur concern, when we depart from the merely descriptive, is with latent sense,' a predilection discriminating us from the 'layman' who, 'we like to think, sees without perceiving, hears without understanding'[28] – this itself echoing Arnold's assertion that 'the practical man is not apt for fine distinctions, and yet in these distinctions truth and the highest culture greatly find their account.'[29] Yet it is not the 'layman' or 'practical man' whom James's *'amusette' (oubliette?)* sets out to ensnare, but sophisticated readers like ourselves, the critically astute and instituted, preferring what is latent to what is manifest because to do so answers to the mysteries of our craft. And in that tendency to invest what is not obviously there with greater value than what is, our *'semblable'* in James's story is not Peter Quint (whose insurrectionary insistence suggests potential kinship with Figaro, another truth-bearing, table-turning valet?) but the rectitudinous Governess.

Mind 'the gap'! The critic interposes himself in two principal modes: as a guardian of morals – a Nahum Tate or a Bowdler – removing noxious matter before it can contaminate the vulnerable; and, in Kermode's account, as functionary of an institution that seeks to influence what should be read, and how. The approaches differ, of course, but both presume the existence of something like a horde of the preterite: who either need their textual food to be rendered innocuous by mincing, to achieve digestibility, or need elaborate instruction in table-manners and the comparative nutritional value of dishes, in order to reach approved standards and become licensed eaters. The Governess, our surrogate, combines aspects of both, embodying a wrong relation toward those in her duty of care, and a trust in the superiority of her own virginal but fancifully bookish understanding that not only fails to prevent disaster but actively conduces to it: her own 'small, smothered life' leads finally to another (metaphor transformed to fact). Unluckily she is her situation, and the energy with which she seeks to nullify the threat of excluded meanings continually augments the force with which they irrupt upon her; so the 'ghosts' gain in minatory definition, and Miles and Flora in corruption. Blatant as he apparently becomes, Peter Quint may be less satanic emissary than the bearer of requisite knowledge ('sin is behovely'?), perhaps achieved by Eliot's process of 'sinking to the most primitive and forgotten, returning to the origin and bringing something back'; for whilst his initials enact inevitable alphabetical progression and, perhaps, the due minding of P's and Q's, his whole name (to an ear less innocent than hers) is slangily decodable as suggesting 'Penis Vagina': a 'necessarye coniunction' that lies beyond her circumscriptions.

Ours too: for we are complicit in her shortcomings, all of us avid respondents to the text's promiscuous invitation to uncover private parts. It catches us whichever way we turn: if we decide she is mistaken, we repeat her own mistake of presuming to have access to the truth; if we believe she actually sees the visible spirits of Quint and her predecessor Miss Jessel, we overlook those elements militating against this; if we think her prey to delusions, and that there are no such things as ghosts, we need at least to acknowledge that our activity as readers of fiction might make us less dogmatically definitive about interchanges between the 'real' and the 'imagined' – categories which, in any case, are less securely separable within the 'package deal' of fiction and fact. The House of Fiction isn't necessarily a very salubrious accommodation: the undead walk in it, and here a man may change into an insect; but we are more its tenants than we care to think. Thus Bob Dylan: 'You ever seen a ghost? No,/ But you have heard of them.'[30]

Kermode puts *The Turn of the Screw* (1898) alongside *The Sacred Fount* (1901) as two of James's works in which the hermeneutic gap 'cannot be closed, only gloried in; they solicit mutually contradictory types of attention and close only on a problem of closure.' It seems appropriate that James should write both around the time when in England the study of English literature was beginning to be developed as an academic discipline; this supports Kundera's sense of sequence, for it would be quite a while before the academy found a language to discuss the games they play – as Kermode observed in 1975, 'literary theory has caught up with the practice of Henry

James.' [31] He has some reservations about *The Sacred Fount* (whose narrator speculates that a kind of vampiric reciprocity underlies the respective ageing and rejuvenation of fellow house-guests); Rebecca West, in the year of its author's death, had more: '(H)e records how a week-end visitor spends more intellectual force than Kant can have used on *The Critique of Pure Reason* in an unsuccessful attempt to discover whether there exists between certain of his fellow-guests a relationship not more interesting among these vacuous people than it is among sparrows.' [32] It is as if in this excess, however, with regard to the professoriate James was getting his retaliation in first; his (doubly) alphabetical cohabitee, James Joyce (Nahum Tate's fellow-Dubliner), would soon enough spend as much intellectual force as Kant producing a novel to keep professors busy for years to come. Q.D. Leavis asserted of Walter Raleigh, first occupant of Oxford's Merton Chair of English Literature, that he was 'an example of the most dangerous kind of academic, the man who hasn't enough ability to set up on his own as a creative artist and bears literature a grudge in consequence'. [33] It could be said that the high-jinks of *Finnegans Wake* (such a novel as Mrs Malaprop – in a sense its Hibernian ancestress – might write, given world enough and time, like a monkey with a tyepwriter), looks, in the spiralling effusion of its puns, like literature's revenge on the acacademy. Just as Wittgenstein clapped his doctoral examiners on their backs and assured them, 'Don't worry – you'll never understand it!', *Finnegans Wake* renders categorically impossible a point of knowing *about* it that is separable from being engaged *in* it. The joke is by no means to everybody's taste, but if we were to turn and face the ch-ch-ch-changes, as per David Bowie's stuttering instruction, we might find an enhancement of being rather than a challenge to it; the sort of thing Stevens envisaged at the end of 'Esthétique du Mal':

> And out of what one sees and hears and out
> Of what one feels, who could have thought to make
> So many selves, so many sensuous worlds,
> As if the air, the mid-day air, was swarming
> With the metaphysical changes that occur,
> Merely in living as and where we live. [34]

Joyce's novel threw down the gauntlet of necessitating elucidation which itself required a different kind of criticism (an 'exagmination round [its] factification', maybe); what was wanted was what Stevens, only a few lines before those just quoted, termed 'the thesis scrivened in delight.' More typically, alas, the institutional response generally evinces itself less in delight than in conferences, where acacademics batten like flies upon the artistic corpus, and the point of creative writing would sometimes seem to be to justify the twenty-minute paper – Larkin's deplorable 'whole business of literature'. In *Finnegans Wake* the principal compositional resource is the pun, whereby a word changes in front of our eyes – further subjected by Joyce to a kind of knight's move into diagonally adjacent and almost uncontrollably incremental orders of signification. As a species of semantic rhyming it does, however, tend to prioritise the aspect of meaning, even in twisting and extending it, thereby perhaps encouraging our attempts to close the hermeneutic gap. Yet if we had its experience but missed its meaning, approach to the meaning restores the experience, that the meaning always will be missed. As Thoreau asserts in *Walden*: 'The volatile truth of our words should continually betray the inadequacy of the residual statement.'[35]

Is it then the case that literary criticism obsesses over the 'residual statement' at the expense of its animating but now evaporated spirit, in a kind of cloddish misrepresentation of what was really the case? (From wrong to wrong the evaporated spirit proceeds . . .) And is such criticism, furthermore, vexed by the impossibility of achieving that Emersonian 'original relation to the universe' embodied in the text, to which it is inevitably posterior? A large part of the threat posed to the Governess by ghostly predecessors is precisely that they got there first: their relationships with the children preceded her own, and their sensed but resented priority powerfully feeds anxiety about the influence they had. As she seeks to arrest their perturbing spirits, so the critic would supplant the author of his cherished text, in quasi-Oedipal uprising. The idea of footnotes crowding out the bardic utterance was taken to comic extremes by Nabokov in *Pale Fire*, where Kinbote the commentator (among other things that he is) uses the pretext of editing his assassinated neighbour's long poem as a means of ensuring that it fulfils the hopes he, Kinbote, had entertained of its true subject-matter: telling, that is, of his life rather than the poet's. It is a model of 'strong misreading' to which we all to some degree conform, I suppose, as we locate our own agendas in the texts that others author; but Nabokov adds the particular twist to this by making the poet John Shade prosaic in his attitudes and assumptions, and his editor by contrast a figure of capable, if distorting, imagination. Although their relationship is hierarchically that of the complacently ensconced, socially-embedded writer and his marginalised, outcast neighbour-commentator, to that extent confirming the critic-as-upstart-usurper model, as a work of fiction *Pale Fire* obviously consists both – it might be a mistake to say 'equally' – of Shade's viewpoint and Kinbote's. In his editorial foreword Kinbote makes some uncompromising assertions: 'Let me state that without my notes Shade's text simply has no human reality at all'; 'for better or worse, it is the commentator who has the last word'[36] – which turns out to be even more valuable than having had the first one.

Although this illustrates the apparently unshakeable *chutzpah* of a self-deluded grandee, it also quietly enforces a true enough point: that any text requires animation by readerly engagement – without which it has merely the inert potential of Dracula in his day-time box: a 'residual statement' requiring human input to conjure up its 'volatile truth'. In an odd but (by him) unintended way, the posthumous publication of Nabokov's unfinished novel *The Original of Laura* (2009) takes a further step in readerly empowerment, allowing us a nearer approach to mysteries of origin and even offering the promise of participation in originality. For, adding to the illicit thrill derivable from access to a writer's secret workshop, the reader is encouraged to emulate authorial powers of disposition, because this edition photographically reproduces the index cards on which Nabokov habitually composed his fiction and, as the editor (his son, Dmitri) explains: 'The photos of the cards that accompany the text are perforated and can be removed and rearranged, as the author likely did when he was writing the novel'.[37] Described as 'A novel in fragments,' it candidly supposes on the reader's part an heroic and indeed clairvoyant labour of defragmentation; subtitled 'Dying Is Fun,' it seems, regrettably, as if in its case being dead is altogether too much fun, and however many blood-multiples of Tony Hancock's legendary 'whole armful!' we donate, the coffined corpse remains inert.

Of course, the vampire is a rather ominous model, albeit one which poses the not-entirely-irrelevant questions of who gives life to whom or who has a stake in whose heart, in such matters? A more playful and no less relevant scenario is that presented by Stevens in his poem 'Earthy Anecdote' (1918):

> Every time the bucks went clattering
> Over Oklahoma
> A firecat bristled in the way.
>
> Wherever they went,
> They went clattering,
> Until they swerved
> In a swift, circular line
> To the right,
> Because of the firecat.

Or until they swerved
In a swift, circular line
To the left,
Because of the firecat.

The bucks clattered.
The firecat went leaping,
To the right, to the left,
And
Bristled in the way.

Later, the firecat closed his bright eyes
And slept.[38]

This poem is like a little machine that starts up every time we read it, releasing complementary energies on the parts of the bristling firecat and the clattering bucks from whom fearful symmetries are elicited. Their apparently bloodless conflict of interests has no issue other than the poem itself and the firecat's somnolent cessation from activity; odd and even fabulous as these encounters seem to be, however, they occur, we are asked to believe, in 'earthy'(?) Oklahoma. This was the poem Stevens chose to open his first collection *Harmonium* (1923) and, thirty years later, his *Collected Poems* (1954); presumably because it hints at the nature of the book that is to follow. We might say that the firecat seems vigorous, quirky, and admirable, and the bucks seem evasive, single-minded and slightly silly; and we might wonder whether the firecat isn't a bit like a poem and the bucks, with their herd-instinct, a bit like reader-critics, who would rather it weren't there and try to carry on around it; but the poem 'Earthy Anecdote' contains each and requires both for its proper existence: a package deal.

'I trust the reader appreciates the strangeness of this,' writes Kinbote in one of his extravagant annotations, 'because if he does not, there is no sense in writing poems, or notes to poems, or anything at all.'[39] Stevens told an enquirer about 'Earthy Anecdote' that 'explanations spoil things': does, then, the construction I have placed on it fatally modify the strangeness and thus condemn its firecat to a permanent slumber? The last line of his *Collected Poems* is 'A new knowledge of reality'; so perhaps the 'reality' to which, all those pages and years earlier, 'Earthy Anecdote' acted as prelude was one that, we see, includes in its package deal the 'strangeness' of the firecat's existence and operations. But, equally, that last line of the final poem outlines – and this is a dread word in Stevens studies – an epistemological position. 'Writing poetry', he once declared to a correspondent (not long after Eliot had been lecturing about the 'hidden depths of feeling'), 'is a conscious activity. While poems may very well occur, they had very much better be caused'; he had told his earlier enquirer that 'Earthy Anecdote,' whilst containing 'no symbolism,' had 'a good deal of theory about it'.[40] What could be a less Keatsian creed – reinforced by those later lines in 'An Ordinary Evening in New Haven' that 'This endlessly elaborating poem/ Displays the theory of poetry,/ As the life of poetry'?[41] This is, perhaps, to offer a different kind of 'strangeness,' one apparently complicit with, rather than hostile to, *post facto* critical recuperations – which is to remind ourselves that 'Earthy Anecdote' contained the bucks as well as the firecat, that *Pale Fire* consists of commentary as well as poem, and that Robert Frost once confessed of his poems, 'So many of them have literary criticism in them – *in* them. And yet I wouldn't admit it. I try to hide it'.[42] The Governess may seem overmotivated, but her interpretative mania is, after all, what enables and indeed constitutes the story: a hypertrophical version of that 'interest' by which, in James's view, facts need to be animated in order to become fiction.

The title of this essay, 'Our never-to-be-slighted "fun,"' is a phrase James uses in his preface to *The Ambassadors*;[43] the word 'fun' occurs several times in the Prefaces, and it may be thought that literary criticism has been particularly bad at finding an appropriate register in which to discuss it. But for James, as a resonant parenthesis in his preface to *The Golden Bowl* makes clear, having 'fun' is not something which excludes the kind of attention to minutiae sometimes tarred with the brush of pedantry:

> (It all comes back to that, to my and your 'fun' – if we but allow the term its full extension: to the production of which no humblest question involved, even to that of the shade of a cadence or the position of a comma, is not richly pertinent.)[44]

An example of the kind of productive detail James might have had in mind is furnished by the unassuming poem, titled 'The Pasture,' which the wily Robert Frost chose, to preface both selected and collected editions of his poetry. Consisting of two quatrains whose inner but not outer lines rhyme, it seems to promise pastoral companionship, a sharing of natural simplicities; but it is worth noticing that the repeated shorter final line, 'I shan't be gone long. – You come too,' is one in which the 'I' and 'You' are separated each time by the chasm of a caesura, whose depth is emphasised by the punctuation which denotes it: a full-stop followed by a dash.[45] To notice this, I'd like to think, is to amplify rather than to abolish the strangeness of a –

to me – increasingly unreassuring little poem. James also defined the act of criticism thus: 'To criticise is to appreciate, to appropriate, to take intellectual possession, to establish in fine a relation with the criticised thing and make it one's own'.[46] For one who deplored the 'great grabbed-up muddle' of Britain's imperial acquisitions that might seem, surprisingly, to describe a violently acquisitive set of procedures; yet this, as well, is part and parcel of 'our never-to-be-slighted "fun."' Seamus Heaney, too, in his essay 'Learning from Eliot,' recalled that as a sixth-former Eliot's seemed a '(p)oetry that was originally beyond you, generating the need to understand and overcome its strangeness'; however, the attempts at critical containment that followed, although they seemed beside the point in their reductive message-making, were part of what eventually made the work 'familiar,' a process which enabled him to set message and music in their proper perspectives: 'I was encouraged to seek for the contour of meaning within the pattern of a rhythm.' Part of what enabled that was the example of Eliot's own criticism, particularly his responses to lines from Dante and Shakespeare; and it is interesting to find Heaney admitting that, although Eliot was not a poet central to his own poetic development as such, 'he did help me to learn what it means to read.'[47]

What I'm trying to assert, then, is the importance of criticism as part of a process of creative reading that is the necessary complement, whether on reader's or author's part, to creative writing. The critic, if you like, is always-already part of the poem, and need not be consigned to the Lazar-house of fiction; indeed, when James diagnosed a weakness in contemporary English writing he reportedly linked it to a critical deficiency: 'He evidently thinks that art is nearly dead among English writers – no criticism, no instinct for what is good.'[48] Criticism, I'd like to think, can be part of the 'fun' of writing and reading, and not a regulatory abridgement of either. I opened by referring to Marianne Moore's 'Poetry,' which she eventually reduced to a mere three lines; she retained the original title but, in enactment of the critical arrogance that has been part of my concern, I want to appropriate it for my own purposes, retitled as 'Literary Criticism': 'I, too, dislike it./ Reading it, however, with a perfect contempt for it, one discovers in/ it, after all, a place for the genuine.'[49] I would, however, like my ending to offer two different visions of the possible outcomes of critical aspiration, respectively suggesting exclusion from and access to interpretative wholeness. I leave it to the reader to choose, or not, from these two writers whose surnames, beginning with 'A,' symbolically return us to the start of alphabeticality, of writing, of 'poems, or notes to poems,' of the whole dreary, exalting 'business of literature.' 'In an epoch like those,' wrote Arnold at the close of his essay on criticism, referring to the times of Aeschylus and

Shakespeare, 'is, no doubt, the true life of literature; there is the promised land, towards which criticism can only beckon. That promised land it will not be ours to enter, and we shall die in the wilderness: but to have desired to enter it, to have saluted it from afar, is already, perhaps, the best distinction among contemporaries.'[50] Against that sense of unentitlement (who would have thought old Arnold to have had so much Kafka in him?), I'd like to refer to the close of Caliban's speech in Auden's 'The Sea and the Mirror,' a work which subtitles itself 'A Commentary on Shakespeare's *The Tempest.*' In doing so, it embraces its – and all literature's – derivative and unoriginal identity, drawn always from a source anterior to itself: the 'I' with which the whole poem ends is, deliberately, an echo. Like Shakespeare's text, Auden's commentary is alert to transformations – not least that of criticism into creativity – and the *coup de théâtre* to which it leads is the metamorphosis of Caliban, whose disposition for cursing transmutes into the poised and polished orotundity of late Henry James. In Auden's ventriloquy the 'salvage and deformed slave' stands centre-stage and assumes the periodical style of one affectionately nicknamed 'the Master,' while poetry and prose exchange identities in an extendedly ecstatic embrace. '(N)ow it is not in spite of [our faults] but with them that we are blessed by that Wholly Other Life from which we are separated by an essential emphatic gulf,' he declares:

> It is just here, among the ruins and bones, that we may rejoice in the perfected Work which is not ours. Its great coherences stand out through our secular blur in all their overwhelmingly righteous obligation; its voice speaks through our muffling banks of artificial flowers and unflinchingly delivers its authentic molar pardon; its spaces greet us with all their grand old prospect of wonder and width; the working charm is the full bloom of the unbothered state; the sounded note is the restored relation.[51]

I wish *I'd* said that . . . What do you mean, 'Get off!'?

Notes

I am presuming that the reader will tolerantly embrace my allusions to Hamlet *and* Emma, *or to the catchphrases of comedians and the critical phraseology of Harold Bloom, without striking the board and calling for exact references.*

1   Marianne Moore, 'Poetry' (1921); here cited in the version from *Selected Poems* (1935), as printed in successive editions of *The Norton Anthology of American Literature.*

2   Samuel Beckett, *Waiting for Godot* (London: Faber & Faber, 1965), p. 75.

3   Franz Kafka, *The Transformation and Other Stories*, tr. Malcolm Pasley

(Harmondsworth: Penguin, 1992), p. 76. The German text of *'Die Verwandlung'* can be accessed via The Kafka Project website.

4 John Gross, *The Rise and Fall of the Man of Letters* (Chicago: Ivan R. Dee, 1992), pp. 205, 206.

5 *Ars est celare artem* means 'art is to conceal art' whilst *ars criticus est monstrare artem* would mean 'critical art is to show art.'

6 Henry James, *The Turn of the Screw and Other Stories* (Harmondsworth: Penguin, 1969), pp. 59–60.

7 *Ibid.*, p. 116. The 'short, smothered life' later cited occurs on p. 24.

8 Matthew Arnold, 'The Function of Criticism at the Present Time,' in *The Oxford Anthology of English Literature* (London & New York: Oxford University Press, 1973), Vol. II, p. 1003.

9 *Selected Prose of T.S. Eliot*, ed. Frank Kermode (London: Faber & Faber, 1975), pp. 72–3.

10 *Ibid.*, p. 53.

11 *Ibid.*, p. 73

12 *See* Valerie Eliot (ed.), *The Waste Land: a facsimile and transcript* (London: Faber & Faber, 1971), pp. 76–7.

13 T.S. Eliot, *The Use of Poetry and the Use of Criticism* (London: Faber & Faber, 1964), pp. 118–19.

14 For these phrases, see *Letters of John Keats*, ed. Robert Gittings (Oxford: Oxford University Press, 1970), pp. 37, 64, 61.

15 *Selected Prose of T.S. Eliot*, pp. 148, 150.

16 *Letters of Wallace Stevens*, ed. Holly Stevens (London: Faber & Faber 1967), p. 361.

17 *Writers at Work* (The Paris Review Interviews, Seventh Series), ed. George Plimpton (Harmondsworth: Penguin, 1988), p. 156.

18 Frank Kermode, *The Genesis of Secrecy* (Cambridge, MA & London: Harvard University Press, 1979), p. 3.

19 Frank Kermode, *Essays on Fiction 1971–82* (London: Routledge & Kegan Paul, 1983), pp. 158, 160, 182.

20 Alexander Pope, *An Essay on Criticism*, ll. 105–7, in *The Poems of Alexander Pope*, ed. John Butt (London: Methuen, 1965), p. 147.

21 Milan Kundera, *The Art of the Novel*, tr. Linda Asher (London: Faber & Faber, 1988), p. 140 (both quotations).

22 *Ibid.*, pp. 160, 132. For Kundera's comment on Gregor Samsa, see p. 112.

23 *Rebecca West: A Celebration* (Harmondsworth: Penguin, 1978), p. 411.

24 W.H. Auden, *Selected Poems*, ed. Edward Mendelson (London: Faber & Faber, 1979), p. 100.

25 Anthony Easthope, *Englishness and National Culture* (London & New York: Routledge, 1999), p. 142 (both quotations).

26 Kermode, *Essays on Fiction*, p. 95.

27 Henry James, *The Art of the Novel* (New York & London: Charles Scribner's Sons, 1962), p. 172.

28 Kermode, *Essays on Fiction*, p. 183.
29 Arnold, 'The Function of Criticism,' p. 1014.
30 Bob Dylan, 'Spirit on the Water', from the album *Modern Times* (2006).
31 Kermode, *Essays on Fiction*, pp. 95, 128.
32 Rebecca West, *Henry James* (London: Nisbet, 1916), pp. 107–8.
33 Q.D. Leavis in *A Selection from SCRUTINY*, compiled by F.R. Leavis (Cambridge: Cambridge University Press, 1968), vol. I, p. 11.
34 *Collected Poems of Wallace Stevens* (London: Faber & Faber, 1955), p. 326.
35 *Henry David Thoreau*, Library of America (Cambridge University Press, 1985), pp. 580–1.
36 Vladimir Nabokov, *Pale Fire* (Harmondsworth: Penguin, 1973), p. 25.
37 Vladimir Nabokov, *The Original of Laura* (London: Penguin Classics, 2009), p. xxi.
38 *Collected Poems of Wallace Stevens*, p. 3.
39 Nabokov, *Pale Fire*, pp. 164–5.
40 *Letters of Wallace Stevens*, pp. 204, 274.
41 *Collected Poems of Wallace Stevens*, p. 486.
42 Quoted in Richard Poirier, *Robert Frost: The Work of Knowing* (Oxford & New York: Oxford University Press, 1977), p. 86.
43 James, *The Art of the Novel*, p. 324.
44 *Ibid.*, p. 345.
45 *The Poetry of Robert Frost*, ed. E.C. Lathem (London: Jonathan Cape, 1971), p. 1.
46 James, *The Art of the Novel*, p. 155.
47 Seamus Heaney, *Finders Keepers: Selected Prose 1971–2001* (London: Faber & Faber, 2002), pp. 28, 34, 37.
48 Quoted in Simon Nowell-Smith, *The Legend of the Master* (Oxford: Oxford University Press, 1985), p. 167.
49 *The Complete Poems of Marianne Moore*, 'Definitive Edition, with the Author's Final Revisions' (New York: Macmillan, 1981), p. 36.
50 Arnold, 'The Function of Criticism at the Present Time,' pp. 1018–19.
51 Auden, *Selected Poems*, pp. 173–4.

The Poetry of Marginalization

John Goodby

'The Critic as Artist' – well, absolutely. But
then again, absolutely not. Or, rather, while

all artistic activity bespeaks prior critical thought,
shouldn't criticism only with caveats aplenty ever

claim to be 'creative.' Though here I
stand, a university lecturer, earning my crust

writing critical articles and books, with poetry
strictly a sideline, appearing to sign up

to the outdated Romantic hokum by which
the genius and his/her expositor are different

in kind. Which is one reason why,
blatantly ripping off Bob Perelman's poem

'The Marginalization of Poetry,' a paper written
in couplets and presented at a Comparative

Literature conference in San Diego in 1991,
this paper is a poem, that is

both, or perhaps it's neither.[1] Its status
as poetry is probably most disputable, so

let me observe at the outset that
I'm writing in couplets, each consisting of

a pair of seven-word lines (Perelman used
six), and these don't establish a 'natural'

rhythm, although I am pausing slightly at
the end of each line. Perhaps, then,

this is the kind of chopped-up prose
that gets poetry a bad name, although

(as Perelman explained) to set a flush
left and irregular right margin inevitably interrupted

me as events as I was writing
by making me think or write something

other than I had in mind. Despite
revision, that problem (or that opportunity) still

recurs every seven words. This perhaps exemplifies
the friction between the critical and artistic

impulses we are here to consider. Meaning
that for criticism the point is generally

making an argument; prose, which is indifferent
to margins, is its medium, even when

it concerns the critic as artist, according
to the discourse of the academic profession –

No salary gradation without citation, and which
leading journal would accept an article in

verse on, say, the senses of inversion
in Edwardian fiction? Lack of a sense

of language as a material medium rules
here, since subjection to norms confers certain

kinds of approval, reward, prestige, and power.
'Aha,' someone will object, 'can you *really*

lump anything written in prose and oppose
it to anything written in lines? Woolf

is a poet or she's nothing; what
about Joyce or Malcolm Lowry? Can they

be usefully discussed under the same heading
as Enid Blyton or *The Radio Times*?

And by homogenising 'prose' in this way
aren't you essentialising poetry? Of course I

may be. But lineation is the prime
marker of the poetic, a visible, premeditated

break with the sentence as dominant unit
of composition, a visible and continual reminder

that different kinds of sense may assert
themselves against the sentence and its

hierarchies of grammatical subordination. While much that
is lineated and called poetry is piss-poor,

it has pointedly chosen to be piss-poor
poetry and not piss-poor something else according

to certain longstanding, unignorable and powerful discursive
codes, as Woolf, Joyce and Lowry chose

to be regarded as prose (prose poems
are Another Matter). Still, some critical writing

signals its aspirations to the creative realm –
although that is a too-loaded word – whether

as fiction, poem, or a hybrid mixture
of both. Usually it deploys modernist / postmodernist

strategies – parataxis par example, collage, parallel texts
wordplay. But if Kristeva's *Stabat Mater*, Derrida's

Glas, the *hommelette* and *père sevère* of Lacan
take their cues from Mallarmé, or Joyce

or Apollinaire, and some royal flushes uncannily
take their cue from these in turn,

as Geoff Ward says, 'even the advance
guard of university criticism (*soi disant*) usually

ignores contemporary poetry in favour of the
distant past.'[2] There's nothing wrong with Jack/ques

meeting London, of course, although as Ward
goes on to say, it's only too

easy to out the hidden subtexts here –
the real question is what to do

with a poet like, say, Frank O'Hara,
who has already made deconstruction *avant la*

lettre part of his practice. Not only
does O'Hara happily splurge 'ambiguities, incoherences,
    discontinuities,

ellipses', he thematises them, and then goes
on to mix this kind of material

with realist-representational stuff, metaphysical with anti-metaphysical
    timbres,
in a way which contains its own

critique of critics aspiring to create – hyper-active
use of hyphens, brackets, slashes, and weak-

end puns isn't going to cut it
here, just as there is more linguistic

jouissance, not to mention more economy, beauty
and poise in one *Wake* paragraph than

the whole of *Neat Chunny*, in which
an ingrown mandarinese seems mesmerised by its

clever-cleverness into believing it has something aesthetically
original to utter. Such belatedness is linked

to deconstruction's canonical conservatism – its practitioners rarely
know that dozens of poets have been

performing dizzying variations on their basic themes
for half a century, because most accept

Faber and Faber's claim that their backlist
equals twentieth century poetry; *mettre en abime*

here seems to mean lack of curiosity
and deafness concerning your own advice concerning

the operations of literary power. Which brings
me to a book by a keynote

speaker at this conference, Valentine Cunningham, namely
his *British Writers of the Thirties*. This

is a sprightly and in some ways
useful account of the field, and yet

as far from the problematising of critical-creative
boundaries as could be conceived; more important,

his book advances an Anglo- and Oxbridge-centric
account of the era wholly antagonistic to

almost any kind of seriously playful writing
where boundaries come under scrutiny (though that

is an awful choice of verb). That
is, he makes a point of trashing

the *Wake* and glibly dissing Dylan Thomas
in his study, which – like Samuel Hynes's –

erases experiment from the decade, and pre-emptively
dismisses the Apocalypse and New Romantic heirs

of Modernism in the 1940s. This reinforces
the dominant narrative of mainstream English poetry

and literary history, of smooth transition between
Thirties social-realist poetry and the Movement across

some unspeakable mess — the myth, in Andrew
Crozier's famous 1983 essay 'Thrills and Frills',

which followed the crushing of a later
recrudescence of native modernism in the 1960s

and early 1970s. Here Crozier argues compellingly
that the dominant poetic tradition is one

in which 'the authoritative self, discoursing in
a world of banal, empirically derived objects

and relations, depends on . . . metaphor and simile
for poetic vitality. These figures are conceptually

subordinate to the empirical reality of self
and objects, yet they constitute the nature

of the poem.' As a result, English
poetry has become 'a reserve for small

verbal thrills, a daring little frill round
the hem of normal discourse.'[3] Simplistic it

might be, largely true it remains, for
all the recent lip-service to pluralism, slight

blurrings at the Salt and Shearsman edges
of the poetry publishing industry. What's required,

still, is more recognition of the Welsh
and Scottish dimensions of British poetry, maybe,

not in the usual ethnic theme-park terms,
but an acknowledgement of what Thomas discovered,

astonishingly, in his teens; how to arrest
readerly perception temporarily at the poem's surface

by the fizzing energy of the words –
not permanently held there, as may now

disablingly be done – so the imaginative space
we gain immediately afterwards is imbued with

'features of the barrier,' in Peter Riley's
phrase, a figuration pushed beyond the bounds

of rational location and poetry set up
as a metalanguage, something that treats language

as materials of the world, like paint
or marble, autonomous, 'an addition to

the world', not a commentary on or
reflection of it.[4] Thomas's images and logics

which link them cannot be verified by
an appeal to the world independent of

the poem (this is what pisses off
those who work in the critical discourse

which insists that poetry observe the dominant
contractual usages of languages and commonsensical

meanings of its time). Figures in Thomas
and W. S. Graham become themselves objects

of attention while retaining traces of their
representative function sufficient to keep a purchase

on empirical and social realities. To follow
Thomas's insistence that his poems 'be read

literally,' as Andrew Crozier notes, is 'to
commit a serious assault upon the empirical

sanctions of meaning. What is crucial is
that language's own inherent instability, its inability

to pin down meaning, is released by
such a practice, while the poet allows

himself to be acted upon by language
rather than demonstrating an (anyway illusory) mastery

over it. Not to mention the anticipation
of Derridean 'slippage,' moral issues are involved

in treating language as a collaborator rather
than as a slave of some ironic

panoptic intelligence, as in Auden; the fixed
authoritative self is replaced by one more

fluid, more marginal. This is the legacy
developed by Graham, who refused to recant

his earliest poetry ('Listen. Put on morning')
but in the one which stretches back

through through him to Thomas, who is
the 'King of Wales' of 'Implements in

Their Places.' And while Graham is more
than Thomas plus Heidegger, credit where credit

is due. It is Thomas from whom
the Paul Celan of *Mohn und Gedächtnis*

learnt, which should give those who read
the poetry through the legend pause, their

bad Leavisite slippage from text to author
as Kate Belsey puts it. Beyond Graham,

of course, are the likes of Denise
Riley and some of the most important

poetry of the last thirty years. And
it is such a refiguring of the history

of figuration in poetry that should inform
our deliberations here, our pedagogy if we

teach creative writing, our critical representation
of modern British poetry, if that's what

we do, our own practice as writers.
My own poetry (yes, we finally arrive

at that crass predictable terminus!) hamfistedly reflects
on the different traditions I've sketched out

unconsciously manifest, from a big Arvon prize
and publication by Faber and *Poetry Review*

to the dawning sense, around 2000, that
this was not what I wanted poetry

to be, was a tithe of its true
possibility, following encounters with the incomparable chopped

Sonnets of Ted Berrigan (how much more
and dizzying sense there than the sedately

'crumbled' sonnets of Paul Muldoon, another favourite),
following soundings of Los Trios Rileys, John

James and John Wieners, Barry MacSweeney, Geraldine
Monk, Ric Caddell. (Lift the mute, let

The full note sound, however imitative unfettered
In some new way!) And so some first

efforts at cut-up in *Illennium*,[5] and cageian
mesostic in *uncaged sea*,[6] a grateful revenge

after working on Dylan Thomas for years,
and the long line of 'Mine arch

never marble . . . ,' which those of you with
an ear for these things will already

have discerned contains 'menarch' and 'monarch',
the real and Leonard Cohen's marble arch,

not to mention the infamous Sophie Dahl
Opium advert, and goes on (this was

my aim and excuse anyway) to under 'mine'
its appropriative male ego.[7] More bizarre, perhaps,

is the phonetic transcription of Pushkin's 'Autumn'
into English, following Zukofsky and Caddell, in

which, somehow, the detergents *Bloo* and *Daz*
become agents.[8] Or how about taking Andrew

Motion's anodyne, offensively consolatory elegy for victims
of 9/11 and switching its nouns for

those nine and then eleven places distant
from them in the O.E.D.?[9] And yet

under the heading of the O'Haran 'mix',
the refusal of any one mode, desire

for the former mode returns, begging indulgence,
forgiveness, use. I may object to our

new Laureate's glib phrasemaking in her poem
'Prayer' – 'truth enters our hearts,' say, 'Leaving

his youth' – any dud phrase that like
so much mainstream or 'High Street' poetry

makes us see what the poet means
before we really know, at the level

of rhythm, timbre, colour, lexis, what actually
they feel – but at the same time

forge them knowingly to make my own
somewhat saccharine prize-winners, another strategy of obliquity

which, if I win enough before judging-panels
cop on, might make a collection of

their own. Call it *Judge for Your
Selves, In/Sincere, Sentiment for Cash*; even though

I like them, too, their shallowness hurts,
the obvious nostalgic heartstring lexis in 'vast',

'slide', 'cool blue dusk' – ah, the uplift! –
in 'The Uncles' being a case in

point,[10] that blatant teary water and memory
gush of realism in '21ˢᵗ October, 1966'

(the date of the Aberfan Disaster if
you want to know).[11] Yet, why tough

it out that I don't do shallow,
sweet, the poems my mother would have

liked? How technocratically macho would that be,
how Cambridge Marxist Prefect preachy as McSweeney

I think put it? These are just
the way my split, spilt, torn subject

happens to be superfly on its dancefloor
at present, and parataxis is fine but

sometimes an anagram of a prat's axis.
Let the poetry prize culture, its commodified

lyric, with its sepia grievance posing as
critique, dissolve in self-adulation and lack

of relevance. I still await days when
in my scribblings at least the different

modes and strategies meet their sutre, their
k/night in shining amour, the unstable fusion

momentarily bringing the broken lines of outlandish
particles together under a mountain – now

there's a trope that has its cake
and eats it if ever there was.

Notes

1   Bob Perelman, 'The Marginalization of Poetry,' *The Marginalization of Poetry:
    Language, Writing and History* (Princeton University Press: Princeton, NJ,
    1996), pp. 3–10.
2   [T]he applicability of . . . deconstructive methods to contemporary poems such
    as [James] Schuyler's is questionable. A poem by O'Hara beginning:

The root   an acceptable condition
ochre   except meaning-dream partly
where the will falters   a screw polished
a whole pair of shutters   you saw it
I went in the door   the umbrella

Seems similarly not to be in need of a Yale key to unlock its "hidden" tendency
to generate "ambiguities, incoherences, discontinuities, ellipses." . . . Far from
wishing to suspend a recognition of that slippage, which would leave the poem
in the thrall of a transcendentalist aesthetics wilfully blind to the rhetoric of
temporality, O'Hara insists on "differential play" and, by the arrangement of
the words on the page, a fundamental deferral / differentiation of any settle-
ment of the wayward energies straining around the bar of the sign. However .
. . [t]here exist other poems by O'Hara and Schuyler that know about that
groundbreaking detonation of signifiers, but which deploy it as one device in
the armoury, while the most exploratory aspects of the writing move on into
a territory which is as hard to characterize as it is vital for their practice. . . .
[T]here may well in the work of any artist be a shifting co-existence of deep
and layered-space forms, metaphysical and anti-metaphysical energies.
    [I]n O'Hara's "How to Get There" obscurity, ambiguity, discontinuity and
the rest are not merely available to the post-Surrealist poet as part of the
armoury of poetic devices; they are the thematic substances on which the work
meditates explicitly. What, then as alert readers, should we look for in the
margins of O'Hara's poetry? Is there a Victorian social-realist novel trying to
get out? And where are the margins of an O'Hara poem anyway? The differential play of language which literary theory strives to expose in texts such as
those treated by J. Hillis Miller in *Fiction and Repetition* or Paul de Man in
Allegories of Reading, Conrad or Hardy, Proust or Rousseau, is so much to the

fore in an oeuvre such as O'Hara's that it needs no special argument or exposure.

[The] blurring of the distinctions between criticism and literature is a common insistence – perhaps, in fact, the only ubiquitous insistence – among those critics whose names have been associated with deconstruction. Their discoveries along parallel tracks concerning the powers of rhetoric and the illusory nature of any claim to a disinterested position have led to a shared elevation of "style" beyond any merely decorative or emphatic function. . . . Ironically, however, the workings of difference may need to be traced inside the dubious assertion that the "difference" between literature and criticism is "delusive." That consummation was devoutly wished by de Man, but the dream of his rhetoric represses their separate development, rooted in the pedagogical associations of criticism as against the marginal positioning of Romantic and modern poetry in society, and (to say the same thing in a different way), the brazen self-distancing of poetry from normal linguistic usage. . . . The critic who quotes from O'Hara rewrites his poetry by excerpting, a parasitical attachment; and dead poets depend on live readers for the survival of their work. But no matter how complex or shifting these relationships, poetic and critical language remain as different in kind as ivy and bark.'

Geoff Ward, *Statutes of Liberty: The New York School of Poets* (Basingstoke: Palgrave, 2001), pp. 29, 32, 67–9.

3 Andrew Crozier, 'Thrills and frills: poetry as figures of empirical lyricism', Alan Sinfield, ed., *Society and Literature 1945–1970* (London: Methuen, 1983), pp. 199–233.

4 Peter Riley reviews W. S. Graham, *New Collected Poems, Jacket* 26 (October 2004), p. 1.

5 From *Illennium:*

IX

Waging Just But Only Just War from two miles up
is like making love to a beautiful woman
'If anyone's going to get hurt it has to be me and
Progress implies it. That succumbs
so Nia & yet so far. Weak
in proportion to power, brutal in its indiscriminations,
a Massive embrace of *The Week-End*
Michelle Scragg Mumbles
for a pearl. I am no thing but affect
out of her cycling shorts hopefully with armed doughnuts.'
So we take but three steps from feathers to iron –
Adulter's dark warmth. A taxi's kryptonite-green dash-glow
and swinging furry dice hurry
to Oystermouth's glittery necklace of bay, & fur below.

XVII

If the person deposed touched the other person's   West
South-Wets inside & out   Drenched
Under the Spelling Wall   a grin-creased filtrum
in wine-dark   that 'Arse!', at Parkway,
from behind!   it scares me that I feel so evil
That is what married men do
the embrace of *The Week-End*   genitalia
Could this never have not-been?
Supernal grinning candour   It is 12.35 p.m.
Sunday, 2 November   ahead of wersh paella.
The Avon Gorge glows jonquil as a Scillies' pre-Spring,
the superhuman cries of the sea
taxi's kryptonite-green
'If you aren't doing it now you won't ever do it.'

> *Illennium* (Exeter: Shearsman, 2010)

6   From *uncaged sea*

golD tithings barren
Off bY
  soiLs
the grAss
  wiNter floods of

faded yard, Teach Me
      threAds Of doubt
  houses wheRe
      signaL
  sap rAn
                Is zero in
that flashed the hedgeS

STature by seedy
fro wHere
  Or
the Mouths
  lAme the air
they with the Simple

                Death, we ring
their fireflY
      belLs . . .

> John Goodby, *uncaged sea* (Brighton: Waterloo Press, 2008), p. 15.

7 'Mine arch never marble . . .'

Mine arch never marble, my on the My oh my, O
pium of the pupil, my sofia Dahling, my purr loined,
my bazooka bust tear, badinager of the wound, my big
best palooka, my sloe hand, my slay belle, my covet
ed covert, my muslined peach waist wasp, my un
lisping eventhong, my all of a huh head, Durdle my
Dor you, my a per se paragon, choux-choo boog
aloo nachts, my M press of mad rabbits, my White Lad
derette to the full stocking star, my fuscia skirty, sac
Red Love (Prof âne my Luve), my spined pen gwyn clas
sic, my www.handbaggista, bramble cottager, my
go via gloucester, swindon, andover, and over my A
303 towards yeovil, my scorched lightshade, Ma Jolie
laide asleepe with Giaconda grin, my face chawer, my
shout, my round, my Primerose Hill strider, my horrors
of tempdom without alyssum, my chattage, you peel
my yore pelt off, my jolly groan giant, exactamente
überbabe of top banana, malaysia my knight in shining
amour, my sketch of the highest magnitude, a tuna s
teak-seared, my dear breath, deep sweetedness, my and-
rotikolobomassophile dream, my key flinger down
in Crawford Street, in Little Sweden, ova my awesome
striped awning, pat Ron of greasy spoons, my waterbed
emporium, Ma rocco letch shop, beef heart havoc
king with the feng shui, my fyi, my ebtg, my play misty
unmusty, my Chardonnay shilling, my floating left
test icicle, my completely floaty date, in right my old
twitch, my old right strop, about my all and sundry,
my Sunday papers at midnight Saturday, my cello-
backed asbo lute, my Canto CXIII and coming ready
or not, my Thou by dark and Du by day, my situ, my sat
you, my satay, my galumph sashay, lower case my
caser, my stone floods, methinks, my monged out post
card, my swimming with monkeys, one of you in my
high heels, my E rhotic nude ashtray astray, my Cant
onese valise of fireworks on a millennium lawn, cult
ure is out and reserved for the next 1000000000 years ho
roar, my Countless of Qui, my conditions of applaus
ibility mr sinfield might say, my young manyoung man,
the azure adze in a field adazzle, not, my beehive hut
ment some total trevor of a day, that trussed fund famili
ar, smarting with my brilliance, my Bhabhling brook, my
britpo pinuppance, my quick squince, my perineum

fingherling, quelle palaver la mienne, my hi hon, hi ho,
my adamant à demain, JUICYMALUCID, my Barbie
of the breezeblock, my hallelu yah yah, my ketch
up with oven chips, tobacco-brown beau weau-it's-all-
my eye, just in time was justice intime, my joue
ster adjuster, my leman 'n' lime I'm, my phallic individ
uation of the single line, embraceletable you pour bais
ermine, heart's rhyme, mynage de tout adultère, car
pe dieming all over the place, my try me true, my peart
Mehitable unbeatable, breaut bute minger-damner, peer
lass jesse Mutt and Jeff's majorly leg muscles, my
flatter-flutter, compleat with wine racks and funghi por
cini, my study/living room is dar blue, very gorgeouse,
and what the bloody hell is experimental writing any
weigh my Shah-owner, bus-holloa with turner's arms,
my minder, bouncer blesséd, my surely chef mocker
astride his Vespa, my toepath emboss'd all and buffy,
my mean green chicken curry, my Thai gruess I don't
want to know but something dark and bloody in me do
es, my Regal purple, jazz mine unlearning curves, snor
ter on kearney's postnationalist ire land, my ingress
of Ingres, Mai Lieda, Venus de Mylilo, my Black
Rod's Garden Entrancer, my hoving of not having-to,
my luff love, my wholed me but not holed, my calm
ness, my cadence, my fou fighter, my whirlybrilliant,
my Morris Minor dancer, depth less me mine all unmine.

Poetry Wales, 42: 3 (January 2007) 3–4.

8   *From* 'Autumn'

> *What does not then enter my drowsy mind?*
> — *Derzhavin*

1.

October is a nasty pill – is a rich author racket,
Puts lead in A-listers, is a nag each voiced vet inveighs;
Doc Neil, has he any? Claddagh ragger promises, yet
Jeer at ya; eschew veggies a melon sees as a rich *Eh?*
No pride is a style, sauce-head, my pop is shit;
Voters hear Paula sock it too, you ('s for ye!)
Estranged it; O see me out West! Channels have a 'V'.
He videoed it lies of a kiss never shed, die bravo.

2.

Temporary my para. Ian halloo, *Bloo* vest, knee
Kitchener money at a pail; void, Gaz – best by Anne Boleyn;
Crave brought it schist vain task, O you sten-nanny.
Sirrah *voyou* zee, Moy labeller, yeah; dabble in
Loo *Bloo*, yeah; yaw, snigger; the priest steal any
Cackle-y orgy; beg sanity's Páidrig goy Bistro Vollen,
Cogged a pod's sob alum, sacked Rita is vag-
Ina and Ricky's kismet, pill layer id Roge!

* * * *

11.

In my sleeve Gulliver volley you to save at baggier,
He riff meal orgy have stretchy him beg it,
He pally to cypress yachts yak perry, per rack be Magyar,
Minuter – is Stickies' very bad nap architect.
Tack dream let Ned be Jim-curable of Ned vision, flaggier,
No *chi* – mattress if drew kidder you to see ya, pal zit
Berk, of knees – he parries an *adiles*, vet rap polly;
Grow madder divine ill as Iras's skate volley.

12.

Plea vote. Kid *Daz* Nam pleat? . . .

Poetry *Wales*, 43: 3 (Winter 2008), 32–4.

9 'The Voidage Lives' is made from Andrew Motion's poem, 'The Voices Live',
written as a response to the mobile phone messages left by the victims of 9/11:

 The voices live which are the voices lost:
we hear them, and we answer, or we try
but words are nervous when we need them most
and stutter, stop, or dully slide away,

so everything they mean to summon up
is always just too far, just out of reach,
unless our memories give time the slip
and learn the lesson that heart-wisdoms teach;

of how in grief we find a way to keep
the dead beside us as our time goes on –
invisible and silent, but the deep
foundation of ourselves, our cornerstone.

 I substituted most of the words in this dubiously consolatory elegy with others
taken either 9 or 11 places away from them (in either direction) in the *Compact*

OED in order to see whether Motion's poem might yield something more interesting. Lines were trimmed in some cases in order to preserve the iambic lull
of the original, and 'always' dropped from the second stanza. *Te* is defined as
'the essence of Tao in all things' and 'in Confucianism, and in extended use,
moral virtue.'

The Voidage Lives

 The voidage lives whid is the vol-au-vent:
we heave it, and we answerphone, or try
but wordiness is nervous when we need,
and Stygian, stoopid, dunnish, slides awry,

so everting they mealmouth to summise
is juxtaposed too farley, just reach-down-me,
unlegged our menacings give time the sloe
and learn the let that heated wiselings *te*;

of howlet in grieve we find a weapon
the debacle besot us as our timekeeper –
invulnerable and sillabub, but the de-
fect fouled of ourseltzers, our cornfactor.

10 'The Uncles'

 Uncles, talking the camshaft or the gimbal connected
to a slowly oscillating crank. The Uncles Brickell,
Swarfega kings, enseamed with swarf and scobs, skin
measeled with gunmetal but glistening faintly, loud
in the smoke. Lithe and wiry above the lathe, milling out
a cylinder to a given bore. Uncles, pencil-stubs at their ears,
spurning ink, crossing sevens like émigré intellectuals,
measuring in thous and thirty-secondths (scrawled
on torn fag-packets); feinting with slide rules, racing,
but mild not as mild steel. Pockets congested, always. Uncles
with dockets for jobs, corners transparent with grease,
with a light machine oil. Time-served, my Uncles, branch-
ing out into doorhandles, grub-screws and the brass bits
that hold the front of the motor case to the rear flange
of the mounting panel. Release tab. Slightly hard of hearing
now, the Uncles, from the din of the shop, slowly nodding.
Uncles in 'Red Square'; uncles swapping tolerance gauges,
allan keys, telephone numbers, deals and rank commun-
ism. Forefingers describing arcs and cutting angles. White
and milky with coolants and lubricants, mess of order. Never
forgetting to push a broom. The missing half-finger, not

really missed any longer, the banjo-hand gone west. My
Uncles still making a go of mower blades, on the road
at their age; offering cigars at Christmas. Uncanny if
encountered in visors, overalls, confounding nephews
in dignity of their calling, their epoch-stewed tea. Stand
a spoon in all their chamfered years, cut short or long. Uncles
immortal in the welding shed, under neon, lounge
as the vast doors slide to a cool blue dusk. My Uncles.

> (1ˢᵗ prize winner [£5,000], Cardiff International Poetry Competition,
> 2006)

11   '21ˢᵗ October, 1966'
They followed their stolen water for miles, the Birmingham
Welsh. Why not? It swelled Rough Road's square tumulus
to which it had flowed 86 *miles without being pumped,*
through tunnels and pipes from the mountains of mid-Wales
the plaque said, and so should flow from their taps too, from Huw's
and Glyn's in Endhill, whose Dad carved lovespoons for *hiraeth,*
as from our own. And it is a little Wales I increasingly
reflect on through the years' glassed depths, the painful, jewelled beauty of a carboy garden, chalk-dusted desks,
endlessly handwritten *m*s, broad beans in damp jam-jars, root-
hairs preternaturally distinct, as if engraved. I overlook it all, now, the crown of Bandywood Crescent – beeches,
wheeling rooks, a vertigo of clouds – and Kingsland Juniors,
fathoms clear in a crystalline drowned valley, as clear
as their escape from mine and furnace with the fervour
impressed on our soft inland minds, thrown into relief
by exile. Mrs Scott, thick-lipped, throaty-sibylline, invokes
her father's hen-coops in Merthyr; Mr Thomas, grinning
through his wife's childlessness, his cowlick falling, his plimsol
for what we called a pump half-heartedly falling, unlike
dark-jowled, beastly Mr Williams's expert welting
action (his beer-and-Woodbines breath a bardic tenor
hoarse across stud-stamped wastes). Is that his string vest, or
an elaborate, blurring retrospect? How, at this distance, anyway to see the hymn-book bound in green, sing a green hill
so distant it is black, below which three boys sat on the playground wall, witnesses recalled, before the tremor minutes
after morning prayers; as we were opening desks and books
together, monitors still at their tasks, milk from the gate trembling in steel crates to classes ignorant of the pulsing well-
spring of the tip; our big clock also oozing towards nine-
seventeen, hands telling time's gravity, a hill waters move

that should move from a hill unbearable as love, reservoirs
filled like our heads with hurt bent in dark rows next day, salt
tears we shed learnt from them also, or do I imagine all of this?

(1st Prize Winner [£200], *New Welsh Review* / Aberystwyth University
Poetry Competition, 2009)

Rage, Rage Against the Dying of Delight

Steven Connor

I write and have written about a range of different kinds of topic, in a range of different professional styles and tones of voice. Because some of the things I have written relate to works of literature, I am sometimes described as a critic. This is odd, now I come to think about it. For, although most people in the humanities regard the capacity for 'critical thinking' as an important part of their range of intellectual accomplishments and therefore an important transferable skill to transfer to their students, not every kind of thinking and writing qualifies its exponent as a 'critic' of the subject in question. Even those, philosophers and sociologists mostly, I suppose, who are apt to regard themselves as engaging in 'critique,' are not generally called 'critics' as a result. Historians are not critics of history, geographers are not critics of space, sociologists are not critics of social forms, and art historians are not necessarily critics of art, in the way that writers about literature are said to be critics of literature.

To be a critic, or to have a critical relation to one's object, means that there is a certain *agon* or antagonism in one's relation to one's object of study. There is always a kind of struggle for supremacy between the work and the one who accounts for it critically. Even the arts of admiration contain and conceal the possibility of denunciation. Nowadays, only journalists, or academics who rely upon the newspapers for their income, really pretend to be engaged in the work of critical judgement, in the old-fashioned sense of a weighing of the merits and demerits of a piece of literary writing. In the academic world, literary criticism has come to mean the forming or inhabiting of argumentative positions, within a field of intellectual antagonism and dispute that is simultaneously a market of professional standing and advantage.

For most other academic pursuits, there are critical relations, not so much between scholars and their objects of study, as between different scholars themselves. Learning and conflict seem to have been indissoluble for centuries. To gain knowledge is not a neutral act of entering into knowing; it is, in some sense, always to win (gaining and *gagner*), to triumph, and therefore, implicitly, to try to create a loser. How can I be right unless there is a wrong to be righted, how can I be in the right unless there is somebody who is in the wrong? Perhaps, indeed, all it will take for me to be in the right will be my demonstration that somebody else is wrong.

Even today the language of critical and philosophical disputation is combative, even martial, through and through. One advances propositions, and defends positions. Beneath the surface of every academic discussion is a scarcely concealed military-juridical apparatus of assault, arraignment, defiance and self-defence, of advancing, retreating, allies and adversaries, struggle, striving, victory and defeat. That the site of a university is called a campus suggests less camp than campaigning. The central term in academic thinking and writing is argument, the meaning of which has shifted from being what appearances or evidences do (the presence of a fever argues an infection) to what human parties do with each other. It is no accident that *Debate* shares an etymological root with battle and combat. There is a seemingly indissoluble relation between truth and torture.[1] Thinking seems inseparable from disputation – literally the pulling apart of thinking. There is no putting of questions without the putting of something or somebody to the question.

Few philosophers have taken the martial law of academic life as seriously, or declined its solicitations as single-mindedly as Michel Serres, who even refused to wear the ceremonial sword that tradition required on his election to the Academie Française.[2] Serres is roused to intellectual anger only to denounce the aggression that is threaded through academic life:

> I have spent enough of my life on warships and in lecture halls to testify before youth, which already knows, that there is no difference between the purely animal or hierarchical customs of the playground, military tactics, and academic conduct: the same terror reigns in the covered playground, in front of torpedo launchers, and on campus, this fear that can pass for the fundamental passion of intellectual workers.[3]

The other side of fear, and often its twin too, is anger, which may be regarded as the libido or tonus of academic thinking, the alloying of thought to will, force and always more or less aggressive intent. Anger is always present in the will-to-thought.

We think far too little about anger, I think. This is an omission and a pity, since so much of thinking itself seems dipped in and driven by it. Peter Sloterdijk is right to see in anger the great blind spot of psychoanalysis and historical sociology.[4] Anger, says Sloterdijk, is to be regarded as the expression of *thymos*, the drive to self-assertion. In a sense, anger is simply will attempting to overcome resistance. But if anger is to be identified with will, we seem also to have inherited from the Greeks a sense that that will comes from elsewhere than us. Less likely than a Hector or Achilles to experience anger as a kind of divine afflatus, we nevertheless accord it the special kind of cautious respect due to something that has arrived rather than arisen, that has come from elsewhere. Anger is always to be referred to a cause. The idea of free-floating anxiety, of a dread unable to identify its cause, and anxiously looking about for objects to which to attach itself, seems familiar and credible enough. It seems similarly easy to conceive of desire detached from its real object, and perhaps detached from all specific objects – thus a desire-to-desire, or desirousness. But it seems much harder to accept or account for endogenous anger. We are more likely in such cases to assume that the rage is displaced from some primary occasion or object, that has for some reason become inaccessible to the raging subject. It seems obvious and unquestionable to us that if somebody is angry, their anger must have been provoked by something, even if we suspect that we may sometimes be better placed than they to identify this cause.

This suggests in turn that we feel we or others are always in some sense right to be angry, even if we are wrong about the cause. When we persuade ourselves or others that we are wrong to feel anger, when we are encouraged, as we say, to manage our anger, it is often by modifying our understanding of its cause, revealing that what had seemed an intolerable affront or injustice to us is not after all so intolerable or unjust. It is much rarer to find somebody who feels that, even though they are undeniably the victim of affront or injustice, they nevertheless have no anger to manage. Anger always has a reason, and where there is a palpable reason for anger, its absence strikes us as unreasonable, immoral, perhaps cowardly, even a shade pathological. We may not be in the right about our anger, since we can always have misjudged the reality or seriousness or intendedness of a wrong or affront, but anger itself is always in the right – in that it always operates within the field of moral force and assertiveness.

Anger is also, more simply, in the right because anger is so often a way of putting yourself in the right, a way of asserting justification in its absence. Like many other apparently spontaneous or unreflective states of feeling, anger is the forming of a judgement. Anger may be regarded as the primary expression of will, as the insistence that my desire is in the right, and that it is right that I should have what I desire. Anger exists in order to give itself the right to be, precisely by being in and for the right. Anger may seem as though it breaks in upon us from elsewhere, beyond or beneath rational choosing, but the impersonality of anger is precisely what the subject of anger, the one carried by it to an incandescent peak of self-presence, uses to justify itself to itself. I can affirm myself as I assert my absolute rights and dignities over those of others, and even over myself, since I may mistake where my real interests lie when I am not purified by anger, only via the absolutely justifying force of what I cannot help or influence, coming as it seems to unfalsifiably from beyond me, and therefore beyond the suspicion that it is mere, vulgar egotistic self-assertion. Anger is a way of giving oneself the law, of subjecting myself to the law of self-assertion, and is the law that decrees that I may, and in the end must, surrender myself up to this law. I am and depend upon the other that is my anger, when I am, as I say, beside myself. The raging subject maintains that its anger comes from the *it*, from the world of things, from the things of the world, in order to justify its fundamental intolerance of the fact that things, and the world, those affronts to my existence, and my insistence that I and I only am the world, in fact also exist.

As the moral affirmation that you cannot help but make, anger is therefore a gun you hold to your own head, especially if, as Stanley Fish astutely asserts, '*the gun at your head is your head.*'[5] The state of emergency that you declare with the onset of rage allows you to suspend your own rights and responsibilities and curtail your own vexatious freedoms. Often, the imperiousness of anger, its demand that 'the inner life of the actor should become wholly manifest and wholly public . . . should become wholly deed,'[6] can turn it from a transporting release from inhibition to a grimly remorseless duty that one must see through to the end. Anger can be a coercive release of purposive intoxication.

But the rightfulness of anger, the fact that anger is thought to be impossible without a cause, also exposes it to a difficulty. For it means that anger will always be heteronomous, since it must always be provoked from outside. Not only am I beside myself in anger, then, but anger is constitutively beside *itself*. Because it can only be depended upon to be right if it does not provoke itself, and can never rightfully be *causa sui*, it can never in fact rely on itself. Anger can only be relied upon to put one in the right, because it can never be regarded as right in itself. Rightness is straightness, the direct, pitilessly unswerving course that, in French *droit*, is even more closely twinned with rightness. Wrongness is twisted, awry. There is pain in this wrongdoing: the wrong wrings, and is wrung. Anger aims always to cut through delay, digression, and aberration, the waste of time involved in taking the wrong path, which is always a deviation from the true, and therefore also a waste, or extravagance. Anger cuts the knot, breaks through the barrier. Anger says no to non-identity, says now to delay. Anger sets the jaw and stiffens the sinews, while, up until the sixteenth century, the word *delay*,

from *disligare*, to unbind, could also mean to soak, soften, macerate or miti-
gate.

As rightness, directness, going straight to the heart of the matter, anger
is an economising and an acceleration. It is what delivers the access of
aggressive power necessary to overcome inhibition and cut through frus-
trating complexity. But, because anger is a means of rushing things to a
conclusion, of bringing an end to intolerable delay, dilly-dally and prolon-
gation, anger is quickly exhausted. Anger does its work by exploding or
dissolving every kind of impediment, but in so doing also hastens its own
dissolution. Indeed, one might say that anger provides 'leaps into the realm
of the absolutely final', as Sloterdijk puts it,[7] precisely through the suicidal
force of its own flaring apoptosis. In this, it resembles and probably sometimes assists sexual feeling. The enemy of sexual desire is not repression,
but rather indifference or, at the other end of things, satiety, which is to say,
exhaustion. Everywhere in our libidinised modern world, the problem is
how to defer sexual discharge, in order that it be available for stimulation,
and to maintain the general imperative, *let there be sexual feeling*. It is for this
reason that sexuality is multiplied into so many different forms, which one
might see as libidinous hedge funds, to minimise the risk of a sudden run
on the sex banks, and consequent libido bust.

Even more than sexual libido, or libido channelled into sexual forms, the
libido of anger – the thymotic drive, as Sloterdijk designates it – is exposed
to the danger of the ruinous expense of spirit. So the problem with anger is
therefore not so much how to avoid it as how, as we say, to 'manage' it –
that is, how to organise, sustain, diversify and husband its energies and
possibilities. Just as sexual desire must be partially inhibited in order to be
universalised, and maintained at a reliably steady mains voltage rather than
being subject to erratic and spasmodic wellings and extravasations, so too
must anger. The Leiden jars which were the first condensers could only
release their electrical charges in spectacular and painful electric shocks that
left the victim prostrate and the water in the jar drained and inert. Only
with the development of Volta's electrical pile was it possible to produce a
steady and reliable current of electricity, which, instead of providing
delight, astonishment and laughter, could be made to do a steady job. Anger
must similarly be managed, not just to keep violence permanently at bay,
but in order to keep it permanently in stock and able to be withdrawn and
put to work in controlled quantities and on judiciously selected targets.
Anger management is maintenance in the literal sense – the keeping of
anger at hand.

Peter Sloterdijk has identified this as the central organising problem of
anger in European history. It may be regarded as an organising problem in

that the various ways in which the problem is solved allow anger precisely to become a kind of organisation, a standing reserve on which to draw for a range of different purposes. Saving anger *from* expenditure allows it to be saved up *for* future expenditure, just as saving surplus resources in the symbolic form of money allows them to be exchanged and deployed in a larger range of different circumstances. Anger, like money, requires mediating systems for its accumulation, exchange and controlled distribution. Or rather, it needs these systems if it is itself to act as a kind of affective currency.

Sloterdijk identifies two historical institutions for the building up and management of capital reserves of anger. One is religion, in particular the monotheistic religions, and in especial Christianity, with the displacement or devolving of its wrathful impulses to a militantly vengeful God and to a *dies irae* that will be the end of time. The other is revolutionary politics, which acts to concentrate and sustain indefinitely mass resentment first of all up to the cathartic act of revenge-taking that is revolution, then beyond it into the managed rage that is permanent revolution, which exhaustingly requires the maintaining of states of alertness against external or, often, internal antagonists. In both cases, with the final reckoning of rage postponed to the end of time, there is a state of martial peace, of an agonism maintained precisely by a kind of cryogenically-cooled rage.

For Sloterdijk, the ever-lengthening interval between offence and payback produces history. Deferred rage gives to time its very texture, direction and tonality; forced to take its time, rage therefore is forced to take the form of time itself. As 'a vector that creates a tension between then, now, and later,'[8] the desire for revenge is the most perfected form of the human sense of project, allowing Sloterdijk to effect another of the *détournements* of Heideggerean slogan that he so enjoys, by substituting for Heidegger's anxiously passive *being-towards-death* a striving, bracing *being-towards-revenge*. Anger, on this account, is a matter not so much of temper, as of tempo. Anger is the name for the rushed or intemperate judgement, or, worse still, the rush to action before the tempering work of judgement has been allowed space to operate. Thus we advise impulsive children to count to ten. Anger, on this account, is simply impatience, the intolerance of any kind of gap between action and judgement. Revolutionaries and millennialists cannot wait until the end of time for their revenge, and want to bring history to an end, or a new beginning, without delay. Perhaps anger is always directed against time itself, against the interminable, world-without-end inbetweenness and ongoingness of history. Anger banks can sometimes act to concentrate enough energy to precipitate just these violent hurryings of history to its ordained conclusion. More often, on Sloterdijk's account, they act to reconcile *Zorn* and *Zeit*, allowing the rage against time to give structure and purpose to time itself. Anger, which is the enemy of time, provides the energy which keeps time going.

I want to propose that there is at least one more area, historically the offspring of theological disputation and the in-law of revolutionary politics, which takes its character from its distinctive forms of anger management, namely intellectual life, especially in the academic forms and institutions in which it is nowadays almost exclusively conducted. As with religion and revolutionary politics, anger provides intellectual life with its moral conation, and sense of justification. Like religious institutions in secular democracies, academic institutions hold out to their adherents the promise of an absolute moral and intellectual freedom while in fact carefully restricting the range of their temporal and political powers. An academic can think what they like, just as an archbishop can believe, or affect to believe, what he likes, as long as those thoughts and beliefs have no consequences. Given the things that archbishops and academics are minded on occasion to think, this is probably a very prudent arrangement.

Anger is both the cost of and compensation for this political restriction. Liberal academics in the humanities and social sciences can easily reroute their anger against their own insignificance into political anger on behalf of the oppressed or victimised collectivities, past and present, for whom they so often and so passionately elect to speak. Across the humanities and social sciences, it is taken for granted that the role of the academic and especially the kind of academic whose function it is to generate forms of what are called 'critique,' is to take the side of the wronged, oppressed, or merely 'marginalised,' against power, or, if not this, then more generally to defend the cause of human value and potentiality against the deadening effects of techno-scientific rationality, instrumentalism, commodification or other forms of self-declaring nastiness. It is the condition of the life that is defended against power that it should be both inviolably and self-certifyingly in the right, which is to say, morally irreproachable and even omnipotent, and yet also apparently without any possibility of standing up against power, the power in general that is assumed to be wielded by ever more generalised forms of antagonist. Actual members of victimised minorities know that, in fact, there is no such power in general, or none that actually matters, and also that there are few victims that are absolutely without power, but when such members of minorities enter into dealings with academics, they must learn to cash in these ordinary experiences and understandings for a more systematic political theology made up of abstract generalities.

Anger in its natural state is intensely local, spasmodic, discontinuous.

The capitalisation of anger aims to smooth out and generalise this thymotic *haecceitas*. Anger can thereby be delocalised, dis-occasioned, unidiomatised. It must be modified from a particular feeling, erupting immediately and spontaneously out of *hic et nunc* wrongs, to a general propensity-to-feel. Where the eruption of anger in its raw and untutored state is the claiming of an exclusive and exceptional right, it must be made into a cooperative reservoir of anger to which nobody can lay exclusive claim, since everybody must be able to have 24-hour access to it.

Systematic analysis is said to make political organisation more rational and effective, but in an academic context its function is to stimulate and lubricate the circulations of academic anger and argument. Power is so often thought of in terms of abstract generality because, surely, talk of power is always an academic allegory. Academics give themselves the right to feel and proclaim vicariously the anger of the wronged against their injustices, because, distributed as investments, hedge funds and dividends through the whole system, this anger enables academic life to maintain, and maintain itself through, its own sense of its thwarted purpose and disrespected virtue. This accounts for the fact that conflict and aggression in academic life are kept under a veil of dissimulation and deprecation, and for the fact that the most characteristic feature of academic violence is its militant oneirism (the irony of this disjuncture producing the comic media spectacle of the academic feud). Our indignation at the pain of others is a perfect opportunity for the investment and deployment of our own surplus capital of rage, a rage that we only intermittently are able to remind ourselves how to feel. Like Mrs Gradgrind, one always knows in an academic conference that there is rage in the room, but it is hard to say whose it is exactly.

All of this will seem implausible and perhaps even inflammatory to most of my colleagues. It seems so in large part to me too. How can all this be true? For surely, if there is one thing we know about academic life it is that it is characterised by the careful and systematic sublimation of violent impulses, the substitution of calm and respectful (and prudently time-consuming) dialogue for the bruising, bragging, air-stabbing laying-down-the-law that the newspapers and daytime television wants to persuade us is the normal mode of human intercourse. Surely, though there are moments of irritation, ill-temper and pique, the predominating ethic of academic life is a dedication to what Habermas famously called 'the unforced force of the better argument'? [9] It's a beguiling idea, to be sure, that the modes of academic argument, expression and interchange allow and require a space in which the impulse to lean on the scale, and to exert illegitimate and partisan interests, is kept in abeyance, so that the true force of things as they are may be isolated, and things as they are permitted to put their own case and proclaim their own cause, undeflected by fantasy, faction or strategic self-interest. The principle behind this is the same as that governing divination. If only we can find a way to set aside human influence, things in themselves will give their verdict neutrally and *in propria persona*. In this respect at least, academic argument has much in common with haruspication, the construing of the flight of birds, the ciphers of giblets or twitchings of the dowser's twig.

But I do not think that we can in fact count on things as they are to exert or assert themselves with this kind of unmistakeable force, once the background noise of human interests is filtered out. Indeed, I am inclined to think that the very notion of the indwelling, unforced force of evidence, or the requirement for being not simply to be, but, as a result perhaps of a kind of assertiveness training, to thrust itself forward as the kind of being it is, conceals a kind of conjuring trick, in which the force of things derives precisely from the desire of evidence or argument for there to be such a force. That things are as they are, and not some other way, is a matter that should and could concern us deeply, but it does not in itself exert any force on us to believe in them, and does not in itself legitimate any secondary exercise of force on their behalf. It may, for example, very well be that an unprejudiced view of the physical evidence points strongly (even, as we sometimes say, 'irresistibly') to the exceedingly high probability that human actions are having a measurable and, as far as our interests are concerned, very dangerous impact upon the world's climate. This is the view held by nearly all the competent people for whom I have the most respect, and so it is one I am strongly disposed to credit. But this state of things does not in itself exert any necessary force. The force that we say is irresistible will always in fact be a reflex of our need for things, and actions based on them, to seem to force themselves on us.

This is a process for which the operations of anger provide the best model, since anger constitutes the strongest performance of the subjection to a force from outside, along with the suppression of any acknowledgement that it is in fact a performance. The unforced force of the better argument is only a force insofar as it borrows from the human will-to-force, or the will-to-be-forced (and the will-to-be-forced cannot long survive without mutating into the will to force others to will-to-be-forced). As soon, or as long, as the state of things in themselves is construed as exerting a necessary force in some direction or other, or enjoining some particular attitude or judgement, even if this extends only to the demand that they be believed in, they have been harnessed to a necessity, forced to act as a force.

As the most forceful form of this forcing of force, anger is also the most militant form of Sartrean bad faith, the stubborn or indignant refusal to recognise our freedom, by which Sartre means the non-necessity of any of our actions, indeed, the essentially unnecessary nature of every aspect of our being. This kind of bad faith is everywhere apparent in academic discourse, especially in the humanities and social sciences, in which the discourse of causes, conditions and determinations has extended its reach so grandiosely and grotesquely, in intriguingly exact synchrony with the retreat from almost every form of absolute determinism in the physical sciences. The forking paths of the Two Cultures have in fact become a chiasmus, in which the hard, or exact sciences have been softened by the penetration of the stochastic and the probabilistic into almost every area of scientific observation and calculation, while the humanities and social sciences, all the while assuming and proclaiming that they represent a lenitive and life-enhancing alternative to the desiccating and objectifying rigours of the scientific world-view, have come to depend more and more implicitly upon the spurious exactitude and will-to-absoluteness of science in its phase of classical determinism. What may strike us (forcibly, as we like to say) about this is the habilitation of the notion of a force in things upon which we can rely because it gives us no choice. For, in truth, that is what it is for, to be relied on, because that is what we force it to be for, to embody force itself. The signature of this vehement choosing not to choose, the longing demand to be able to subject oneself, and others, to unquestionable force, is anger, the anger that is the inner lining of every religious obedience.

And, notoriously, comically, academic life is a matter of what is called 'infighting,' the turning inwards on one's peers and contemporaries of the instincts of aggression and self-aggrandisement. The battle is always an endogenous one, a matter of sibling rivalry. All human beings prefer the intimate enemy and the narcissism of small differences to the encounter with what we call the 'other,' whom it is in fact exceedingly hard to know how or why to hate. The introversion of academic disputes is a clear sign that what is at stake is not actually victory, but the continuing dominion of struggle itself.

Anger is self-assertion through harnessing the force of impersonal necessity, the aggrandisement of the self by the pretence of opening it to destiny and the absolute. Anger insists on the intolerability of complexity, and on 'bringing everything down to the number one, which tolerates no one and nothing beside itself.'[10] This impersonal One is then made the guarantee of the necessary and unadulterated oneness of the one through whom it exerts its unforced force, the one who, putting nothing in the way of this elemental force, then becomes it. Anger is therefore the alpha and omega of monism. It is always the affirmation, or the justification of the thrilling, chilling Lutheran affirmation 'Here I stand. I can do no other.' It is the disavowal, nearly always, soon-or-late, homicidal, of the possibility of being and doing otherwise from what one insists one absolutely and singularly is and must.

Because anger wants to annihilate every ambivalence, its aims are not only totalitarian but also territorial. Totalitarianism is so often expressed in territorial terms, since space, unlike time, allows for exclusive occupation. Where natural anger explodes absurdly and unpredictably in all directions, concentrated anger-to-the-second-degree takes a stand, occupies a particular place. The metaphors of containment that we use to express the organisation of anger point simultaneously to the enfeebling effect of diffusion and the necessity of fixing anger in place, which is achieved by the assignment or occupation of place as such. This is to say that anger expresses itself in the taking and holding of territory, precisely because anger itself requires to be held in place for its continuance. Territory is also the guarantee of temporal persistence, of the possibility of continuing in being. The rage at the fact that there should be a world that has no need of me, and offers no apparent acknowledgement of my humiliating need of it, finds refuge in the idea of a world that consists only of me – or of me, shadowed by the fuzzy, infuriating residue of what I cannot assimilate to myself. As Michel Serres has maintained in his *Genesis*, anger is always the location of *furor* in a particular position, the fixation of space in general into a matter of places and positions – of the *thesis*.

> Thesis is the action of putting something in a place. What is important is the place, and only then the manner of occupying it. Of taking it, holding it, setting oneself up there. Setting one's foot on it. The foot, here, is the trace of a thesis, and the wall of colors, the noise, is at once battle and racket, the two strategies – material and logicial, hardware and software – of taking place and getting a foot in the door.[11]

We may, I think, be reasonably sure that the government of the academic tongue in the humanities and social sciences by military metaphors of territory – sites of struggle, margins, subject positions, and all the rest – along with the erotic preoccupation with the thematics of space itself, is the reflex of the impassioned struggles for *Lebensraum* that drive academic discourse.

The most important and perhaps the most dissimulated form that anger takes in academic life is in the forming of consensus. This by no means entails unanimity of view on everything, or anything. In fact, it is necessary to develop forms of consensus that precisely allow the localised emergence of apparently contrary opinions on a large range of topics. The way in which the thymotic impulse, cooled now close to absolute zero, maintains and expands its territory is through the establishment of univer-sally-applicable consensus on the form of the questions about which it might be possible to have diverging opinions. Hence, for example, the near-total dominance, developed over the last thirty years, and holding good in almost every discipline of the humanities in the parts of the world where there are functioning universities, that the humanities exist to articulate forms of critique of 'power' – to speak on behalf of the oppressed, the marginal, the excluded, the exceptional, the unintegrated, the idiomatic, the unpredictable. It is possible, and indeed desirable, for there to be disagreement about almost every aspect of this work of critique – who it is who embodies the operations of power, who are its most oppressed victims, how and where that power operates and how it is to be most effectively denounced. Critique, of course, requires endless reflection on forms of symbolic tactic and strategy. But it is scarcely thinkable for anyone to suggest that critique of this kind is posturing, purposeless and thus a preposterous waste of our intellectual lives and, insofar as we systematically tutor them in these modes of operational anger-management, our students' lives too. Those who decline the work of critique have the option of course, in engaging in what is called 'celebration,' which accepts all of the terms of critique, especially the universal dispositions of impersonal power and that which it ruthlessly subdues, but substitutes a wish-fulfilling fantasy of minor, symbolic triumph for the more senior and sovereign vocation of various kinds of struggle. Anger is the proof that academics provide for themselves and for others that what they do is serious. I think that academic work is serious, but, as I will try to say by the end of this essay, not in the way that academics think

Critique and celebration come together in the practice and identifica-tion of what is known as 'resistance,' of which the celebration of various kinds of approved virtues or powers (carnival, difference, contingency, plurality, idiosyncrasy) is the mildest form. The really disadvantaged or victimised social group, the intemperately angry, see little use for resist-ance, or only as a means to a greater end, namely the ending of their suffering, which may very well entail the annihilation of its cause or agent. Resistance, Nazis used to hiss at the pictures, is futile, which is precisely why it is academically indispensable. Since critique is necessary to the life of the academic, resistance is the currently unbetterable means for the homeostatic sustaining of grievance and the formulaically aggravated responses to it. Anything else would risk either the possibility of victory, or the recognition of the footling uselessness of the struggle conducted in this fashion. In either case, there is the danger of a depletion or devaluation of the anger reserves, with the associated prospect of wheelbarrows piled high with the waste-paper of thymotic promissory-notes which nobody will any longer cash in.

An academically conventional thing to say at this point would be that the internalised and bureaucratic fractiousness of academic culture is a parallel to the conditions of advanced consumer capitalism, which similarly require individuals to join together in a kind of solidarity of mutual antagonism, so that we live in a state of glumly genial war of all against all. Liberal academic culture in the humanities and cultural studies currently finds it hard to imagine any kind of radical criticism of existing political arrangements that does not in the end pin the blame, with weary, resigned, pseudo-indignation, on the entity known as 'capitalism,' with the suggestion that no real improvement in anything is possible without some way of instituting or, better still (because much less effective), of imagining a radical alternative to capitalism, despite the gloomy, yet exhilarating recognition that capitalism has already, tarnation, assimilated to itself every form of radical critique.

I seem to have worked myself up into a bit of a state about these matters, do I not? And yes, yes, I know, if this is not itself critique, what on earth does it take itself for? What I have been saying is, I concede, critical through and through, of course, and somewhat irritably so. I recognise and own up to an inability to detach myself from these delights or reason aside from these affective tonalities, which seem to give academic life its force and function. Perhaps I should simply acknowledge that this is a game that I have got too fond of and good at playing for me to give it up now; take me by the hand old rage, that sort of thing.

But I don't want to end without trying to find a way of saying that there is a way of doing academic work that might not simply further the managerial dominion of critique. For the last fifteen years or so, I have found the pluck here and there and on lucky occasions to dissent from the culture of coercive systematic critique and dissension in academic life, and have found myself blurting out in more and more public places the fact that I am motivated in the reading and thinking and talking and writing that I do, not by any commitment to a putatively greater good, or desire to confound wickedness and expose error, or desire to get myself and others in the right and in the true, but by the prospect and presence of joy – the joy that lies, for me, in thinking and writing about things. This has gone along with the realisation that, however else I may be describable, I must think of myself as a kind of philographer, an amateur of writing. There is striving in this enterprise, though it is not, not really, a striving against competitors, but a striving to outdo myself in the pleasure I devise from the ways I try to invent to think and write about the ways in which others, in similar and different circumstances, have written about things. This means I find myself writing about the ways in which human beings have for the last two or three millennia, been engaged in the work of respeciating, or despeciating themselves through the particular way of entering into the things of the world that writing affords. Writing has a particular role in this, perhaps, because, as Walter J. Ong reminds us, oral cultures, for all their warmth, intimacy and immediacy, are also subject to savage and ungovernable transports of rage. Oral cultures are, he says 'agonistically programmed.'[12] The joy of writing, and indeed of thinking about what writing does, depends upon stepping outside the charmed, autistic circle of social relations and antagonisms, of tussles for turf and standing-room, into the history of human worldliness, with an accompanying relief and delight that comes from recognising that we are not, after all, locked up alone with our angers and resentments.

I will not try to deny that this sometimes prompts a kind of reforming motive, if only because it is hard to keep entirely quiet about joy of this intensity and abundance. But I am convinced of the futile silliness of trying to argue myself or my friends out of their dependence upon the arts of cold war and into something else by means simply of critique. I have changed my mind about many things over the course of my immense and ridiculous life, but have never once, I now realise, been persuaded to change my mind by the fact that I was wrong (despite having been with glorious monotony almost continuously wrong, about a cornucopia of things). In fact, like most people, or most academics, the demonstration of the untenability or contradictoriness of my beliefs, or the demonstration that my views were 'problematic' (as though academic life did not in fact depend for its continuance upon an unbroken supply of problems) has never made any difference at all to them; I have in fact always been steadied and confirmed in every stubborn assurance by the very fact that it was under attack, and stiffened by the thymotic jolt of indignation this assault on my self-love gave me. If you really want to persuade people (I am not really sure I do), then you will seek not to convince but to seduce them. The only reason that people change their minds is because they see more profit and pleasure, all things considered, in the prospective new mind than they saw in the old one. You change your views not because you are persuaded that they are wrong, but because you encounter some new views that it will be more delightful and fulfilling to hold than the old ones, very often, of course, just because they are new.

This is to say that I agree on the whole with Michel Serres that the purpose, or at least the best use, of intellectual life is invention rather than the securing of truth – or, rather, lest I should seem, heavens, to contradict myself, that thinking of intellectual life as invention itself seems more inventive, more pregnant with the kind of possibility that, for the time being, I most like the sound of, than thinking of it as the austere pursuit and defence of truth. This will have no impact at all on my capacity for the forming of true rather than false propositions or the arriving at warrantable as opposed to mistaken judgements, for these will depend, as always, mostly on a mixture of good luck and the judgement of others, rather than on the thymotic warranty I provide for their truth or utility by the intensity of my belief in them or conviction of the wrongness of others. I, like my ideas, like everything else, are just going to have to make their way, uncertified, in the light of their perceived utility, or not, in changing circumstances.

I have said that anger is an effort to assert the One against intolerable plurality. The most important thing that happens during the course of an argument is similarly a diminution of number. An argument between two parties that begins over some cause or object will, the longer it goes on, gradually tend to leave behind the object in question, as the point of the argument begins more and more to be to win the argument, now a matter exclusively of the relations between two combatants. The presence of the object in question and the intensity of the anger felt by the two parties are therefore in inverse ratio, the less object, the more anger, and vice versa. Like a rocket lifting into space, an argument burns up and discards the module that has launched it. The winning of the argument will involve either the annihilation of the opponent or, more satisfyingly, their annihilation plus the assimilation of their point of view to that of the victor. Thus, like fish being consumed in a goldfish bowl, three becomes two becomes one.

Of course it is far too late in the day to have done with academic disputation, and, as you can obviously tell, I for one have no intention of giving up its gratifications. But cancelling-out or rounding-down contention of the kind I have just characterised is not the only kind possible. I think Michel Serres is right to suggest that the humanities and social sciences are particularly liable to this kind of autistic anger because they have so weak a sense of objects, and so dangerously overdeveloped a sense of 'culture,' constructedness, intersubjectivity and the determining force of human relations. Following Georges Dumézil and René Girard, Serres has suggested repeatedly that the only thing that human beings have reliably found to bring the escalation of anger and violence to an end is the formation of objects. The object, the third thing that is neither me nor my opponent, is a kind of buffer zone, which can absorb anger and turn it into – absorption itself. This might help us become less acosmic, less taken up in the enchanted circle of interhuman relations and antagonisms, and so less, in the Heideggerean sense, poor in world.[13] A more worldly kind of argument, one that includes and bears on the world, rather than attempting to ignore or annihilate it in the finalising ire of rightness, would be one that would keep the things of the world in question, available and necessary to be thought, and would make it possible more and more to be, as academics in their best moments have always known how to be, in joyful ardour, taken up in things.

Notes

1 See Page DuBois, *Torture and Truth* (London: Routledge, 1990).

2 Michel Serres, *Genesis,* trans. Geneviève James and James Nielson (Ann Arbor: University of Michigan Press, 1995), p. 23.

3 Michel Serres, *The Troubadour of Knowledge*, trans. Sheila Faria Glaser and William Paulson (Ann Arbor: University of Michigan Press, 1997), p. 134.

4 See Peter Sloterdijk, *Rage and Time: A Psychopolitical Investigation*, trans. Mario Wenning (New York: Columbia University Press, 2010).

5 Stanley Fish, *Doing What Comes Naturally: Change, Rhetoric, and the Practice of Theory in Literary and Legal Studies* (Oxford: Clarendon, 1989), p. 520.

6 Sloterdijk, *Rage and Time*, p. 9.

7 Peter Sloterdijk, *God's Zeal: The Battle of the Three Monotheisms*, trans. Wieland Hoban (Cambridge and Malden MA: Polity Press, 2009), p. 141.

8 Sloterdijk, *Rage and Time*, p. 60.

9 Jürgen Habermas, *Between Facts and Norms. Contributions to a Theory of Law and Democracy* (Cambridge, MA: MIT Press, 1996), p. 305.

10 Sloterdijk, *God's Zeal,* p. 96.

11 Serres, *Genesis*, p. 53.

12 Walter J. Ong, *Orality and Literacy: The Technologizing of the Word* (London and New York: Routledge, 2002), p. 44.

13 Michel Serres, *La Guerre mondiale* (Paris: Le Pommier, 2008), p. 139.

ON THE WALL

ON THE WALL

Mene, Mene, Tekel, Upharsin*

Michael Symmons Roberts

One by one, would-be interpreters
are pushed at gunpoint through the hall,
distracted as they walk past rows

of toppled chairs, rioja pools,
half-eaten rolls, concave terrines;
detritus of a fast-abandoned meal.

Led to the wall, each reads the runes.
Some ask if they can catch
this ghost graffiti on their cameraphones.

No flash, just meanings. As such:
'A mineral in the plaster leeching out /
lover's vengeance / rebel with a brush.'

The words warn what to do, *or not,*
yet within hours the king is dead, his lands
carved up, as meat curls on his plate.

* The title refers to the mysterious 'writing on the wall', which foretold the demise
of King Belshazzar's kingdom in the biblical Book of Daniel.

The writing on the byre beams

Helen Farish

In a John Menzies A6 notebook (40 leaves
ruled feint) which my father used to mirror
English with French and to safeguard
the foreign language (to me) codes
of his profession, finally I copy down
the writing on the byre beams. Already
twenty years (more) since my father said
Look, read, imagine: here I am.

Crossed out – *1945 white cow bulled*
10th May. Dates the following year
for the light cow, the dark and the heifer.
2nd July 1947 is legible despite being
crossed out whereas what happened
on that day (though uncontradicted)
is too faint. And on 25th Dec something
(what?) was *Due* with a capital.

I find myself writing
on one of the beams *This is History*
and then try to sign the name of a man
I never knew and tell how he made
these records the decade before
(in the same building) he looped a noose
like he looped his *L*s despite that year's light,
white and dark calves bawling.

My father's typically neat A6 notes
now are next to mine which fail
to follow the rules, accustomed as they are
to unlined space. It was never the intention
of the 1940s farmer to be read, but his impulsive
pencil and wood logbook has become
his *J'etais ici, J'etais ici*: a message
to death – don't cross out me.

Dithering

Mark Ford

'Let Spades be trumps!' she said, and trumps they were; it leaves
us free to cry, and whisper to their souls to
go. Nor wilt thou
then forget where are the legs with which
you run, Hurroo! Hurroo!, or wake
and feel the fell of dark. Like an angel came
I down,
when my dream was near the moon,
the crux left of the watershed, and the stars that usher
evening rose. He
is not here; but far away – o'er Bodley's dome his future labours
spread. 'Have you been
out?' 'No.' 'And don't want to, perhaps?' Men shut their doors
against a setting sun, and high
the mountain-tops, in cloudy air, and instantly the whole
sky burned with fury against them. They
like to drink beer, and each one had
a little wicker basket, made of fine twigs, entrailed curiously:
patient, look, thou watchest the last oozings hours by hours,
etherized
upon a midnight dreary, where no flower can wither; many
a spring I shoot up fair, the book on the writing-
table, the hand in the breast pocket.

'Dithering' is a cento, i.e. a poem composed from lines by other authors. This form originated in the 3rd or 4th century – *cento*, in Latin, is a term for a patchwork cloak. 'Dithering' is a cento with a difference, however, in that it is also an acrostic. It was inspired by the opening lines of T.S. Eliot's 'The Love Song of J. Alfred Prufrock.' Read down as well as across.

Histories

'Broken Hallelujah'

Kevin Mills

Stepping into the hall is akin to walking through the back of a wardrobe into Narnia: a whole new world is there, peopled by strange new kinds of beings who speak their own languages, sing their own songs, and meet with their own destinies. You can feel it coming out to meet you as you approach. It is not just the wave of exultant sound, the strange, unconstrained, free-form singing of more than six thousand God-possessed voices; it is an energy, a power, a force-field of Holy-Ghost electricity that unweaves your flesh and scatters your mind. As you step across the threshold into a tangerine light, you hit a wall of solid essence. You encounter in a single moment the awe of Sinai, the confusion of Babel and the afflatus of Pentecost, and nothing has prepared you for this moment. Nothing ever could.

Sceptical and post-Christian, you still feel the nap of your skin bristle when you think of it. You have no rational account to offer. You describe that moment to many people over many years, in the hope that they believe you, but can never be sure quite what it is you are describing. In that instant you feel your life change. Already the other side of a river you do not remember choosing to cross, you find yourself already having decided. It seems like a sound heard only in the echo. It is always already too late not to have done it.

Histories of Wales disagree about whether or not the religious revival that took place between 1904 and 1905 actually qualifies as history at all. Accounts of the religious movement appear in historical works written from a number of different perspectives, ranging from brief descriptions in secular or general histories, such as A.H. Dodd's *A Short History of Wales*,[1] and Prys Morgan (ed.), *Wales: An Illustrated History*,[2] to whole volumes dedicated to describing the events as evidence of divine intervention in the affairs of the nation – for example *The Welsh Revival of 1904* by Eifion Evans[3] and *Fire on the Altar* by Noel Gibbard.[4] There are also those histories of Wales that do not mention it at all, such as David Williams' *A History of Modern Wales*,[5] Philip Jenkins' *A History of Modern Wales, 1536–1990*[6] and Dai Smith's *Wales: A Question for History*.[7] While some secular historians fail to mention the affair, others, such as John Davies, consider it to have been of enormous significance. In his *A History of Wales* – a work which covers a huge time span – he finds considerable space for the revival, which he calls 'one of the most extraordinary happenings in twentieth-century Wales'.[8]

Maybe the problem with the representation of revival underlying such diverse responses is that most histories are written from a materialist perspective, whereas most accounts of the revival that survive from the time of its actual occurrence speak of it in terms of spiritual experience – whatever that might mean. So, if it is to be written into a *secular* history with no specific interest in religious matters then both the events and their causes have to be rendered in a way that is at odds with the very documentary evidence upon which that history (ostensibly) is based; at odds, in fact, with historiographical principles as such, principles that preclude divine intervention, or spiritual causes for material effects. The historian of Wales, then, is in an impossible position when it comes to the years 1904–5. According to the documentary evidence from the period something happened, but it appears to have been something that cannot be described in its own terms without falsifying the laws of historical cause and effect. On the other hand, it cannot be ignored without discounting the documentary evidence that survives from the period, including personal testimony, first-hand accounts, a great deal of journalistic reporting, and even fiction.

The difficulty that materialist discourses find in registering experiences identified by their sufferers and sympathetic interpreters as 'spiritual' makes of the revival a kind of historical edge or margin: some historians write it in; others write it out.

Even among those who think that the series of events that constitute the revival deserve to be included in the annals and narratives of Wales, there is little agreement about what kind of history it belongs to, about how it should be framed or contextualised, or about the character of its cultural, political and religious significance. It has been viewed by secular historians as a minor detail in the story of the south Wales coalfield, as an adjunct to the rise of the Labour Party, or as an admixture in the tale of the cultural flowering that produced the national university, national library and national museum. It has been seen as a reaction to the demythologising movements of the Victorian era; as a killjoy movement that disapproved of Welsh passions for rugby, beer and socialism; or as the swan song of Welsh non-conformist culture, dying a prolonged death in the jaws of modernity.

On the other side of the great divide are those sacred historians for whom the revival of 1904–5 is one of the most important moments in a spiritual saga that defines the divine significance of Wales in the wider world as a conduit of revelation and transformation. Such writers take for granted the reality of divine interventions in history, and they write for believers in the argot of the spiritually initiated. For such people the revival was a work of the Spirit of God, causing sinners to turn away from the besetting vices of alcoholism, gambling, swearing, lead-swinging, neglect of the means of grace, and less specific forms of defection from the will of God.

Somewhere between these two poles are the accounts that belong (broadly speaking) to the category of Church History. Books such as J. Vyrnwy Morgan's *The Welsh Religious Revival 1904–1905*[9] and R. Tudur Jones' *Faith and The Crisis of a Nation*[10] attempt to tell the story of the revival as a chapter in the history of the church in Wales, of interdenominational conflict, of the dominance of the culture by Nonconformity, and of the processes that led to disestablishment. Devoting three chapters of his book to the revival, Jones is open in his criticism of those historians who choose to ignore it:

> Perhaps it is not surprising that it is not included in such wide-ranging volumes as *Christianity in a Revolutionary Age* by K.S. Latourette or *The Church in an Age of Revolution* by Alec R. Vidler. But the fact that David Williams does not discuss it in *Modern Wales* does demonstrate the way in which the judgement of historians can be distorted by deep preconceptions and prejudices.[11]

This is religion as you have never experienced it. It involves no intellectual assent; it does not address your mind at all, nor yet leave it vacant. It is as if the mind has been translated into undifferentiated light. In place of the thinking you, is a cloud of diffuse sensation and energy that has no focus or centre. A cloud of unknowing, you become, instantaneously, something other than a cogitating subject, something other than an individual, something devoid of location or definition. It is some kind of transcendence. Or submergence.

Novelists have tended to be more willing than secular historians to dwell on the movement, but usually in a broadly negative way that psycho-pathologises its prime movers, its converts and its propagators. Offering counter-historical perspectives, they interweave fact and fiction, focusing on repressed desire, on relationships between those caught up in the movement, and on the conflict between the apocalyptic urgency of revivalism and the stolid endurance of traditional nonconformity. Published in the immediate aftermath of the revival, Allen Raine's *Queen of the Rushes* (1906) depicts the revival as a kind of brief emotional storm through which her characters pass; some are damaged by it, others survive with an older, less evanescent form of faith intact.[12] The revival, then, is a bone of contention for Raine, and is characterised in mixed terms. On the one hand the two exemplary lead characters are little engaged by the impassioned meetings and the fervid activity of their neighbours. The verbose, histrionic and emotional tone of the meetings is contrasted quite pointedly with the spirituality of the two main characters who find a closeness to God and a sense of consolation in an almost animistic communion with nature out on the atmospheric moorland of west Wales. The revival is sometimes seen as divisive and productive of social and domestic disharmony. Women are absent from the domestic hearth at religious gatherings when they should be caring for their menfolk. This divisiveness extends into the broader community when the people of the village at the centre of the story shun and suspect the key male character precisely because he refuses to be a part of what they believe to be the work of the Holy Spirit. On the other hand, some characters seem to be genuinely reformed by the influence of the revival, while others remain unreformed and yet, at times, respond to the music and the energy of the movement in positive terms, however vague: 'Converted, no!' said Captain Jack, 'I am the same bad lot as ever, I'm afraid! Hark ye, mate, *there's something in it*. As sure as I am sitting here, there's something comes into those meetings besides the people.'[13]

Is it the wonder of novelty that shifts gears in your brain? Or is it the sheer volume of humanity gathered with a single purpose and sharing a nebulous desire that powers the flight? Under such circumstances do we become something other than atomic beings – a super-being with the corporate will of a flock of starlings or a colony of ants? You will try on many occasions to re-capture the experience as a member of smaller congregations, or when you are alone, but will never quite manage it. Something similar, perhaps, but always marked by a lack, a loss or a disappointment. The closest you will come will be the post-religious, unlooked-for transport of being in the audience at a Leonard Cohen concert, thirty years later, when he reads the lyric of 'If It Be Your Will'.

Later novels such as those by Rhys Davies and Tom Davies are far less willing to see anything positive at all in the events of 1904–5. Rhys Davies offers a Lawrentian version of the revival's star performer (Evan Roberts, renamed Reuben Daniel). In his novel *The Withered Root* (1927), the protagonist is sexually frustrated, his urges effectively disabled by guilt and shame.[14] A harsh and unforgiving nonconformist evangelicalism is depicted as attaching negative emotions and social sanctions to sexual desire, and these debilitating forces crush the life out of a potent and charismatic individual. The spiritual empowerment he appears to exude is more-or-less equated with the return of the repressed libido. When Tom Davies revisited the period and the character of Evan Roberts in *One Winter of the Holy Spirit* (1985), he seems to have taken his cue from Rhys Davies; the energies at work in his story are decidedly sexual and his revivalists are both disturbed and disturbing.[15]

The revival, then, is something that happened and that did not happen, the effects of which were both good and bad. It was a process that can be attributed to political, economic, cultural, emotional, psycho-sexual, or spiritual causes. It may be a sign without a referent, or a sign whose referent is best understood as fictional, or, at least, as counter-historical. Religious discourse is replete with such terms, of course – lexical items that positivists would dismiss as nonsensical, rationalists as irrational, materialists as immaterial. Like its experiential and exclamatory counterpart – 'hallelujah' – 'revival' is a broken word, fractured by history and counter-history.

Some people are standing, their eyes closed and their arms raised, singing unintelligible syllables in free-form melodies around the impromptu weavings of the musicians. There are three guitarists, a bass player, a keyboard player, a drummer and a flautist. The Holy Spirit is conducting. The stage, erected at the midpoint of one of the long walls, is bordered with extravagant blooms and foliage – a gang of suited men scattered across it, some standing, some sitting. One is on his knees. An intense calm flows across the crowd as the singing grows quieter, and the flautist steps forward. An ethereal woodwind voice drifts out above the gathered thousands, and every face you can see appears rapt. The entire congregation would follow that sound off the edge of a cliff, and cry 'hallelujah' as their bones shattered on the rocks below. You feel it as an exquisite, violating presence that insinuates itself at the ears, dodges the brain, and winds itself around the solar plexus. You close your eyes and let the sinuous music do to you what it will.

There are intermittent cries of 'Hallelujah' and 'Thank you, Lord' coming from all around you, uttered in breathy stage whispers, like expressions of sexual joy. You begin to pick up unintelligible sounds in a soft, female voice, close by. You turn around, and directly behind you is a girl, her face is lifted and wears an expression that looks iconic. Her skin is bathed in the tangerine light that fills the hall, and she wears a picture hat made of straw. It clings to the back of her head, so that with her face lifted, the brim appears around her visage as a halo. Her eyes are closed and her lips move like two little flames, forming beguiling sounds that make no sense: 'Shanda roothia, el esta marabuteo. Porunai shevuneth, castinos aduto borunara.' It is pure language, flowing like milk and honey. Perfectly meaningless and quite beautiful.

The language of revival, the talk of those dwelling in the hidden realm of spiritual truth, is often perfectly meaningless beyond the confines of its human territory. Meaningless and uncomfortable. Perhaps this is because we feel ourselves to be sullied by the encounter with unreferring signs, as though we were listening to, or even speaking, baby-talk in adult company, as though the fantasies that keep us sane had become visible to unknowing eyes. Because it speaks another, conceptually alien, language, religious experience is the antithesis of the critical, everything that criticism is not, everything that it inveighs against, its unspeakable other. It cannot be spoken of in the critical voice. Another voice is called for, one that we cannot hear with the same ears. Another kind of writing is demanded that evades, or that dreams of evading, the critical eye.

We might say, then, that an occurrence such as the 1904–5 revival in Wales forms a kind of Lyotardian *differend*, in the sense that history and criticism cannot register the testimonies that do not confine themselves to recognised categories.[16] The historical causes and effects of the revival must be traced in economic, political, cultural and/or psychological processes, and the voices of participants will thus necessarily appear to be naïvely ideological or self-deceiving – ignorant of their own meaning. They will root their comprehension in the mystical, in the direct experience of spiritual inundation, conviction, revelation, conversion, afflatus – and so will be unable to speak to, or within, the historical record or the critical response.

The converse of the case is that the discourse created from the perspective of the believing historian will be unable to recognise, or to acknowledge, material causes. For example, in *Voices from the Welsh Revival 1904–1905*, Brynmor P. Jones quotes and then challenges the opinion of the French psychologist and sociologist Rogues de Fursac.[17] De Fursac argues that outbreaks of conviction, repentance and subsequent euphoria such as those typical of the Welsh revival are the effects of unconscious operations building up silently and over a long period of time, then suddenly exploding into visibility.[18] The manifestation of psychological and emotional effects without apparent causes, the argument goes, create for their sufferer the illusion of external influence – a belief that the sudden changes have been produced by powers outside their own ego. This is Jones' reply:

> Such an explanation ignores the divine factor altogether and leaves no room for the Spirit . . . It would be safer to trust the instincts of the converts themselves, who somehow saw clearly that it was not from within their souls but from the dynamic pressures of saving grace that they had come to the end of their rebellion.[19]

It is tempting to sneer at Jones's apparently naïve assumption that the subjective experience of those he calls 'converts' is a more reliable guide to the truth, or at least the meaning, of revival than is the more objective psychological analysis of such phenomena offered by de Fursac. What does Jones mean by 'the instincts of the converts'? Since it suggests a certain function of the unconscious, the term 'instinct' rather plays into de Fursac's hands. Does not his use of the vague term 'somehow' undermine, or at least cast a shadow over, the clarity that he wants to claim for the instinctive insights of his converts? These are easy targets, yet to hit them is not without significance.

But while the sympathy of the critical reader perhaps lies with de Fursac, his claim is little less problematical than Jones's because it depends upon a tacit assertion that the *hiddenness* of the psychical operations is *open* to the scrutiny of the psychologist. The convert is necessarily, and by definition, confined to a darkness that only the analyst can penetrate. This is a self-involving assertion that is devoid of empirical proof or even support from the subject of the analysis. Furthermore, de Fursac's claim is psychologistic: it seems to deny the influence upon the ego of forces outside of, or beyond itself. In this sense it is no less naïve an argument than Jones's objection to it.

Jones and de Fursac each mount arguments that depend upon conditions that the other cannot possibly admit. When Jones says that de Fursac ignores the divine factor, he says nothing at all, since 'the divine factor' has no meaning within the discourse of psychology; it does not signify. Similarly, when de Fursac speaks of the illusion of external influence, Jones's position would be that the real illusion lies in de Fursac's own failure to see beyond the realm of the ego and its internal dynamics.

The keyboard begins to tinkle a mellow tune, like piped music in a restaurant. The bass comes in with a visceral rumble, and the drummer takes up brushes. A hum rises from the congregation. Thousands of people are singing quietly, just inventing stuff – singing 'Hallelujah' in a thousand ways, or 'I love you Lord' in hundreds of variations. Others are singing in tongues. Arpeggios, and unrehearsed harmonies drift across the crowd like incense fumes. It seems organic. The entire crowd has been woven into a single organism with six thousand heads, and twelve thousand raised arms. A spirit and a motion rolls through all of them, impels all of them.

Other than an internal dynamic, yet inextricably interwoven with it, is music. Music is ubiquitous in the realm of spirit. The journalistic reports, the sacred histories and the novels of the revival are full of it. The secular histories are silent about it. The sacred histories and the novels characterise it as an influx of external influence: a disruption of the internal dynamics of the ego. Brynmor P. Jones devotes a chapter to the subject (Chapter 3).

In Eifion Evans's work it pipes up irresistibly. W.T. Stead observed about Evan Roberts' meetings: 'Three-fourths of the meeting consists of singing.'[20] According to the newspaper reports, the singing was a key element in the effectiveness of the meetings, and their accounts of events hardly ever (if at all) fail to mention the hymns used and the relative enthusiasm with which they were sung by the different congregations. On 17th November 1904 the *South Wales Daily News* carried a short article headed 'Is it a Singing Revival?' 'A wonderful feature of the meetings,' the article insisted, 'is the hymn singing, which is very impressive, and at times goes on for nearly an hour without interruption.' The *Western Mail* occasionally printed the words for hymns in its pages as an aid to the cause, and the edition for 5th December 1904 referred to the movement once more as 'the singing revival.' On another occasion, the paper lauded the 'musical genius of the Welsh' as an element in the spread of the revival (18th Dec. 1904).

The singing and its power were why Roberts toured with a group of women, of whom the *Western Mail* (15th Nov. 1904) opined: 'The young ladies . . . are not professional singers; but they are manifestly touched with the spirit of singing pilgrims.' In a gesture that does not lack credibility in the light of manifold evidence, Tom Davies has his fictional version of Evan Roberts say to his fictional version of W.T. Stead: 'The ladies must go with me wherever I go . . . I can never part from them without feeling that something is absent if they are not there. Their singing is the most important key to this Revival.'[21] A book devoted to these singing women, Karen Lowe's *Carriers of the Fire*, includes a chapter entitled 'Unending Song,' and she characterises their charismatic performances as a kind of portal to the realm of the spirit – a means of transcendence that released what she calls 'the flow of heaven's grace and love.'[22]

The music changes, and now people begin to sing a real song – one with words and a tune, but one that you have never heard before: 'Jesus, Jesus, Jesus, your love has melted my heart'. That is it. That is the whole lyric. You are used to the hymns of Charles Wesley, sung to sombre but stirring Welsh tunes. A Wesley hymn is a three course meal of theological niceties, outlining divine policy on crucial issues such as salvation by grace alone, the redemptive work of Christ, or the division of responsibilities within the Trinity. This song comprises nine words, sung twice over. The melody starts softly, with the second 'Jesus' echoing the first, a tone higher. The third Jesus is melismatic, and falls gracefully into 'your love has melted my . . . ' sung almost in a monotone, then 'heart' is sung in another lower melisma. Second time around, the third 'Jesus' is the focus of a crescendo, as the melody reaches its highest point, before coming down with the sobbing bursts of the melting heart. The music carries the words into body and breath, so that they consume the singer with effort and rhythm, with an irresistible inbreathing that physically binds the individual into the corpus.

It is time for a song. I have one in mind. You will have heard it often in recent time, I suspect.

Leonard Cohen's song 'Hallelujah' has become very familiar. Although it was first released on the *Various Positions* album in 1984, it became a record-breaking hit only in 2008. This is how Cohen's official website tells it:

> . . . a version performed by Alexandra Burke, winner of the . . . 'X Factor,' rocketed to the #1 slot on the UK singles chart, becoming the fastest-selling single by a female artist in UK chart history . . . Jeff Buckley's rendition bulleted to #2 while Cohen's original version entered the singles chart at #34 . . . With versions of the song holding down three Top 40 UK Singles Chart positions simultaneously, 'Hallelujah' became the fastest-selling digital single in European history. [23]

Before that, the song had been popularised by the soundtrack to the animated film *Shrek* which used a melancholic, soulful rendition variously ascribed to Rufus Wainright, Jeff Buckley and John Cale. It has been covered, though not necessarily recorded, by a number of other artists including Bob Dylan, K D Lang, Willie Nelson, Allison Crowe, Kathryn Williams and Bon Jovi. Recently, Welsh popular classics diva Kathryn Jenkins has produced a silky smooth arrangement that strips the song it of its barbed peculiarity and its sexually charged edginess. Popularisation has turned what was once a counter-cultural blending of the religious, the frankly sexual and the subtly blasphemous into – in Jenkins' version, anyway – an anthem of deracinated spirituality: a psuedo-mystical confection of toy emotions. But then the song itself tells us that this doesn't much matter: we are welcome to hear the holy song or the broken one.

The key to this distinction lies in the universality of the word 'hallelujah' – one of very few that needs no translation whatever language we speak. Like Coca-Cola it is a word that has travelled the world keeping its phonetic shape more-or-less intact. But if the word is pretty impermeable to formal alteration, it is not immune to semantic deviation. It can be used to praise God ('praise God' is, roughly, the meaning of the original Hebrew exclamation), but also to express a sense of joy or relief that is not specifically attributed to any divine intervention. It can also be used as an ironic expression of irritation or impatience. The word 'bloody' (or even 'fucking') can be let into the middle of it in order to accentuate a sense of annoyed relief that a long overdue result has been reached: halle-bloody-lujah! The worshipful connotation of the original expression is lost in such uses so that the term is broken, severed from its religious or devotional roots. And this, I suspect, is Cohen's point – or part of it anyway.

There is a verse that suggests that we should also think about the word as embodying the impossibility of blasphemy:

> You say I took the Name in vain
> I don't even know the Name
> But if I did, well really, what's it to you?
> There's a blaze of light in every word
> It doesn't matter which you heard
> The holy or the broken Hallelujah

Language here is divided between implication and inference by a 'blaze of light' – a sublime something that remains impenetrable. Therefore to accuse a speaker of blasphemy – to say that they have taken the Name in vain – is to claim a knowledge that one simply cannot possess. Cohen's Judaic heritage shows in the refusal to know the Name, of course, and this adds another layer to the poetic effect: it is both a profoundly religious gesture that respects the Jewish prohibition on pronouncing the Name of God, and at the same time a wilfully sacrilegious gesture that denies all knowledge of religious value and refuses to accept the terms imposed by the addressee.

For a short while – the moment is all too brief and yet infused with a sense of timelessness – you enjoy an absolute certainty, though you could not say of what. You know that you know something ineffable, something that defies expression even within your own thoughts. And in this state of mystical abstraction the only word that comes into your mind, or onto your tongue, is 'hallelujah'. Hallelujah, hallelujah, hallelujah. Over and over again you say the word, repeating it like a mantra, singing it in as many ways as your limited musical capacity can fashion. You know what it means, but somehow you do not what it *is*. It means 'praise the Lord,' but it flows through you as though it were a word incapable of translation, as though it were not a word at all so much as an irresistible current of some-thing non-linguistic coming from far beyond you and going on far beyond you, carrying with it an infinity of space and light.

This issue of what must (paradoxically) be called blasphemous worship has an unexpected echo in the revival of 1904–5. On 31st January 1905 a letter was published in the *Western Mail* condemning the 'sham Revival' as 'a mockery, a blasphemous travesty of the real thing.' And the 'chief figure in this mock revival,' the letter runs, 'is Evan Roberts, whose language is inconsistent with the character of anyone except that of a person endowed with the attributes of a divine being.' It goes on to suggest that Roberts gave every appearance of ordering the Holy Spirit in his meetings – commanding the presence and the activity of the third person of the Trinity, as though he were himself the fourth. The letter was written by Rev Peter Price, BA, a Congregational minister from Dowlais, near Merthyr Tydfil, and it served to highlight the fact that even while the revival was underway, in its very heartlands and among those directly affected by it, opinion was divided over its character. Subsequent letters sent to Price, and published in J. Vyrnwy Morgan's book, illustrate just how deep the divisions went: some outraged by Price's audacity in questioning the work of divine Grace, others relieved that at last someone was breaking the illusion of spiritual authority worked up by Roberts and his band of itinerant charlatans. [24]

For Rev Peter Price, there were two revivals – one genuine, the other a blasphemous imitation:

> It is this mock Revival – this exhibition – this froth – this vain trumpery – which visitors see and which newspapers report. And it is harmful to the true Revival – very harmful. And I am horrified lest people who trust to what they see at Evan Roberts's meetings and to newspaper reports should identify the two Revivals – the true and the false – the heavenly fire and the *ignis fatuus*.

What seems to terrify the educated Reverend is the apparent similarity between the two opposed phenomena, the difficulty in telling them apart. That is the trouble with blasphemy – it looks and sounds like true worship, and one sometimes has to work quite hard to tell the one from the other. For those troubled by blasphemy the peril is that the devil can always appear as an angel of light, as St Paul put it.[25] But for those with a will to blaspheme the obverse is no less troubling: to indulge in blasphemy is always to run the risk of accidentally glorifying a God in whom one does not believe, or for whom one feels contempt.

So the music plays on and people begin to move toward the front of the great hall – ones and twos at first, but soon there seem to be hundreds thronging forward. You want to go. You know you have to go, but you cannot bring yourself to do it. What is holding you back? You fall to your knees, sobbing, and call on God to have mercy on you. You stay in that posture for some minutes weeping with joy, and with a kind of exquisite agony, desperation like acute hunger. A power not your own has seized you. You are hardly aware of where you are. All of your self-consciousness is focused on an inner space where you are meeting with a nebulous God, present as a searching thought at the heart of which is a warm and welcoming darkness.

You pick yourself up. Your insides have turned to bright liquid. You feel a hand on your shoulder, and look around to see the young madonna in the picture hat.

'Thank you for kneeling just then,' she says. 'That meant so much to me to see you kneel before Father.'

There are tears in her eyes. She throws her arms around you, and you feel her cheek brush softly against yours. Momentarily, you are in love with her and with God in equal measure and with the same desire.

Perhaps more fundamental to Cohen's 'Hallelujah' than its concern with blasphemy, but not unrelated to it, is the song's refusal to distinguish between the religious or spiritual and the bodily or sensual. One verse of the song runs:

> Your faith was strong, but you needed proof
> You saw her bathing on the roof
> Her beauty and the moonlight overthrew you
> She tied you to a kitchen chair
> She broke your throne and she cut your hair
> And from your lips she drew the hallelujah

It is the sustained allusion to the biblical story of King David and Bathsheba that underpins the wicked brilliance of these lines. 'Hallelujah' becomes the expression of sexual joy, all the more potent because the utterer is that legendary author of orthodox worship material, the psalmist David. In Cohen's lyric he becomes the author of the double hallelujah that is both sacred and profane. Well, David and not David: the song addresses the implied hearer as 'you' – you are put in David's place. It is accusation and it is foreplay, guilt and ecstasy. Cohen gives you an orgasm, implicating you, drawing you into the biblical story, and, simultaneously desacralising the scripture by throwing open that which is definitively closed. So the movement by which the exclamation of spiritual fervour is translated into the moan of sensual pleasure, and vice versa, is also that by which the sacred text is paradoxically earthed in the experience of the here and now.

Rhys Davies's fictionalised version of Evan Roberts (Reuben Daniel) would (albeit grudgingly) recognise the condition Cohen's song diagnoses. Troubled by his own carnality, Daniel is uncomfortably aware that the spiritual experience empowering him is not unrelated to his sublimated libidinal drives:

> A dark shadow seemed to cast itself on Reuben's mind. Somewhere in his consciousness a hateful knowledge brooded, like an evil fume over the bright pastures of his soul. He remembered how sometimes in his most exalted visions a certain flame of desire leapt with searing and blinding force within him, and he would see within stretches of dark night the naked white bodies of women.[26]

Tom Davies has to be a little more circumspect in the way he depicts the eroticism of pneumatic religion since his fictional revivalist bears the name of his real-life model, but he too allows sensuality to mingle freely with religious fervour:

> He rubbed his cheek against the side of Beth's arm. 'God has chosen me to shoulder this burden in the same way that Jesus took the full force of human sin when he was on the cross . . . '
> He began sobbing again, hands still clutching Beth's wrists and eyes open as he ran his wet parted lips up and down the length of her forearm.[27]

Since the hallelujah in Cohen's lyric (like Reuben Daniel's vision and the fictional Evan Roberts's 'burden') is both spiritual and sexual, both sacred and profane, what we hear is always and necessarily the broken hallelujah rather than the holy one. Multiplicity, or choice, forces the break. Once there is choice then the hallelujah is already split, and the holy hallelujah loses its connection with any kind of transcendence by virtue of its embeddedness in its material other. Entrammelled in its simultaneity with the ironic and the sensual, it is no longer able to function as a marker of transcendence.

The brokenness of the hallelujah can be read in the song's most insistent rhyme strategy which involves following an /uː/ sound with the word 'you.' The presence of the word hallelujah as rhyme for 'overthrew you' or 'to you,' for example, invites the pronunciation of 'you' as 'ya' – 'overthrew ya', 'to ya.' This makes the informal 'ya' (you) phonetically indistinguishable from the name of God (Jah), and the two are constantly juxtaposed in the lyric. So the speaker's insistence on not knowing the Name both valorises and devalues it, as the multiple repetition of the forbidden becomes both blasphemy and the expression of an atheistic ignorance of the prohibition.

As a pop phenomenon, then, 'Hallelujah' is an expression of what might be called a postmodern religion: an unstable discourse that encodes and perpetuates diametrically opposed values, an athesitic insistence that the 'hallelu' or praise can be yoked with 'ya' (you), or with a more conventional 'jah' (as a signifier of a superhuman agency of indeterminate character), or even with a conservative understanding that connects 'jah' with the God of Judeo-Christian belief.

Thus the song refuses to let go of the 'holy' hallelujah – as though the broken version did not erase, eradicate or undermine its holy twin. This is perhaps grounded in the fact that the very idea of brokenness depends upon a prevenient wholeness or holiness. That which is broken can be identified as such only by comparison with a prior state of integrity. That, of course, is the original meaning of holiness.

After the long journey back to Wales, you enter an empty house. You slog tiredly up to your room, drop your heavy bag, grab your guitar and sit on the bed. Automatically you play 'Bird on a Wire.' 'I have tried in my way to be free,' you sing. Then, gripped by a spasm of conscience you can neither understand nor control, you stop halfway through the second verse. Something runs through your soul like a tear through paper. Two versions of yourself now seem to lie either side of a rift. You are neither one nor the other; you are the rift itself – a torn thing.

In an effort to relive recent experience, trying and failing to lose yourself again in the power of an awesome presence, you try to make worship happen until weary with the effort and with a long day's travel, you feel your chest convulse with a nameless sorrow. Tears rolling down your face, you put down the guitar and stretch yourself out on the bed, two songlines competing in your brain until you fall asleep: you have tried in your way to be free, but you are broken by the hallelujah.

As you know, original meanings never last. Words split apart and reform. Version gives way to version. Voice replaces voice. The song is rearranged. Hallelujah.

Notes

1 A.H. Dodd, *A Short History of Wales: Welsh Life and Customs from Prehistoric Times to the Present Day* (London: B.T. Batsford, 1977). Previously published as *Life in Wales* (Batsford, 1972).

2 J. Graham Jones, 'Wales Since 1900,' in Prys Morgan (ed.), *Wales: An Illustrated History* (Stroud: Tempus, 2005), pp. 211–44.

3 Eifion Evans, *The Welsh Revival of 1904* (Bridgend: Evangelical Press of Wales, 1969).

4   Noel Gibbard, *Fire on the Altar: A History and Evaluation of the 1904–5 Welsh Revival* (Bridgend: Bryntirion Press, 2005).

5   David Williams, *A History of Modern Wales* (London: John Murray, 1950).

6   Philip Jenkins' *A History of Modern Wales, 1536–1990* (London: Longman, 1992).

7   Dai Smith's *Wales: A Question for History* (Bridgend: Seren, 1999).

8   John Davies, *A History of Wales* (London: Penguin, 1993, 2007), p. 490. Originally published in Welsh as *Hanes Cymru* (London: Penguin, 1992).

9   J. Vyrnwy Morgan, *The Welsh Religious Revival 1904–1905: A Retrospect and a Criticism* (London: Chapman and Hall, 1909).

10 R. Tudur Jones' *Faith and the Crisis of a Nation: Wales1890–191*, ed. Robert Pope, trans. Sylvia Prys Jones (Cardiff: University of Wales Press, 2004). Originally published in Welsh as *Ffydd ac Argyfwng Cenedl: Cristionogaeth a Diwylliant yng Nghymru 1890–1914* (Swansea: John Penry, 1981–2).

11 *Ibid.*, p. 348.

12 Allen Raine (Anne Adaliza Puddicombe), *Queen of the Rushes: A Tale of the Welsh Revival* [1906] (Dinas Powys: Honno, 1998). Originally published in 1906.

13 *Ibid.*, p. 195.

14 Rhys Davies, *The Withered Root* [1927] (Cardigan: Parthian & Library of Wales, 2007).

15 Tom Davies, *One Winter of the Holy Spirit* (London: Macdonald, 1985).

16 Jean-François Lyotard used the term *differend* to indicate a kind of impasse between diverse language games. It occurs when there are no agreed procedures or protocols by which divergent ideas, principles or conceptual formations can be presented within a single discursive field. It can therefore be said to indicate a silencing of some particular voice, causing or precipitating an injustice.

17 Brynmor P. Jones, *Voices from the Welsh Revival 1904–1905* (Bridgend: Evangelical Press of Wales, 1995).

18 J. Rogues de Fursac, *Un Mouvement Mystique Contemporain: Le Réveil Religieux du Pays de Galles, 1904–5* (Paris: Alcan, 1907).

19 Brynmor P. Jones, *Voices*, p. 232.

20 Eifion Evans, *The Welsh Revival*, p. 127.

21 Tom Davies, *One Winter*, p. 139.

22 Karen Lowe, *Carriers of the Fire: the Women of the Welsh Revival 1904/05* (Llanelli: Shedhead Productions, 2004), pp. 68–9.

23 www.leonardcohen.com/bio.html. Accessed 10.05.2009.

24 J. Vyrnwy Morgan, *Welsh Religious Revival*, pp. 141–62 (pp. 115–38 in the 2004 edition). Includes the text of Rev Peter Price's letter as well as correspondence he subsequently received.

25 St Paul, *2 Corinthians* 11:14.

26 Rhys Davies, *Withered Root*, p. 234.

27 Tom Davies, *One Winter*, p. 218.

Criticism and Creativity

Graham Holderness

The very title and its various permutations – 'with,' 'and,' 'versus' – concatenates these activities as differends, even sets them up in binary opposition, one against the other. They are generally thought of, both in theory and practice, as alternatives. When we look at the ways in which we construct critical writing, in the curriculum and in everyday pedagogic practice, this is understandable. It is almost *de rigueur* to open a discussion of these issues with parallel columns of descriptive terms that we apply respectively to critical and creative writing. Criticism is discursive, analytical, logical, clear, argumentative, impersonal, objective. Creativity is intuitive, evocative, expressive, performative, personal, subjective. And so on.

And yet criticism, or at least literary criticism (no longer, as it was for Matthew Arnold, a kind of humanist master-discourse that could, and should, speak with authority on anything and everything: but now restricted, professionalized into a limited cultural sphere), is surely nothing more than an effort to explain and account for creativity, as it is manifested in writing. There is, at the very least, continuity between the two, since the one is a means to knowledge of the other. Typically the critical incorporates the creative into itself, by the device of quotation. At the very best, one might claim that criticism is the precursor of creativity, criticism's John the Baptist to creativity's Christ, announcing its imminent advent. Like John the Baptist, criticism is 'not itself that light,' but is 'sent to bear witness of that light.' The best criticism ushers creativity into human knowledge, so that the light need not shine in darkness; but then eclipses itself in favour of a greater one who is to come. As creativity waxes, so criticism wanes. Having prophesied creativity's imminence and its own demise, criticism faces a kenotic evacuation of meaning as it renders the creative intelligible and accessible in its own right.

However, in reality, things are not that simple. Notwithstanding his deference and deferral to Jesus, John claimed considerable authority in his own right too, not least the authority of tradition, of the Old Testament prophets; and many people (including Herod Antipas) could not tell the difference between Jesus and John. A few Christians still follow John, believing him to be the true Messiah. And some have argued for a systematic replacement of literature by literary theory.

I want to suggest a different relationship between criticism and creativity: to suggest that the best criticism is actually creative writing, and that the two are not really binary opposites at all, but more like non-identical twins (as Jesus and John are often represented). Criticism that separates itself off from literature, linguistically and discursively, is producing something else, philosophy or critical theory. The most perfect harmony between criticism and creativity is where they become almost indistinguishable. And possibly the best criticism of all is that which succeeds in using language in the way it is used by creative writers.

There are many examples of this holistic critical-creative practice. Think of all the criticism written by creative writers. Think of the kind of Aesthetic criticisms practised by, for instance, Walter Pater and Oscar Wilde. Think of the examples that abound of modern theoretical writing that seeks to replace or substitute for literature, only to find itself mutating into a quasi-creative kind of eloquence: Roland Barthes, Jacques Derrida, Maurice Blanchot. But I don't at the moment want to get into these controversies at the theoretical level. Instead I propose to restrict myself to a few very pragmatic and personal remarks about my own practice as a critical and creative writer.

I have often been asked what prompted me, after so many years of writing criticism, to embark, around 1995, on a programme of creative writing, producing a novel, a verse anthology, short stories and so on.[1] Suffice it to say that, having started out with the aspiration of being a writer – and beginning with a writing practice that recognised little formal distinction between poetry and the critical 'appreciation' of poetry – I managed in the course of my career to invest considerable productivity into forms of critical analysis that stand at some remove from the 'creative,' and were actually read, at times, as hostile to creativity. I think this is a misreading, but I am not disposed to defend that kind of writing. I'm content, in fact, to allow my poetic and fictional writing to be read as the return of a repressed creativity. Let's say, for the sake of argument, that one way or another, I've put myself into writing on both sides of that binary divide. The key difference, I would say, is not that one is objective, the other subjective. It's much more a matter of where, in the writing, the personal is placed *vis-à-vis* the reader: whether it's enfolded within layered integuments of learning, rhetoric, irony; or much closer to the surface, exposed, vulnerable to readerly explication.

But the difficulty remains: how do these apparently disconnected kinds of writing practice co-exist? This problem I addressed by putting criticism and creativity together in the same text: *Textual Shakespeare: Writing and the Word,* published in 2003.[2] The book opens with an attempt to resolve what still remains an intractable paradox: is literature something *made* by an originating act of imagination, *created*; or is it something *produced* by subsequent acts of reading and appropriation, *constructed*? Both invoke major theories of literary production; both entail different practical approaches to the interpretation of texts. What I try to argue in the book is that both are true and indispensable: that writing is made, imagined, created, and yet re-made, appropriated, constructed. The initial act of making creates something that lends itself to re-making; and all subsequent acts of re-making pay homage to that originating creative act, even when they seem to be completely reconstructing the original, and stretching the limits of iterability to extremes.

> The processes of remaking the text are shared in common between textual study, editing, critical interpretation, indeed all our various 'reading' practices . . . 'A real reader,' says Hélène Cixous, 'is a writer.' (p. 14)

It seemed to me that in composing this argument, it was impossible not to enter a creative response, a creative commentary, into or alongside the critical arguments. There were different ways of doing this: by trying to write a critical language with aesthetic properties, making the true beautiful; by looking at the creativity implicit in critical readings by other critics, often buried beneath the surface; and by mining works of fiction, poetry, drama, that in some way could be seen to parallel the critical arguments.

Hence the first chapter ('Text') concludes by discussing Tom Stoppard's play *The Invention of Love,* about A.E. Housman, which is what I called a 'rarity,' 'a play about textual criticism.'[3] Stoppard presents Housman as two people. When the dead Housman arrives at the River Styx, Charon asks him if there's anybody else there, having been told to pick up 'a poet and a scholar' (he thinks they must be different people). The naivety and sentimentality of Housman's poetry does not seem to fit with the rebarbative arrogance of the classics professor. But textual scholarship spends all its time self-defeatingly trying to find things as romantic and personal, as pointlessly beautiful, as *A Shropshire Lad.*

> In the play's second act the 22 year-old Housman, not yet an academic, defines scholarship as 'useless knowledge for its own sake.' Although already confident in his ability to ferret out hidden corruption (he is sure of what Horace did and did not write), it is the poetry, and the poets' 'invention' of love that really counts. Against the robust academic confi-

dence of his older self, the young Housman asserts a belief in the random and accidental survival of poetic riches, miraculously enduring the wholesale destruction of a much larger cultural heritage, the wreck of ancient literature:

HOUSMAN   …have you ever seen a cornfield after the reaping? Laid flat to stubble, and here and there, unaccountably miraculously spared, a few stalks still upright. Why those? There is no reason. Ovid's *Medea*, the *Thyestes* of Varius who was Virgil's friend and considered by some his equal, the lost Aeschylus trilogy of the Trojan war … gathered to oblivion in *sheaves*, along with hundreds of Greek and Roman authors known only for fragments or their names alone – and here and there a cornstalk, a thistle, a poppy, still standing . . . (Stoppard, *Invention*, pp. 72–3)

Those miraculous survivals (and incidentally our ability to revive them through translation) are what matter, not the futile attempts of scholarship to establish what an author really wrote. AEH extrapolates this critical position to a philosophy of life:

AEH   You think there is an answer: the lost autograph copy of life's meaning, which we might recover from the corruptions that have made it nonsense. But if there is no such copy, really and truly there is no answer. (Stoppard, Invention, p. 41)

AEH is ultimately reconciled to the Stoic position, accepting the permanent value of chance fragments in place of an attempt to reconstruct the lost totality.

AEH   In the Dark Ages, in Macedonia, in the last guttering light from classical antiquity, a man copied out bits from old books for his young son, whose name was Septimius; so we have one sentence from The Loves of Achilles. Love, said Sophocles, is like the ice held in the hand by children. A piece of ice held fast in the fist …

HOUSMAN   Love it is, then and I will make the best of it.4

As AEH knows only too well, in that romantic aspiration he signally failed. (pp. 30–32)

The quotations from the play flow naturally out of the preceding chapter's discussion of textuality, and relate directly to its major themes. Scholars try to find out exactly what an author wrote, because they believe that writing to be a unique and originating act. However, in the course of establishing the texts, the scholar can get caught up in his/her own methodology, and lose sight of the point of the exercise. But if a scholar is genuinely involved in re-making the work, as a kind of co-author: then isn't it vital that he/she makes every effort to connect with the imaginative origins of his text?

> All the key issues that pertain to 'textual Shakespeare' are explicated here: the complex relations between poetry and scholarship; the rationalist attempt to construct order out of evidence that in the end amounts only to accidental, miraculous survival; the final acceptance that there is no 'lost autograph copy' that would, if rediscovered, answer all our questions and resolve all our problems. Instead there are only fragments, documents, texts, that choke us with an awareness of what we have lost, while simultaneously prompting activities of reconstruction, re-imagining, translation, that can fill empty space with words and music. (p. 31)

So if the scholar, critic, or editor, is going to connect with the source, that must surely involve a creative as a well as a critical response. The chapter is, therefore, followed by an attempt to fill in the gap left by that lost poem of Sophocles, in the form of an original poem improvising on the remaining fragment:

Fire and Ice

Sophocles said
That love's like ice
Held fast in the fist
Of a child's warm hand.
Squeeze it tight,
And it slips through the fingers;
Open your palm
And it melts, evanescent,
Absorbed in the empty air.

Michelangelo made
A statue of ice
That stood for a day

Then lapsed into liquid
A pool on Pietro's floor.

Yet it's more near to me now
That shimmer of shards
Than David's abstracted gaze
Or the Mona Lisa's
Mockery smile.
Sophocles' line
Lies on my lips
Tasting of snowflakes
Echoing silent speech.

Lovers never forget
The chill in the palm,
Cold's shiver on shrinking skin
The dampness where love has been. (p. 32)

Each chapter of critical and theoretical discussion concludes, in a similar way, with an anecdote, or an example of creative writing that rehearses critical issues, supplemented by a poem or translation, or some other example of creative practice. A chapter on Shakespeare bibliography (Ch. 2), which concludes that we need to understand literary text as both Platonic idea and material object, is illustrated with an Anglo-Saxon riddle about how books are made, how an irreducibly material process produces a sacred object (p. 56). A chapter on materialist criticism (Ch. 3) ends up talking about Gary Taylor's imprudent use, in the Oxford Shakespeare, of a phrase from Pinter's *The Homecoming*; and concludes with a translation of Catullus's politically-incorrect *Carmen* 63 (p. 85). A chapter on the Bad Quartos (Ch. 4) closes with a discussion of what Derrida calls the universal 'principle of contamination,' which is that, however isolated, texts are always infringed by traces of the manifold influences that impinge upon them. I illustrate this with a passage on Dante Gabriel Rossetti's manuscript of poems, buried with his wife Lizzie, and later exhumed, and reflect on what that incident might tell us about the relations between body and text, love and death (pp. 110–112). The MS can be seen in Jerome McGann's Rossetti website, with a gaping hole in it, caused by the autolysis of Lizzie's corpse, the 'textual traces' she left in the work. Then a further comment is inserted by a translation of the famous Old English riddle on the 'bookworm': the worm that destroys language by destroying its material substance; and the worm that destroys the source of language, the human body, after death (p. 113). How does literature survive such destruction, except by reproduction that means alteration? What survives human existence after the destruction of death?

Let me offer another example. The book has a chapter on *King Lear* (Ch. 5) which reviews the 'two texts' debate. At the end, I contrast the redemptive and nihilistic versions of *King Lear*, and ask whether we can find these perspectives somehow differentiated between the two texts. The lines, 'Do you see this? Look on her: look, her lips/Look there, look there' are only in the Folio text. But they can be, and have been, in any case interpreted by critics as 'blessed liberation' or as 'cruel delusion.' I then give an example of a new kind of conflated text, the Arden 3 edition, edited by R. A. Foakes, which puts the texts together, but shows the joins.[5]

> The Arden 3 text is also a conflated edition. But … it introduces a set of bibliographic codes that call the reader's attention to the text's hybridity. The sutures joining one text with another are not concealed, or partly disguised at the foot of the page as a collation, but obtruded upon the experience of reading. Instead of the invisible mending that normally stitches together the disparate materials of Q and F, Foakes's text boldly displays the joints, brackets, or hinges that weld the text together into a construction. They further adumbrate the activity of the editor as craftsman or artisan, a collaborator in the process of composition. He does not make the material from which the text is fashioned, but as the superior indicators show, he has decided or agreed that this is how it should be put together; the design of the piece is his. The raw material has itself in any case been produced by collaboration, at the very least of the author with himself in a dialogue between different and discordant aesthetic choices ('Two texts, two hands, two ways of listening'), and more probably in a collaborative economy involving the activity of others. (pp. 147–8)

This notion of the 'collaborative' text is then applied to the editor's own 'collaborative' experience:

> Inside Foakes's text is signalled to the reader another kind of collaboration. In his list of acknowledgements to colleagues and predecessors, Foakes mentions 'the gracious librarians of the Shakespeare Centre Library in Stratford-upon-Avon', and especially Mary White, who became my wife; it was a joy to have her help and her sustaining presence while I was working on this edition. (Foakes, *Lear*, p. xvi)

> Mary White is evidently the same person who appears in the edition's dedication:

> For my beloved Mary
> *Thou'lt come no more,*
> *Never, never, never, never, never . . .*

From this we learn that underlying this text is a history of personal bereavement, to which Lear's words on the death of Cordelia give eloquent utterance. Mary is inside the text as a collaborator, a 'help and sustaining presence'; but also as an absence, a sign of loss. The 'joy' that accompanies the editor's remembrance of the 'gracious' gift of her (which perhaps echoes Bradley's 'unbearable joy'), co-exists with despair at an absoluteness of separation: 'Thou'lt come no more.'

So it will always be. We love, and lose, and are lost. But we never lose what Stephen Greenblatt called our 'desire to speak with the dead' . . . (pp. 148–9)

Here we see the personality of the scholar emerging from the editorial text, both in terms of his co-authorship of the work, and in terms of his personal engagement with key philosophical issues of the text. Again a creative response seemed appropriate, so I went back to Stoppard's play, which makes much of Housman's translation of Horace's elegy *Diffugere nives*. And here is that beautiful poem, with its paradoxes of finality and cyclical return, newly refashioned:

Thou'lt come no more
(Horace, *Odes* IV.vii)

Snows slop to slush, but growing greenery graces the fields,
Trees toss their hair;
Streams subside, obedient to their banks, earth tilts
In a different direction;
Nature strips off, nymphs and graces unashamed bare
Their skin to the vernal air.

Hours devour the day, the days the year. Fair warning:
Nothing's immortal here.
Spring splits the ice-age, summer scorches spring;
Hard on the heels of
Apple-bearing autumn's profusion of fruits
Back comes the killing snow.

How quickly the crescent moon recovers lost light!
But when we go down
To the dark where the great and the good and the brave
Await us, dust we are, and dreams.

You can pray to the heavenly gods to add to tomorrow
The grace of another day;
Spend all your wealth on delighting your soul, and cheat
The avarice of heirs. But
When we shrink in the shade, and the dreadful judge
Delivers his verdict, there's nothing
Not eloquence, not birth, not virtue, nothing at all
Can bring us back here.
Pure as Hippolytus was, not even huntress Diana
Could drag him to light;
And loving Pirithous still sits in the dark, his chains unsheared
By Theseus' invincible sword.

One final example. My chapter on *Henry V* ends with some observations on the Chorus's image of the hour-glass ('jumping o'er times'), which figures the inexorable passage of time, dust to dust. History is irrecoverable. On the other hand it is possible to just flip over an hour-glass, and replay the past, over and over again. Yet this remains still a process of annihilation, an encounter with loss: ashes to ashes, dust to dust. This paradox is then focused by using an extract from a translation I did years ago of the Old English elegy *The Ruin*.

But Destiny doomed them,
Dealt them a double blow: pillaged by plague,
Battered by battle, the flower of the folk
Fell. This fort fragmented, and fell to waste,
To rack and ruin. The masons melted away,
The valiant men vanished. Hence are these halls
Desolate and dreary: tiles are torn
From the red roof.

'Dust,' as metaphor, is what holds all this discussion together. We move from the sand of the Chorus's hour-glass, to the 'toppled towers' of Anglo-Saxon England, to the ruined towers of 9/11, and thence to a discussion of writing, focused on the biblical story of the Woman Taken in Adultery (John 6), where Jesus stoops down and writes on the ground. I contrast this with the writing of the Ten Commandments, on tablets of stone, as an alternative model of textuality. All these resources of metaphor and symbolism are drawn into the critical conclusion:

> Modern bibliography proposes that all writing is writing in the dust. 'Writing that won't last, something exposed to dissolution' (Rowan Williams). This is either because the material foundation of writing easily disintegrates, so it survives only in altered copy, or not at all; or because, in its elusively iterable nature, writing more closely resembles a continually dispersing dust-cloud than an indelible inscription on a tablet of stone. (p. 244)

It will be apparent, from the examples given above, that *Textual Shakespeare* is an unusual book, an idiosyncrasy that perhaps accounts for the fact it is the only one of my books never, to my knowledge, to have been reviewed. It mingles criticism and creativity together in a promiscuously hybrid discourse. Its arguments operate, as do the creative works it studies, as much by metaphor as by logical argument. And it penetrates into areas where criticism normally dares not go, deep into the subjectivity of the critic and editor. It proposes, in short, a new and fundamentally re-orientated relationship between criticism and creativity. And I am waiting, like a man who long ago dropped a stone into a well, and is still listening for the splash, to hear the sound of an impact.

Notes

1 *The Prince of Denmark* (Hatfield: University of Hertfordshire Press, 2001); *Craeft: poems from the Anglo-Saxon* (Nottingham: Shoestring Press, 2001).
2 *Textual Shakespeare: Writing and the Word* (Hatfield: University of Hertfordshire Press, 2003). All subsequent reference to this book appear parenthetically in the essay.
3 Tom Stoppard, *The Invention of Love* (London: Faber and Faber, 1997).
4 Stoppard, *Invention*, p. 43.
5 *King Lear*, ed. R. A. Foakes (London: Thomas Nelson, 1997).

The Critic as Fiction, or Dr King on Sheds – an Entertainment

Simon King

The Preamble

I'm not sure what the following is, exactly: an entertainment; an anti-paper, an antidote; an exercise in the absurd; a signed confession; a forgery; a suicide note; a letter of resignation – why don't *you* decide. As well as all of this, it's also a manifesto, of a kind, though I'll never explain how or why, so don't ask me.

> *How splendid it would be, if I was saying all this about myself!*
> OSCAR WILDE, *De Profundis*

> *The Doctor is not here; he is rarely here. I speak for him. I perform him. As ever.*

I can't tell you about the first time I came across the Arcane Scribbler, Doctor King. He seems always to have been there, like the weather – mostly overcast, with intermittent sunny spells and sporadic showers of acid. I *can* tell you that he's put in more regular appearances over the last five years or so, and he's even published, albeit a slim book, no thicker than a drinks coaster, about ants of all things, a slight, seemingly random work that made him a very local celebrity for a while – the Antman, the Ant King, Doctor Ant, etc. On the publishing front in general, however, the Doctor has yet to astonish the world, and this is largely due to the fact that his mode of thinking is not best suited to the monograph. Rather, he is a virtuoso of the fragment, whether scribbled on scraps of paper, the backs of envelopes or, indeed, lavatory walls. And yet rumour spread of a Great Work in preparation, admittedly a rumour started largely by the Scribbler himself, but one which found me, against my better judgement, agreeing to meet him with a view to becoming the editor of the project. We were to meet in his 'office'; not, as you might imagine, a donnish room on campus, but any one of a number of seedy backstreet boozers. The boozer chosen was known to lowlife cognoscenti as The Tight 'Ole; we were to meet at noon on a bright sunny day, though you'd never have guessed it from the interior twilight of the pub. In the crepuscular fug, the Doctor's looming shape, dressed in customary black, glass and fag in hand, was unmistakable. How shall I describe him? Imagine a random assemblage of charcoal sticks, topped with a head filched from a Punch and Judy show – he's all nose and chin, and even at his most animated there is something paralysed, immobile about his features, like carved wood. Well, there you have the Arcane Scribbler. He was standing, as usual, at the bar, and I joined him. There were, as usual, no preliminaries; immediately, the Scribbler discoursed, waving a hand-rolled cigarette as he did so, creating a kind of calligraphy in the air, a purely retinal text: like his spoken words, forever lost. I could never look Doctor King directly in the eye; instead we would peer at each other, each reflected in the grimy mirror behind the bar, my eyes set in affected, eyebrow-raised nonchalance, his gimlet-inscrutable. He had with him a plastic shopping bag that I understood to contain 'the Work,' which he handed over to me without much ceremony. Clutching the bag, I was about to make a quick escape, when he detained me a moment, scribbling something on a cigarette paper, which he then offered, as 'a kind of key to it all,' he said. I looked at the paper; it read, simply, *'Teufelsdröckh'*.

Back at the house, I gutted the shopping bag. Inside were half a dozen fat buff envelopes, and inside those were the usual scraps of cuttings and diverse slips of scribbled-over paper, one of which, I noticed, without much surprise or enthusiasm, being an old *Kit Kat* wrapper. All of this shabby confetti offered a fair representation of the Scribbler's mind; not for the first time I reflected on what a poor showing such waste paper would make in the RAE. Just as well that the Doctor remains untenured – but then what *does* he do? Doctor King has never been forthcoming about how he spends his time or how he earns his living; if pushed, as he once was in my hearing, he'll mutter something about being 'in semiotics,' but that's about all (it turned out that he was, apparently, working for a local sign-writer at the time).

The Scribbler is an enigma, then; that's why, in spite of myself, I couldn't help but be interested in the contents of those fat envelopes. I was about to discard the plastic carrier when I noticed something stapled to the inside, a narrow slip of grey card, scrawled over with what looked like a shopping list. On closer inspection, I found it to be an index of sorts, a list, I supposed, of chapter headings: 'Men in Sheds'; 'Children's Sheds'; and, most tantalising of all, 'My Shed Memories'. Checking the shopping list against the fat envelopes, I discovered that there was, indeed, one with 'My Shed Memories' inscribed upon it. Inside I found this:

> It wasn't until I was fourteen or so that I discovered what my grandfather did in his shed every Sunday morning: precisely nothing. He would smoke his illicit cigars and listen to Radio Three while my family's powerful triumvirate of women would squabble over Sunday lunch. As Conrad's Marlowe might say, the women were out of it. Or rather, my grandfather was out of it, which comes to much the same thing.

Curiously, this reminded me of *my* granddad, although he never owned a shed; it was a garage, rather, home to an old Austin 1300, sand-coloured, polished until it was virtually frictionless. And he never listened to Radio Three; he was a Radio Two man, although he did smoke cigars, and drink cans of Sainsbury's own make of beer, the first beer that I ever tasted; and checking his tyre pressure and cleaning his wheel hubs was the first job I ever had, the first wage I ever earned. Surprising that Doctor King and I should have so much in common.

In the same bundle of scrawled-over papers I came upon a kind of general overview of the Work: 'My theme is one of sheds and related structures,' the Doctor had written, 'such as shacks, huts, lean-tos, dens. Not garages, however, nor gazebos, and certainly not conservatories.' It was characteristic of the Scribbler that he did not provide any rationale for his value judgements: such-and-such are fit objects for study, while such-and-such are not. The sheep and the goats, the raw and the cooked, the damned and the saved – each is divided from the other in the court of the Scribbler's imagination, with little justice and no transparency. But perhaps I'm being unfair to him; all of us, surely, are entitled to extra-judicial rights over our own minds. We all have, inside, a court of no appeal, in which we grant indulgences to the seemingly undeserving – it's called *taste*. And in any case, I can, I think, detect *some* logic in this instance; a garage, after all, is a building with a particular and limited function, a gazebo, generally speaking, is a ghastly suburbanite folly, and a conservatory is an extension to the house, the rightful domain of that 'triumvirate of women' to which the Doctor referred. Here I should, I suppose, mention something about the Doctor's relationship with women, which is a mystery. Of course, he was born of woman, and he has, amazingly, been married, once, presumably to a woman. And yet I can't imagine anyone more removed from the female half of the species. It's not that Doctor King is consciously sexist – he's not; it's just that he seems to have no interest in the whole male/female question, whether in a chauvinistic or a feminist sense. However, in one of the envelopes I managed to find the Doctor's single and presumably definitive statement on the sex issue, as it relates to sheds:

> The house, which properly belongs to Woman, is the anti-shed; the shed is the anti-house. The shed must stand apart from the house, related but separate, in that courtship common to all matter, and to the cultures which arise from matter. To utilise the terms of that most gendered and seductive of games, chess, the shed is a pinned piece. Divorced from the house, the shed is merely a shack, a shanty-habitation; married with the house, it is a conservatory, a part of the house, absorbed by Woman, tidied and rationalised by Woman. Thus the shed is pinned, and cannot be moved, nor can it be taken. But in her soul Woman hates the shed, and would smash it all to pieces.

There was a footnote: 'See Cornelia Parker, *Cold Dark Matter* (1991)' – a reference to a modern, conceptual piece of sculpture on a theme of exploding sheds. The influence of Structuralism is fairly plain (didn't Saussure talk about chess somewhere?). Overall, however, I wouldn't dare comment on this passage of the Scribbler's, other than to suggest that he may have been reading quite a bit of Lawrence when it was written.

But why *sheds*? Perhaps that hastily scribbled word on the cigarette paper might offer some clue: 'Teufelsdröckh.' I googled this mysterious word, and discovered a certain Diogenes Teufelsdröckh. German, of course, Teufelsdrokh was a minor nineteenth-century *savant* who achieved some notoriety thanks to the efforts of a British editor – namely, one Thomas Carlyle. My reactions on learning this, no doubt, were perfectly understandable: 'My God,' I thought, 'the Scribbler wants *me* to be his Carlyle!' Need I tell you that at that moment I refused, point-blank, to be anyone's Carlyle. Austere, Presbytarian discipline doesn't come naturally to me; nor, I might add, does it come naturally to the Doctor himself. There is, unremarkably enough, a tinge of The Yellow Book to the Scribbler, a tincture of green and purple Decadence, which is probably the most appealing thing about him. Doctor King is a dilettante, or, as he puts it, a 'pissabout,' a 'fartaround'; he would have been languid in the nineties, and would have fallen apart completely come the twenties. Then again, it sometimes pleases me to think that had he been killed at Ypres, leaving behind a few hastily scribbled fragments, he might have cut quite a figure. But we can't choose our own era. I'm rather partial to the forties myself, Fitzrovia, the blackout, Julian Maclaren-Ross, you get the picture.

Thanks to Project Gutenberg, I was able to get hold of the text of Teufelsdröckh's work, in Carlyle's edition, overloaded to a spine-breaking extent with editorial commentary. After a fairly cursory skim, I realised that the Doctor's identification with Professor Diogenes Teufelsdröckh almost makes sense; in fact, in many ways the Professor's *magnum opus*, a study of the symbolism of clothes, is echoed quite nicely by the Doctor's study of sheds. Both are concerned with coverings, with outsides, and, I guess, with the 'essential-within-the-provisional', and both are, in a word, bonkers. In his edition of the Professor's work, Carlyle regrets that Teufelsdröckh's 'talents . . . have been so much devoted to a rummaging among lumber-rooms . . . [and] to a scavenging in kennels.' One might say the same about the Scribbler; to the proverbial 'bloke on the bus,' the fact that anyone had paid serious attention to old clothes and damp old outhouses would be bewildering. Critics – what can one say? 'How could a man,' Carlyle asks, 'occasionally of keen insight . . . [and] who had real thoughts to communicate, resolve to emit them in a shape bordering so closely on the absurd?' How, indeed.

I have to say that Carlyle has a greater esteem for his subject than I do for mine. For Carlyle, Teufelsdröckh is 'a wonder-loving, a wonder-seeking man,' while my Scribbler represents little more than a nine-day's wonder. The Doctor, as it happens, doesn't have a particularly high opinion of Teufelsdröckh. Carlyle, Teufelsdröckh, Doctor King, and me – what we have here is a near-perfect circle of disregard; you could set it down in an equation, always assuming you could be bothered. C sort of disregards T, I disregard C and K, and I'm sure that T would disregard me, as would C. It's a near-circle because we can never know *what* Diogenes or Tom would have made of the Scribbler, more's the pity.

The Doctor's opinion of T is contained in a series of notes on the Professor's work that I came upon in one of the bulky envelopes. The tendency of these notes is to argue – and I quote – that 'within Teufelsdröckh's misguided and confused study of clothes, there is, in embryo, a study of sheds, waiting to be born.' In short, the Doctor thinks that Diogenes had taken the easy option:

> To talk of clothes is no real labour, for clothes already speak; when we dress do we not make a statement? But think of the silence of the shed! It creaks and moans but does not speak, nor has anyone spoken for it. When criticism encounters non-discursive things or practices, Michel de Certeau writes, 'when, instead of being a discourse on other discourses . . . theory has to advance over an area where there are no longer any discourses . . . [then] there is a sudden unevenness of terrain: the ground on which verbal language rests begins to fail.' The critic who speaks of the shed, who speaks for the shed, is in the rough, on the wreck; he occupies that piece of waste

ground without a name or purpose, that is, nevertheless, familiar to us all
– but 'of all the things everyone does,' as de Certeau puts it, 'how much
gets written down?'

But does *everyone* 'do' the shed thing, or even step into a shed from time to
time? I don't. Doctor King confuses common experience with the fact that
sheds are fairly common-or-garden; but not everyone owns a shed, or wants
to. I'm sure the Scribbler knows this, but he never mentions it. *Pace* Stella
Gibbons, there's always something nasty in the woodshed – there's always
something nasty in any shed: spiders, mould, decade's worth of accumu-
lated rotting shite. You could turn this into a metaphor for the Nation, if
you could be bothered. I can't. In common, however, with a lot of critics,
when the Scribbler is unsure of his material, he attacks someone else's –
thus, he goes back to berating Teufelsdröckh:

> Look at the way he throws his clothes about! Teusfeldrockh is little more
> than an intellectual slut, a slattern, a slovenly teenager who refuses to tidy
> his room. Rather than clothes, T would have done better to think of the
> wardrobe which should contain them.

The upshot of this passage, which continues at some length, is that the
Scribbler regards Teufelsdröckh's work as lacking in clarity, 'a confused
jumble-sale,' as he describes it. 'In contrast consider the purity of the shed,'
the Scribbler continues:

> Ask a small child to draw a picture of a house. They will invariably draw a
> shed, for the image will be without drainpipes or porticos or satellite dishes
> or all of the necessary, unnecessary things which the modern house requires.
> To the childish mind the shed is the Platonic Ideal of the house. The shed
> is simply a sketch, a geometrical arrangement of lines drawn in space
> dividing inside from outside. As such, it is the fundamental achievement
> of culture, because it creates that interior space, echoing thought itself, in
> which human work is performed; in the words of Teufelsdröckh, 'a hut is
> . . . the visible embodiment of a thought.'

I should, at this point, record something about Doctor King's style of
writing, which is to fire out information like bullets from a Maxim gun,
mowing down his readers like so many rebellious tribesmen. To give an
example: at one point the Doctor finds himself all at sea, almost literally,
and embarks on a discourse concerning 'boat-sheds,' and 'shed-boats,' and
'shed-boat-sheds,' the last being another reference to modern conceptual

art, Simon Starling's *Shedboatshed*, which won him the Turner Prize in 2005. From there he goes on to talk about the Irish currach house, the upturned herring-boat sheds of Lindisfarne, the Peggotty's upturned boat-house in *David Copperfield*, and the beach huts at Brighton and Hove, finally ending up with a description of Noah's ark as a sea-going shed, on a vast scale, 'the length [of it] . . . three hundred cubits, the breadth of it fifty cubits, and the height of it thirty cubits.' These abbreviated words of the Lord trigger, in the Scribbler, a chain of thought about religion, which ranges from a general argument that all churches, temples, and mosques are merely sheds for storing God in, to a particular discussion about a shed in darkest Norfolk that has been transformed into a 4th century Roman church by a group of Orthodox believers. You get the general idea, I'm sure – Doctor King has a mind like a gadfly, and has never knowingly written anything in a reasoned, linear fashion.

The magic of religion brings him, by some mental shortcut unknown to the normal mind, to the magic of childhood, and the child's relations with the shed. In the envelope marked 'Children's Sheds' there is a fair amount of material in this vein. He talks of the cowshed which was home to the planet of the Clangers, from Oliver Postgate's animated children's series of the seventies. He talks of naughty uncle Roald Dahl's writing shed. And yes, as I thought he would, for the umpteenth time the Scribbler talks of *Doctor Who*, and of the TARDIS, that 'most wonderful shed of all,' he writes, 'which contains within it all of time and space.' Elsewhere in the same envelope, there is an old postcard upon which the Scribbler had written what was obviously a critical sketch:

> The child's shed contains marvels beyond categorisation. In the shed young Michael, in David Almond's novel of 1998, meets with Skellig, who is 'something like you, something like a beast, something like a bird, something like an angel . . . Something like that'.

'Something like that' just about sums up the Doctor's method. And he goes on – he *does* go on. The Scribbler talks about Wendy-houses and the penchant small children have for squatting in large cardboard boxes, as representing an early onset of sheddism. And elsewhere in the bulky envelopes the Doctor offers us the shed as an antidote to Modernist architecture, 'a Romantic opposition to uniformity and conformity,'[1] and he recalls witnessing the construction by some renegade young aesthetes of a cardboard shanty-shed in the courtyard beneath the Pompidou Centre in Paris. And the shed can never be complete, the Scribbler argues, but is always a work in progress or decay, for ever and ever, amen, and he quotes, in support, poor old Teufelsdröckh: 'all things wax, and roll onwards; Arts, Establishments, Opinions, nothing is completed, but ever completing.'

And on, and so on, and so forth. Despairing of this after a while, I turned once more, with relief, strangely enough, to *Sartor Resartus*, Carlyle's edition of Teufelsdröckh, and I stumbled upon a passage which pulled me up short. Halfway through the text, Carlyle reports that he started to feel a 'painful suspicion' concerning Herr Teufelsdröckh; what, he wonders, if 'these Autobiographical Documents are partly a mystification! What if many a so-called Fact were little better than a Fiction!' – in other words, what if old Diogenes was pulling Carlyle's leg. A further thought struck me, one which doesn't seem to have occurred to Tom – what if Teufelsdröckh himself was a 'mystification,' a fiction? After all, Carlyle never says that he had actually *met* him. The implications of all this for my position vis-à-vis the Scribbler became clear. I've never really believed in Doctor King; he's too much of a fragmentarian, a patchwork man who belongs in the pages of Professor Teufelsdröckh. Clearly he's a fiction, then, cobbled together somewhere – possibly in a tailor's shop, possibly in a shed. And yet I *have* met him, which is worrying; if someone is writing Doctor King, then who's writing me? Are we writing each other? With these thoughts I felt as though I'd abandoned the world of Carlyle for the territory of Paul Auster, the universe of Philip K. Dick.

I imagine going to the same seedy, backstreet boozer, meeting the Scribbler at the bar, and putting all of this to him; I imagine him pausing in his cascade of talk, as if discovered in some practical joke, only to flash me a Forsyth grin, chilling, like a death's head. Comedies rarely end with a death, but they often end with a tableau, like this one: the Scribbler at the bar, hand-rolled fag in one hand, book in the other. Like an action figure – or, in this case, an *in*action figure – the Scribbler comes with accessories. What's the book? Wodehouse of course. Or 'Wood –house.' Christ. Enough said. Slow fade to grey. *Fin*.

Note

1   Later, I discovered that these words were drawn from a volume entitled *Shed Men* by Gareth Jones, that 'pioneering anthropologist of sheddism', according to the Scribbler. You can find this work in any major bookshop, in the Humour section.

OFF THE WALL

Days of 1989

Helen Farish

A metallic blue hearse returns to base, empty.
A spiritualist says I have psychic gifts.
A man with blond hair has hurt me.
I'm reading *The Alexandria Quartet,*
Julius Caesar. It's spring again.
Lizards scratch roof tiles. The woman below
checks drying clothes. Bellini. Donizetti.
At night wild dogs roam the steep street,
the bare bulbs that fail to light the way home
swing in the wind. Almond blossom
in the room-sized garden holds me
in the dark as the courtyard door
closes behind. Trying to see
into the future. What about those gifts?

The Ghosted Interpreter

Geoffrey Hartman

1

Wherever I go is Claudius. Wherever
I turn, breathe, look, Claudius.
Love has no greater presence
as memory and ashes.
Here, here, o here, what a mole of a ghost
reality is! Between me
and love, me and a royal doom,
me and my mother – behind the arras,
in the oratories, Claudius and clones
dally: I see their fathering strings.
Only the heart I do not see, my heart
knows the worm better than itself.

2

Beauteous Ophelia fished from the waters,
old maid, violet, amazonian heart,
wiping the rheum of passion quietly,
smelling of death to bachelors:
Analyze her new mortality.
The unwieldy shield of disaffection
is garnished daily by contemptuous shafts
of selfhood; stroke after brazen stroke
she parries with ex-beauty's art
makes every straight a sevenfold smart
who has only herself to martyrize.
She is the oblique, or like a knight in chess
goes crooked straightly, and her armory
creaks with right angular submissions.
Yet I am grateful, belle heaulmière,
that, living again, or by me filched

unto life, you wing my mind's death with yours,
and let me gaud a moment's entrails.

3
Now Gertrude, poor soul, mutters in the wings.
Her love had long before that fatal month
parted its bed, childed subaltern courses,
flowing forsaken among pieties.
She married strength, then weakness to her nature,
enjoyed the royalties of both and passed
as right is, to a masque of gracious dotage.
Then comes this mad, corrosive son of words
kills subterfuge, strikes into curtains,
revives a ghostly greatness. She shudders at
her image, in his eye the broken beam:
an ardent basilisk transfigures her.

4
A last time, and a last, great bloods, become
gilt with the guilt of knowledge, and before
the lechery of time scatters you quite,
alive again in corruptible verse.

Six Children

Mark Ford

<blockquote>
'Though unmarried I have had six children.'*

WALT WHITMAN
</blockquote>

The first woman I ever got with child wore calico
In Carolina. She was hoeing beans; as a languorous breeze
I caressed her loins, until her hoe lay abandoned in the furrow.

The second was braving the tumultuous seas that encircle
This fish-shaped isle; by the time a sudden rip-tide tore
Her from my grasp, she had known the full power of Paumanok.

One matron I waylaid – or was it *she* who waylaid
Me? – on a tram that shook and rattled and
Rang from Battery Park to Washington Heights and back.

O Pocahontas! You died as Rebecca Rolfe, and are buried
In Gravesend. Your distant descendant, her swollen belly
Taut as a drum, avoids my eye, and that of other men-folk.

While my glorious diva hurls her enraptured soul to the gods,
I sit, dove-like, brooding in the stalls: what in me is vast,
Dark and abysmal, her voice illumines and makes pregnant.

Some day, all together, we will stride the open road, wheeling
In an outsized pram my sixth, this broken, mustachioed
Soldier whose wounds I bind up nightly. His mother I forget.

* 'My dear Master,' John Addington Symonds wrote to Walt Whitman
on 3 August 1890, two years before the poet's death,

I want next to ask you a question about a very important portion of your
teaching, which has puzzled a great many of your disciples and admirers .

. . In your conception of Comradeship, do you contemplate the possible intrusion of those semi-sexual emotions and actions which no doubt do occur between men? I do not ask, whether you approve of them, or regard them as a necessary part of the relation? But I should much like to know whether *you are prepared to leave them to the inclinations and the conscience of the individuals concerned?* . . . It has not infrequently occurred to me among my English friends to hear your 'Calamus' objected to, as praising and propagating a passionate affection between men, which (in the language of the objectors) has 'a very dangerous side,' and might 'bring people into criminality.' Now: it is of the utmost importance to me as your disciple, and as one who wants sooner or later to diffuse a further knowledge of your life-philosophy by criticism; it is most important to me to know what you really think about all this. I agree with the objectors I have mentioned that, human nature being what it is, the enthusiasm of 'Calamus' is calculated to encourage ardent and *physical* intimacies.

Whitman was appalled, and responded in a letter of 19 August in the following terms:

About the questions on Calamus etc: they quite daze me. L of G is only to be rightly construed by & within its own atmosphere & essential character – all of its pages & pieces so coming strictly under –: that the Calamus part has even allowed the possibility of such construction as mentioned is terrible – I am fain to hope that the pp themselves are not to be even mentioned for such gratuitous & quite at the time undreamed & unrecked possibility of morbid inferences – wh are disavowed by me & seem damnable . . . My life, young manhood, mid-age times South, etc, have been jolly bodily & doubtless open to criticism. Though unmarried I have had six children – two are dead – one living Southern grandchild fine boy writes to me occasionally – circumstances (connected with their benefit & fortune) have separated me from intimate relations.

Not a trace of evidence relating to these six children has ever come to light; in this poem, however, I take the liberty of imagining the great poet's getting of his fictitious offspring.

Allusions in 'Six Children'
Line 6: Paumanok, or Paumanake (land of tribute), was one of the many names used for Long Island by its Native American inhabitants. Nearly all of the island's original tribes, who included Canarsies, Rockaways, Nesquakes, Matinecocks, Setaukets, Patchogues, Shinnecocks, Montauks,

and Manhassets, had been displaced by the time Whitman was born in West Hills, near Huntington village, in 1819. He frequently calls Long Island Paumanok in his poems: 'Starting from fish-shaped Paumanok, where I was born, / Well-begotten, and raised by a perfect mother . . . ' ('Starting from Paumanok')

Lines 7–9: Whitman was a great traveler on New York's trams or streetcars, and one of his closest friendships was with the conductor Peter Doyle.

Line 10: Pocahontas was made famous by John Smith, an adventurer who played a leading role in the establishment of the colony of Jamestown in Virginia in 1607. In his *General History of Virginia, New England, and the Summer Isles* (1624) Smith claimed that Pocahontas saved him from being executed by her father Powhatan; just as Powhatan's warriors were about beat his brains out with clubs, Pocahontas 'got his head in her arms and laid her own upon his to save him from death'. She later converted to Christianity and married the Englishman John Rolfe, who brought her to London in 1616. She died the following year and is buried at Gravesend. Whitman's most extended tribute to the original inhabitants of America comes in 'The Sleepers,' in which he recalls an incident from his mother's childhood:

> Now I tell what my mother told me today as we sat at
>   dinner together,
> Of when she was a nearly grown girl living home with her
>   parents on the old homestead.
>
> A red squaw came one breakfasttime to the old homestead,
> On her back she carried a bundle of rushes for
>   rushbottoming chairs;
> Her hair straight shiny coarse black and profuse
>   halfenveloped her face,
> Her step was free and elastic . . . her voice sounded
>   exquisitely as she spoke.
>
> My mother looked in delight and amazement at the stranger,
> She looked at the beauty of her tallborne face and full and
>   pliant limbs,
> The more she looked upon her she loved her,
> Never before had she seen such wonderful beauty and purity;
> She made her sit on a bench by the jamb of the fireplace . . .

she cooked food for her,
She had no work to give her but she gave her remembrance
and fondness.

The red squaw staid all the forenoon, and toward the middle
of the afternoon she went away;
O my mother was loth to have her go away,
All the week she thought of her . . . she watched for her
many a month,
She remembered her many a winter and many a summer,
But the red squaw never came nor was heard of there again.

Lines 13–15: Whitman adored the opera, and in 'Song of Myself' writes:

A tenor large and fresh as the creation fills me,
The orbic flex of his mouth is pouring and filling me full.

I hear the trained soprano . . . She convulses me like the climax of my
love-grip;
The orchestra whirls me wider than Uranus flies,
It wrenches unnamable ardors from my breast,
It throbs me to gulps of the farthest down horror.

Lines 15–18: Whitman spent the Civil War visiting and tending wounded soldiers in hospitals in New York and Washington. He brought them food and gifts, wrote numerous letters to their families and sweethearts on their behalf, and administered what he called 'the medicine of daily affection'.

IDEAS

The Bruise that Heidegger Built

Drew Milne

> *. . . in architecture it is the visible*
> *material, and spatial mass on which*
> *the inmost heart itself is so far as*
> *possible to be brought before*
> *contemplation. Given such a*
> *material, nothing is left to the artistic*
> *representation but to refuse the*
> *validity to the material and the*
> *massive in its purely material*
> *character and to interrupt it*
> *everywhere, break it up, and deprive*
> *it of its appearance of immediate*
> *coherence and independence.*
> G.W.F. HEGEL

hacker dwelling meniscus how go liquid   just
spans modular thrown open to open plan
no part in it nor no evolutionary prompts   as
that natural that rain yet ultimately social
will hold great matter of experimentation   love
then collective work in its own right how
united they stand the coop of landscape   collects
all easeful living to which spirit answers
are aspired said chain of endeavour skin   interiors
spar did it round the table a wood sickle
adventuress of native culture indigenous   become
and ever so modern fit with it landscapes
the post and beam construction here then   home
kitimat and kwakutl village (fig. 73) new
spine spire song dies an odd totem pole   shutting
the thing ranging playful to premonitory

the bruise that Heidegger built so tied up   every
set to pour concrete image or allotments
no kin or inhouse engineers according to   other
the Parking dress code c/o buff brickster
purred concrete slob edges expressed in   then
flamboyant canopy adding serene flairs
boasting to curved doubters to embrace   shells
thus first ever plastic chairs on autoclave
dancing using steam under pressure sing   of
it's all happening or volume accentuated
to lozenge shapes ache to massing bulk   each
do dominion cities coining in definitions
mirage on parking penumbra as an only   finite
unanimous choice to go go electrification
to the blast it's all the same to yes amen   elevation
bastards torn through smooth talk medals
but so promoted into the sacred newness   hold
forced far up cry stark oh clean stocking
as markets proliferated so too modernism   shed
annuals donning bib & tucker and giving
it's hey ho slinging the beaux pants into   skin
a dust bag on on into over-bearing detail

stall city literally bound to margins slang
ltd. star if liberal attuned euros to scream   so
note in transatlantic moults to superbs the
geographic spray yields high proportions   arch
irregular & sloping building lot cum idiom
from west coast style to entrenchment how   its
genocidal mutiny an island of anglosaxon
field trips even after alienating suez crisis   fill
the fruit of the international go local flavor
all widening a whole field of architecture   of
on climbing frames late of imperial hubris
landscape dense or lush and majestic barf   estates
till remarkably luminous grey light downs

a figure loot sublime profile of mountain   bitter
the hills that Hegel scorned till modernism
so bereft of utopian innocence felt boner   grows
leaving slash bowl for the local poor spilt
societal need in material slash such ethos   dishes
zip cuts and wound in very barked strain
a faded gasp of universal legitimacy hark   shifts
the grain elevator on oceangoing Empress
all without irony numen whiter than Ethiop   body
the perfection of efficients giving the evils
stream logged in kinds enslaving to techno   and
whereas the lyric fund growls design motif
spelt out diminished leaves respecting hush   soul
dainty but bluff geometer built in the USA
beaux part cum art deco craft predilections   cutlery
as world war had run the yonk redundant
stucco upon stucco over the killing shelves   how
severs purity further evident in rendering
God the façade were to kill for so optimum   ideally
no fairy castle over a pointy headed peak
the bridge the shovel the briar pipe to bed   crashing
metonymy of pumice in the skirting boards
he want a machine to live in and less clutter   sounds
but still married to the earth works straying
for want of caryatid to cop off load bearing   flimsy

actually cramped in standardized quarters   firm
draped asbestos ranked statuesque in situ
its figurate living mind whose nature strolls   feet
within the floor area the budget will afford
pace Mayakovsky's pacing breath stretcher   then
atop a concrete slab laid upon minimalists
whose song of the box or cupboard draw   slippery
drives a coach and fiat through the whole
will to reside in architectonic vocabularies   tops
no bulky buffet arrangement needed here

later deployed in low brow configurations   nature
all hail Ikea and the stripped soul flooring
the cause economy in light brown parquet   makes
strung out vacantly over gypsum lego sets
till vermiculite sheathing holds each whole   no
of resin-bonded wood chips in rigid ranch
the blue-collar coffee set dreaming a buck   bounds
this is plywood world on the verge of MDF
frankly each kitchen victory requires care   etc.
a legacy of military design in every trainer
slash freedom's no blank indeterminateness   merely
but the expressive slash (since demolished)
how goes it bonnie maid versatile linoleum   trenches
under which circumstances a double want
as a counter-poise to the absolute standing   puckered
partly too for something fixed and secure
feet up on the picture thinking homemaker   lips
while glamour steals a march on the bath
before sitting pretty up on executive foam   in
every picture window brought to you by
technology sanctified in modernist points   furrows
yonder the hum of happy wrecking crews
and the inherent problems of angular form   faces
giving way to the revenue view or upkeep
left to run from elegance to stark brutalism   come
hey you stop roaming in empty abstraction
keep your eyes open for lay Althusserians   physic
then there's the horizontal cadence calling

throttle squall so pulp sentiment pouring
scorning crisp to home of the year combo   drip
raised slab Miesian slotted into rocky crop
ample gives every bosom high rising utility   trickle
if residual neo-gothic articulate in masonry
was compact but glass block enjoying view   down
vista front cast concrete de l'esprit nouveau

as a model for inexpensive 'social' housing   harping
as if there's another kind you house banker
spreading parks in euphuistical clerestory   scam
only the best for patio sets glazed gloomily
into middling distances where poor folk go   how
amid wheely bins spanking tame angularity
turn up cape cod retro styling to historicos   beds
set for cheerful living what is pulls tongue
the reflex gag in sheer concrete weeping   backs
mourns charm suffused torture up and up
bespeak don't namely don't architecturize   rifts
pick the wage scope demanding finer stock
mineral spec molybdenum high-tensile glue   middling
and above all the tree and columnar spray
showering acanthus over bushy carpet and   still
bring me the head of estate management on
a plate and talk of sad suits in Bloomsbury   even
it comes out on wasp bombers c/o Boeing
apparently limitless cheap gaz in structural   your
minimalism it will do many rivers to syphon
the feral report source taking hard headed   extended
low rise pokey do the multiflex said to be
the holy grill of prototypical cheap guilded   limb
before burnt professional saturation smarm
forcefully yet amicably like staid intellects   for
shuffling up through the mollusc categorical
as talk of creative energies leaves the room   family
spinning in concealed mirth the gauche do
sparks trend drainage from growing spots   kids
tangle torn the elite corps looks down upon
hovel dance set baking a black polo sweat   car

the bond's as secure though
effected by different means
for said family on a streeper
site a tricellular stressed-skin

elliptically vaulted building
conceptual variations further
    disposed
    among   spills
    eating
    bathing   staining
    and
    sleeping   loved
    with
    grades   parts
    nesting
    existing   well
    owner
    occupied   broken
    foliage
    breathing parts
    steely
    larkssuch
    gridpark
    frames   that
    snoozing
    through   sinking
    winding
    wires   pulls
    settling
into the raised slab solution
in admittedly flatter locution
intent in their no less purist
pavilions of instinctive glory
urging lyricism over rations

boxy-wood frame and concrete
ranged around a modesty pack
lately doubled in upon circulars
for the more angular deep cave
pitching a mythic dog or domus
including a special custom fitting

graphite	
down	heart
vellum	
textured	spanner
where	
plains	fittings
depend	
stimuli	buckled
expanded	
volume	down
therefore	
moody	among
respect	
naturally	cuttings
setting	
sublime	frosting
northern	
environs	each
broads	
bricking	killer
artificial	
fireplace	cabinet
focals	

the cross-axial kitchen in liquid
plane form volume and facture
showering the polygonal drones
and arcs around a central pool
the texture to the exposed wing

the house of ideas is life as lived
use what is there to lend meaning
and memo to blend varnish cedar
a building should celebrate a site
its should as divine functionalism
disturbs the natural to a minimum

    scoops
    affordable   light
    imaginary
    bank   facing
    managers
    expendable   streams
    livings
    reflecting   flexed
    pooled
    strands   along
    ruthlessly
    screened   industrial
    from
    intellectual   cartilage
    fabric
    therewith   such
    proletarian
    golfers   privacy
    televised
    declining   priced
    locals
    while   to
    fieldstone
    hearth   die
    roasts
    colored   for
    wallpaper

growth spoke of as western scene
for people not for plants creatures
until sold on the golf course circus
sing climate milieu technics encore
once more puppet imaginary client

but warned of looming urbanicide
the trend embraces half measures
dunked in pure opportunism slurp
ironically barely captures the half
acceptable face of countless crazy
stone dykes in Inca parody stacks
    spaced
    between   prefab
    living
    then does
    sleeping
    spaced   screen
    between
    structuring the
    material
    projecting   work
    concrete
    modernism life
    through
    class simples
    dividers
    tongue   your
    and
    groove   glass
    sharing
    laterals   half
    bordering
    upon   full
    sterility
a gambit reflecting military gear
marshalled among said enfilade
to spatial freedom where dusting
the reliable barometer of public
sky bungalow such unlikely term
being the wood generated vistas

cognitive architecture involves the prop in   notes
stays low mental skeletons that don't vary
to those most sceptical of its representation   screwed
suck in the causal draft buttressing events
otherwise done municipal verily Maecenas   to
cometh the pool and cabaña oer the hydro
as starry fire takes a collegiate gothic look   skirts
giving curtains of glass the once standing
pool of lit ennui throwing up the exposed   choked
beam overhanging eave shingle pitch roof
laughably called for genuine regionalism   linen
here plagiarists roam over the old carcase
rather than patch up a mouldy design tort   analogy
bleat bleat comes the all new humanismus
enamelled till the flush bridles to scholarly   masker
decline one time capitalism all but killed
architecture as a decent profession herald   you
tide tilted into breeze block import domes
yours to do with as urban litter honk honk   were
the more so how far far-reaching ever so
talks up ¥ $ down neo-modernismus way   joys
head in hand to face the built environment
simmers over ground once marked to clear   in
be concrete dressed in concrete universals
with Prada conduits well pure Tudorbethan   all
while surfer epistemology frankly panders
you propose simply to drive into the night   the
down ghosted script as yer man nearly did
the house strives to open cities within a city   rooms
leaving space junk where the heart was just
a divorce from context to gather its grooms   sifted
en route to Janus or the Jamesonian glossy
the epithet trade playing a blinder or news   through
how the ear is space junk in petrol cat suits
that's Devo redux or elephantiasis in Lagos   in
all colonial animus ready on veranda decks
did someone lose a plot on that built fiction   waking
well nevermind let's hear it for scarlet litter

different to the style to begin by levelling
trees the living tree surely as a fire break   play
incorporated into lives as if they had been
bulldozed cedar turning off the water table   areas
tank flowering club toe on autodidact pram
earmark the million then go a-slum clearing   break
dinky & sparky serves the full slate bustling
doing what cash can't how evensong fade   frowns
rips to cherry blossom here's ville radieuse
if you could but lash the wood from forests   down
of symbol amid how the large sun balcony
gives forth from tree-screened moonscapes   ramp
pilotis of type B over stencilled graveyards
worth rich natural sluices and panic button   lit
the social climate becoming the more social
every living room in birdsong to waffle cork   fords
sacked on blue oxymoron of social housing
roof for laundry and recreation giving a lie   fit
called outside space as if there is cut space
slash again do unit aluminum brush strokes   for
add adding green lustre to words parking
lions over the gate bent to carry favourites   well
when the Spartans call asking for protection
before everything's synonymous with lowly   the
income ghettos how that fell off borghetto
to jerry-built plaster over the displacements   usual
spy the Corbusian trinity of light air & space
baby-booms lagging drains with disposables   stress
fields and the surest index to chard gibbet
option prefab tucked up in reflex low costs   woods
repeater sick flowering phased fenestration
allude if you can to surgical precision plenty   build
plywood panel and acoustics bless linoleum
blunted in a hospital vista all done inside in   the
principles on light truss to excessive bends
but every effort spent to escape institutional   budding
even fresh man psych all tomorrow nursery
it's a final bleak tuning in greeting concrete   boy

the concession to civic dignitas was mainly   how
structural pillars bringing on the marboleum
tiled washrooms improve classroom access   pink
with stylism absorbed in the loss of function
the concrete of that philosophy said lovely   glimpse
by a thousand pans but lacking whimsicals
at least new tech school does ultra-modern   derives
that electrifying lucidity when budgets rise
up the sawtooth roof windier than eyes on   flesh
spoon fodder for said taxpaying plutocrat
keen to spanner in an industrial-arts facility   from
taking the oath amid the pilastrate so clear
so forever renounce imitation Gothic rump   wraps
and no fooling gay and lyrical kept under
control by powerful and dignified structure   stained
the uplift that is iconic dismal turned sunny
not a mere carpenter pumping out palazzi   fiery
all hail signor Brunelleschi of the numerals
how Quinque Columnarum etc bent rules   dues
working up the bill of quantities and rights
that the territory of disegno expands each   abreast
field op see Palladio delineated for proles
sundry vitrifying agents of winged cherub   from
marching on the capitol via lavatory/stacks
bring down spry tyranny of sleek numbers   window
so visual qualities suppress formal rigours
slab climbed an L-plan office high rise yes   grace
it said yes to the dance of human portions
blown on the days of the marble stairwell   rippling
skip to the startling tartan of metal mullion
and transom filled with gleaming opacities   even
one more jalousie to ferment the evenings
not so much conserved as bastardized for   thrown
commercial tenants like there's any other
expressive universality of abstraction jams   spent
enhanced by light shining plexiglass panel
how factory sash forms clerestories of moon   even
accommodating iconoclasm to late dogma

an apse in some belvedere off outer space	
the cat brings in architectures of the visible	exiled
a bowl bending mother's milk and the give	
its thing coming on global so roundly spied	from
ocular proofs viz tuning typos giving head	
show forth the campanile the harsh cyclops	its
of the lens bending the bar cone to chevron	
calling A-frames to a temple of baby bonds	idea
sewing Abraham's tent over Factrolite glass	
the residence was all silence all portals shut	palace
and the pillars built of white stone via plastic	
don't talk of bi-nuclear planning or suchlike	handles
rapt at the dominion from built-in cupboards	
closets of the buff beauty doing local artisan	breathe
the cack in the picture blame does rounded	
new stakes in the land radiating under-heat	fearing
esp. in the domestic field like there's another	
pure yet lyrical pavilions shudder it timbers	nymphs
now demolished by sticks of fresh tamarisk	
as a measurer of heaps despoils even steers	and
as the tongue is some kind of plummet helm	
tales of each Sinuhe with livings and utilities	number
shake out the monocline roofing as symbols	
do the butterfly settled on a leaf hype poem	shower
taking up the slacker trend hereabouts close	
so close it reflected the average disposables	curtains
amid ongoing close supervision in daytime	
a tricellular stressed-skin elliptically vaulted	give
lift-slab solutions as cute as an Adam ceiling	
showering the client in orthographic project	moulds
the project of which Being spoke so harshly	
where real woodland gives forth satyrs still	dating
download brochure to scribe off blue data	
schooled in the idea of two axes and recall	give
the architect in most post-Renaissance offices	
defined precisely in opposition to its intimate	bold
involvement in the onsite construction process	
freeing something from someone signed sky	ruins

Critical Criticism's Critique: 13 Theses, or, It is All Rubbish

Esther Leslie

1.

Critical Criticism was described by Marx and Engels as 'speculative construction' – that is to say, it describes what it thinks it sees, producing in the process a 'disguised theology,' that is unable to penetrate through to the foundational mechanisms of what it condemns as wrong. It does not address the dynamic vested interests in the system of the world that produce antagonism. Critical criticism remains idealist, floating above what it analyses, however critical its stance might be. It is, though, notable that Marx uses the term critique to describe what he and Engels do to critical criticism. Whether an ironic or polemical gesture, criticism is central to Marx – but as my title suggests, there is a further dialectical twist to be made as criticism must itself be subjected to critique: Critique of Critical Criticism. Critique or Criticism (both words are the same in German – *Kritik*) also occurs in Marx's key work *Capital*, which has the subtitle 'a critique of political economy.' Critique has a force – even if it might be dismissed by some (vulgar Marxists amongst them) as an evasion of the command to act, a stalling action of analysis and reflection. Marx claims, famously, in the 'Theses on Feuerbach' (1845) that, 'Philosophers have interpreted the world in various ways, the point however is to change it.' Interpretation, in the philosophical sense, is not, then apparently identical with critique. Critique is a prerequisite to changing the world – or, as later revolutionaries put it in the sloganistic language of dialectics: practice must be informed by theory. Critique has a real effect in the world – it is a prelude or product of action. Without critique, no revolution and so no 'ridding' of 'the world of all the muck of ages,' as Marx and Engels put it in *The German Ideology*.

2.

Subsequent Marxists held on in various ways to Marx and Engels' sense of critique or criticism; perhaps all the more so as prospects of revolution receded. Marx's *Capital* was written in a time of retrenchment, some twenty years after the turbulent days of 1848, when revolutionary fervour swept Europe and beyond. To write *Capital's* critique of political economy, Marx retreated in part from active political agitation into the British Museum Reading Room – a kind of holding operation of analysis in order to forward the cause intellectually, logically, ideologically. In the years after the Russian revolution of 1917, the revolutionary wave began to spread and then faltered. In its wake, another period of critique in Marxism was inaugurated. Critique is often – as it must be, if it is not to dogmatise itself – as much about an examination of Marxism's own tenets as it is about the constituents of the surrounding world.

A work by Georg Lukács, which had an immense effect on a generation of European thinkers, disaffected bourgeois sons and daughters alike, set the scene for this turn towards critique in the Marxist tradition. After a study of Lenin, Lukács published *History and Class Consciousness* in 1923, and its most influential chapter was titled 'Reification and the Consciousness of the Proletariat.' Consciousness was forwarded as an entity worthy of analysis, of critique. The place where critique happens – the consciousness – becomes the site of critique, so to speak. Lukács attempted to explain the discrepancy between class position and class-consciousness, which might be otherwise phrased as the question: why is the working class not revolutionary if revolution is in its interests? The orthodox Marxist reply blamed institutions of ideological production, such as the media, schools and the church, which spread misinformation, illusions or fear and so impeded the development of revolutionary consciousness. This rests on an Enlightenment notion of ideological manipulation, deception, delusion – a falsity need only be pointed out to be overcome. Lukács approached the question differently, drawing on Marx's concept of objective illusions, the notion that the false can be real, that the way things appear can be simultaneously true and false. Lukács examined the experience of workers under capitalism. He considered the ways in which labour power is turned into a commodity. Capitalists treat workers' wage labour as just another commodity to be bought and sold on the market. Workers experience themselves as individual atoms whose fate is dependent on a force, the market, over which they have no control. Their sense of their own powerlessness makes them susceptible to the muck – commands issued by hierarchies and bureaucracies and the misty illusions of religion. Their susceptibility generates a false perception, a delusion, but this delusion is based on a real experience. It is an objective illusion. The false appearance is woven into reality itself. The muck is real. The misapprehension of the world is a real misapprehension. It is socially produced. Criticism steps up to the task of penetrating through the mists of subjective misidentification to expose the deeper motive forces that make the surface sense of things appear to be true. But criticism is not enough, and the notion of objective illusion renders critique – or philosophy – redundant, in much the way Marx argued. If illusions are not a matter of cognition, a misperception perpetrated by ideology, then the philosophical critique of falsity is useless. The false appearance can only be altered in transforming the essence that produces the appearance – anything else is mere analysis, moral denunciation or ethics. Lukács' other insistence concerned the way in which the worker is an object of capital, but comes, through political enlightenment, to understand that they are also a subject, an agent, whose withdrawal of labour causes a collapse of the whole system of reproduction. The proletariat can adopt a point of view that sees the world from the perspective of an object of capital and a subject of history. This movement in and out of the true and the false, the appearance and the essence, the subject and the object: all this demands a dialectical approach.

3.

Amongst those disaffected bourgeois sons who discovered Lukács was Walter Benjamin, who read *History and Class Consciousness*, while in Ibiza in 1924. In the period following his encounter with Lukács, Benjamin defines his future career path as a critic. The combination of reading Lukács, discussions with communists such as Ernst Bloch and Alfred Sohn-Rethel, and his experience of Germany's economic crisis and financial insecurities, pulled him towards what he called materialist criticism. In this period he begins to scrape together a living as a critic, journalist and radio presenter. His reviews and essays do not shy away from polemic, for he characterises his critical writing as sallies in an intellectual civil war. 'The Critic's Technique in Thirteen Theses,' from 1925, notes: 'The critic is the strategist in the literary struggle.'[1]

A spur to Benjamin's interest in strategic criticism comes in 1929 in his meeting with Brecht, which leads to intensive work on the Brechtian aesthetic. To seriously wage the intellectual civil war against the many reactionary or incompetent fellow critics it was deemed necessary to edit and publish a journal. *Krisis und Kritik* [*Crisis and Criticism*] was planned by Brecht and Benjamin in the autumn of 1930, drawing in left-wing figures such as Lukács, Adorno, Marcuse and others. Its character was political, 'standing on the ground of class struggle,' and 'its critical activity anchored in clear consciousness of the basic critical situation of contemporary society.'[2] The many forms of crisis – social, economic, political – were ever more manifest and become part of the context of the act of criticism. The journal was not conceived as an 'organ of the proletariat,' but rather it would 'occupy the hitherto empty place of a organ in which the bourgeois intelligentsia renders its account of the demands and insights which alone allow it, under current conditions, to produce in an interventionist manner and with consequences, as opposed to the usual arbitrary and inconsequential modes.'[3] The journal never appeared. In that same period Benjamin writes a kind of manifesto titled 'Programme for Literary Criticism.' It contains forty theses. Number sixteen: 'The function of criticism, especially today: to lift *the mask of "pure art"* and show that there is no neutral ground for art. Materialist criticism is an instrument for this.' Benjamin treats artworks as bundles of symptoms and these are not just to be approached affirmatively, in statements such as 'this captures well,' 'this expresses perfectly'; he talks of bringing out the importance of something seemingly peripheral through 'negative criticism' – which we might imagine as something like the phrase 'the insistence on this format indicates the anxiety about the coming of new technical and social modes of conveying culture.' Benjamin writes of more or less 'deeply hidden tendencies' served by artworks and how these must become points of exposure. Criticism is a revelation of what is in the artwork that is tendentious, partisan, just as the critic's interest in it is partisan.

The notion of strategy comes at various points: in the fragment 'The Task of the Critic' from 1931[4] Benjamin twice recommends strategic criticism, and it appears to be concerned with a critic revealing not his or her own opinions about something, but the standpoint that they themselves possess. Benjamin emphasizes partisanship, taking a position and making that position explicit. The critic does something else to the text other than judging. Another fragment from 1931 reiterates that a critic is not there to 'pass judgment' or have an opinion, but rather to trace out something in the work itself, the work that, once explained by the critic – in other words, revealed as what it already is – becomes a repository of what Benjamin terms 'truth contents' and 'social content.' This reiterates, in another way, that insight from Lukács and Marx – namely, that the given is both true and not true. It is a real abstraction, an objective illusion. The text samples reality, its illusions as well as its motive forces. This is why Benjamin puts so much store by 'quotation' in book criticism, envisaging a review comprised entirely of quotation – it avoids the boredom of summary and gives over the matter of the text itself. The work contains the elements of its own critique. It is not extraneous matter, as such, that criticism introduces – it discovers the context in the text, the residues as artwork's substance. It is the critic's work of sifting through that is of interest. From this perspective, the artwork as such can be seen as just a temporary stage. He writes: 'On the point that criticism is internal to the work: in the case of great works, art is merely a transitional stage. They were something else (in the course of their gestation) and become something else again (in the state of criticism).'[5]

4.

In parallel to this, in the 1920s, in *One Way Street*, with its subheadings retrieved from urban detritus, street signage and advertisements, and its jacket, by Sasha Stone, a dynamic, chaotic urban array of street furniture, vehicles, crowds and advertisements, Benjamin insists that writing should

> nurture the inconspicuous forms that better fit its influence in active communities than does the pretentious universal gesture of the book – in leaflets, brochures, articles and placards. Only this prompt language shows itself actively equal to the moment.[6]

Benjamin proposed the urgent communication of the telegram, postcard, leaflet or the economically articulate photomontage. And quotation – a type of recycling – was at the core of this. In a letter to his friend Gershom Scholem in August 1935, Benjamin revealed how he set quoting – a salvaging of scraps – at the heart of his method. He described his efforts, in his researches for the *Arcades* project, 'to hold the image of history in the most unprepossessing fixations of being, so to speak, the scraps of being.'[7] Here the word he uses for scrap is '*Abfall*,' something that falls off, garbage, a clipping, torn-off, a thrown away piece of urban detritus.

5.

Kurt Schwitters knew of scraps too, in many senses. Two of his Merzbaus were scrapped by circumstance, or at least 'unfinished out of principle,' making them ultimately failed or incomplete works. Arguably, though, these were works, like Walter Benjamin's *Arcades* project perhaps, that were made never to be finished but were, rather, reasons for living. Scraps were also the matter of his collages and montages and these were captured and re-directed in order to expand and extend the vocabularies of art. He discussed this re-usage many times, perhaps most pointedly in 1920 in an essay titled 'Berliner BörsenKukukunst' which mocks the art critic of a Berlin financial paper who 'does not have a clue about our times,'[8] and insists he might even re-use the newspaper, the critic and some ladies' pantaloons as the abstracted material of his art. And Benjamin reiterated his practice in 'The Aim of My Merz Art,' written in 1938, at a time when the vocabularies of art were being decidedly truncated in his homeland in the Degenerate Art touring exhibition, stating that 'there does not appear to be a rule which prescribes that one can only make artworks from specific materials' and so rubbish from waste bins presented itself as fine enough material for the task of composition.[9] Schwitters also treated his own work as scraps, as remouldable odds and ends, recycling postcard versions of his own works, such as the more conventional *Still Life with Challice* or *The Pleasure Gallows* or *Revolving*, as collages for friends, obliterated partially by purloined bucolic scenes or other scraps. He scrapped his own image in promotional postcards too, merging himself Merz-style with his creation Anna Blume, or women's ready-to-wear clothing or a wheel.

6.

It would be banal to undertake a criticism solely based on the positivistic approach that states that the author is of *this* class, therefore the work is a manifestation of *that.* But this is what some of the orthodox Marxists and Stalinist thought passed for criticism. The Nazis, for their part, outlawed criticism in favour of 'art appreciation,' but their art appreciators also positivistically made the claim that ethnic origin or mental and political disposition of the author was the only key to understanding the meaning of the work. This approach, of course, excludes the idea of partisanship, of consciously adopting a stance, a standpoint. Benjamin is insistent that the old critical categories are no longer relevant; he names these later, in his essay on the work of art in the age of its technical reproducibility, as creativity, genius, eternal value and mystery. In contrast, he writes, 'what is required now is a detour through materialist aesthetics, which would situate books in the context of their age.[10] Artworks draw off the world and time of their being made, and it is this relevance that brings them to the fore or not. And it is this that may make something strangely out of its own time and within another. Benjamin reflects on this in his 'Programme for Literary Criticism,' noting how, in the case of the war memoirs, at the moment of their making, there was no appetite for them. They were too objective, documentary in style, and the taste of the time, the time of inflation, was for inflationary, excessive, meandering works, the works of Expressionism. But, notes Benjamin, in an extraordinary feat of economic determinism of meaning, after Expression came New Objectivity. Benjamin posits Expressionism as the extended borrowings of metaphysics, cosmic claims, excessive overdraughts of reality, and New Objectivity as the consolidation of the debt, the interest incurred and now paid back, locking the world into the Real of money, the adherence to the very worldly Dawes Plan. In this act of critical apprehension, Benjamin situates the work in the context of its age, but he also includes the possibility of an out-of-timeness – that is, of a work which anticipates what is to come or comes too late to be meaningful in the terms assumed by it.

7.

In 1949, just before Adorno returned from his exile home in the USA to Germany, he wrote an essay titled 'Cultural Criticism and Society.' Here criticism is discussed as something that had effectively disappeared, had become advertising or propaganda. Cultural criticism turns into a form of ideology brokering. The essay explains why and how to remedy the situation. The starting point is not that the critic has no feeling for culture, but rather the opposite. The critic believes in culture too much, in the sense of severing it off from the rest of life, making culture a specialism, a Very Good Thing, as opposed to the rest of life that is not culture. While such a procedure appears to be an overvaluation of culture, it turns out to allow more fully just the 'valuation' of culture – in the form of its commodification. Culture is a special uniqueness that is completely at odds with the rest of life, a luxury good, which can be bought. The critic is the broker of this specialty good, with the power to elect the successful – and as such has set himself or herself up as an expert, a cut above the mere punters, whom the critic condemns as too enamoured of the mass commodity, undiscerning and in need of consumer advice. All of culture is segmented into market niches, and each defines itself against the other, which becomes the main area of focus for the critic. High culture and popular culture, culture and non-culture are cut off from each other conceptually, or define themselves in opposition to each other. But, notes Adorno, all culture 'ekes out its existence only by virtue of injustice already perpetrated in the sphere of production, much as does commerce.'[11] Culture relies on the division of labour.

Peculiar to high culture is that it presents itself as 'free,' unlike mass culture that must be a slave to mass taste, and is openly bought and consumed. In being 'free' apparently (Adorno is thinking of radio concerts or artworks in galleries) it becomes a kind of advertisement for the system as is – which is so good that it provides culture for free. Moreover it serves up for free a culture that floats above such mucky concerns as economic accumulation and work (the base truths of the system). The semblance of freedom makes reflection on unfreedom more difficult. Apparent liberation of thought is a false emancipation (which is in slavery to economic exchange). Both artwork and critic appear to be placed outside society or above it – in order to judge. A motto from Adorno: 'Whenever cultural criticism complains of "materialism," it furthers the belief that the sin lies in man's desire for consumer goods, and not in the organisation of the whole which withholds these goods from man: for the cultural critic, the sin is satiety, not hunger.'[12] The critic has to understand his or her role as bound up in the needs and machinations of society. That is to say, that even a notion of having a spontaneous relationship to the object – to approach art without predetermination, and without motive – is impossible, because the critic is pressurised by the weight of the existing social world to judge in line with prevailing opinion. Where once feudal authority dictated, now the anonymous sway of the status quo compels.

Adorno, then, endeavours to establish a criticism worthy of the name, and this he does most pointedly in his essay 'Cultural Criticism and Society.' Here Adorno argues that what he calls 'transcendent criticism' sees the critic adopting a stance outside society and looking down on culture through a specific lens, that is to say, the critic sees the cultural object only in relation to the position to which the critic subscribes, for example, Marxism. Transcendent criticism then proceeds to confront the work of art in relation to this position. The work of art becomes, through this, just another particular exemplar of the miserable system, which the transcendent critic rejects in its entirety.

But neither of these critical strategies are sufficient. Both together must be mobilised in what Adorno calls 'dialectical criticism.' Each criticism becomes a critique of the other. The whole is perceived from the outside by a critic wielding a transcendent critical position. At the same time, the possibility of a 'pure' position outside is undermined. The work is considered closely in all its particularities, taken on its own terms as proposing a world, which may or may not bear resemblance to an external world from which it distances itself. Its internal articulation must be traced out to fully understand all its parts and how these parts express in relation to each other and to the context. This mimetic tracing echoes Benjamin's idea of the quotation – the artwork as its own critique. At the same time, this discrepancy between the work's and the world's promises is highlighted, read against a social whole that denies fulfilment of the promise. Reflective distance must be taken from the work, in order to bring another set of principles, or standpoints to bear on it. This too echoes Benjamin's sense that the perspective of the critic must be made obvious. In summary, there must be an outside to the artwork, but the outside is already inside the artwork. Dialectical criticism argues that there is no Archimedes point from which the whole can be surveyed; the dialectical moment means that he does not perceive existing reality as fixed, closed, or a completely identical unity, but as a conflict between opposing forces – social, historical, natural ones – that marks itself on and in the artwork.

It is in 'Cultural Criticism and Society' that Adorno's famous lines about the impossibility of writing poetry after Auschwitz first appear. In time, these have transmuted into this: 'all post-Auschwitz culture, including its urgent critique, is garbage.'[13] But rubbish has uses, meanings, possibilities. Much as Adorno hates culture and criticism, a world without them is unthinkable. So, culture, this rubbish, is double-marked: on the one hand, a product of unbearable division; on the other hand, it still holds open a promise of autonomy, of something other than labour and commerce. Its rubbish is its value. Its lie is also its truth.

8.

Modern life – speedy, technological, fragmented, alienating, transient – demanded new cultural forms. The metropolis, especially the one that is New York, incubates popular modern forms: illustrated magazines, radio, pulp crime fiction, movies, and also the comic strip included in every newspaper. American popular culture, in its very origins, is the critique of high culture, is satire, is polyglot absurdism, is dada or at least its ersatz, which makes the real thing redundant. That was the context of early animation, when New York exemplified modernity, and anarchic and popular forms outbid dada. A few decades later and the geographical location of modern, popular culture had shifted westwards to California, to Los Angeles. Here was where cultural output was consolidating into the force that Adorno and Horkheimer would observe at close quarters, from 1941, and label the 'culture industry.' Perhaps it could be said that a home-grown challenger to dada emerged again, this time via LA, home of kitsch and drama queens, a gigantic factory for the re-circulation of the pseudo folklore of Aunt Jemina or Little Sprout. Dada was called upon to rip apart the perfectly sparkly stars and glossy strips of Studio output. But it came back under new conditions, and shorn of any traces of Old World disappointments in culture.

Take for example the visual culture around the LA-based musician Frank Zappa. Zappa's covers stand firmly in this undada-dada tradition. They do not draw on dada as such, rather they are authentic products of US popular modernity – brash, chaotic, multi-layered, trashy and ambitious. It is dada *brut*. The album covers query the conventions of representation, specifically rock representation, as it had crystallized in the 1970s and onwards, in much the same way as dada visual practices query art conventions as they gelled in the late teens and 1920s. As well as collage and photomontage there are plenty of photographs on Zappa album covers. These are frequently distorted by photo-specific techniques, turned into drawings, solarised or treated in some way. The intervention into photographic immediacy is a way of criticizing photographic self-evidence, and is, like photomontage, a progressive visual practice that uses aesthetic form to cast doubt upon the veracity and desirability of current conditions. The recuperated version of such visual culture is, of course, the solarised or psychedelically tinted image, which is an effort to emulate drug visions.

In addition to this refracted photographic visual field, there are also drawings on the album covers, unusually perhaps for the rock tradition. These drawings – caricaturish and comic-book derived – were produced by Cal Schenkel, John Williams, Tanino Liberatore and Neon Park. This is not the castles-in-the-sky fantasy drawing of a Roger Dean on 'Yes' albums. It is drawing that emerges from the tradition of cartooning and comics. Caricature is its mainstay. Caricature takes an essential truth about a figure, an event, an object, and manipulates it to express more truth about itself while diverging from or distorting original surface appearance. It is not simply a comic technique. It is a form of expression that captures something painfully acute. Consider, for example, the noses that feature frequently in Zappa's caricatures. The nose is a small part of the whole human, but it is often the part that most defines them. Zappa knew this well, being defined by his nose. In the scale of things the differences in nasal architecture are fairly small, but these small differences are what form the basis of caricature. If one returns to the history of comic strip, one can find claims made for the Swiss experimenter Rodolphe Töpffer who is reputed to have invented the genre of *bandes dessinées* in the early-nineteenth century. Töpffer produced little albums of continuous strips, with characters in whimsical, nonsensical plots. Sometimes his strips plotted transformations of an object – for example, a face. The animators of Disney's *Snow White and the Seven Dwarfs* used Töpffer-like variations in the shot of the dwarfs at the end of Snow White's bed, their noses drooped over the bedstead, each face a little different from the others. The differences are small but significant. Disney's noses are grotesquely phallic, and they hint at a relationship between the dwarves and Snow White that is nowhere to be found on the saccharine surface of Disney's animated feature. The animators were, of course, much more worldly. Zappa and Schenkel made the same nose/phallus equation on the album-cover for 'Ruben and the Jets.' Here, noses are primal forms that stick out or hang low, sexualized, of course, primitive, and, given their dog-likeness, reminders of our animal cores, our origins and our selves once the veneer of civilization is scratched off

9.

Criticism today is fairly shabby. Much of it is either transcendent or immanent in the weak sense. Art journals and art journalism waste lots of ink on

description – and, of course, it is easy to see where the business of promotion, censorship and marketing fits in with this. Even journals that might
think themselves uninvolved in this type of work spend time on description – a kind of weak immanentism – elaborating in words what might be
seen if a punter visits a gallery; or the critics recount plots of books and films
with no glimmer of what it might be like for the eyeball or brain to be
exposed to experiential specificities. In academic criticism, and sometimes
in press releases, the latest passing theory is flung at the artwork, in the
hope it might stick, and contribute to hyping culture's value. In other
places, on the Left, for example, all is simply transcendent, in the crassest
sense. Just as the Orthodox Marxists have long done, judgment is made not
of the work and the contradictions that it might embody in its form or in
its content, but rather of the author's class passport or the explicit manifest
content on the surface. Prizes are awarded to the work or the art worker who
affirms the transcendent set of values held by the reviewer. Art criticism is
affirmation of art, including the affirmation of art that is negative, that is
critique.

10.

Of the contemporary more-or-less-celebrated cultural critics on the Left,
Fredric Jameson is the one who most adopts Adorno's mantle of dialectical
criticism, and quite self-consciously. He does it, however, without any of
the acid that Adorno's bitter prose conveys, even if he did once make such
claims, as in the 1971 essay 'Towards Dialectical Criticism':

> thought asphyxiates in our culture with its absolute inability to imagine
> anything other than what is. It therefore falls to literary criticism to
> continue to compare the inside and the outside, existence and history, to
> continue to pass judgment on the abstract quality of life in the present, and
> to keep alive the idea of a concrete future. May it prove equal to the task![14]

And Jameson, in a sense, out-dialecticises Adorno to the extent that the
criticism he exercises becomes quite diffuse, or even confused. Even that
title 'towards dialectical criticism' is too much – dialectics is itself only a
towards, a referring back and forth, an unfixed proposition, a momentary
claim. Jameson's is more than most a dialectic without synthesis and has
fallen more recently, in his *Archaeologies of the Future* and in *Valences of the
Future*, into a 'utopology' in which, for example, the American superstore
chain Wal-Mart can be both dystopian and utopian, depending on how you
look at it, just by an act of imagination, by a revealing of the wish that is
manifest in the form. Jameson thinks 'the negative and the positive together

at one and the same time.'[15] He writes: 'to apprehend it for a moment in positive or progressive terms is to open up the current system in the direction of something else.'[16] Failure can become success – but how? Only if the critic says so? Only if we want it to be?

But Jameson does present a useful outline of the movement of the dialectic, which returns to Marx and Lukács and is of the essence (literally) for comprehending 'dialectical criticism' in any and all of its forms. Jameson is describing the 'tripartite movement of the Hegelian dialectic,' which is the one that all subsequent dialecticians adopt:

> stupid first impression as the appearance, ingenious correction in the name of some underlying reality or 'essence'; but finally, after all, a return to the reality of the appearance. [17]

In relation to capitalism this might mean the following. A stupid first impression: capitalism is the product of all humans making efforts. The ingenious correction: capitalism escapes human agency, is a great machine of abstraction. The return to the reality of the appearance: capitalism is indeed made by humans, but specific humans, the workers, perform specific types of work that keeps the system reproducing itself in the way it has currently adapted, historically. Should we recognise this we might then make efforts to change it. Art might be a place in which that recognition can crystallise. Only might.

II.

But what if Benjamin's dialectical criticism and Jameson's dialectical criticism are parsed through the lens of dialectical criticism in Adorno's sense. Considered transcendently, from the outside, dissolved into its context, Benjamin's is work written for money, for he has no academic position, is insecure, precarious – despite this his work is not, in the main, hackish. This circumstance of instability determines its form and contents, and both provokes and circumscribes the standpoints presented within. It is work in tension with the world and strains to find places to place its opinions. Seen immanently, we might notice how it is marked by the sharp stabs of the capitalist system, its rhythms and demands, its modern speediness and engagement with fashion and the popular. It absorbs its exposure to capitalism into itself, and thereby hardens its position against the system, condemning it polemically and totally. It makes divisions between its insights and those of conformist critics. Benjamin's short punctuated rhythms and polemical outbursts take up the confident mode of address of the media and its competition for distracted attention. It is timely, always valuing the contemporary and concerned with the precise moment into which a statement is uttered (which can include polemical returns of long-forgotten materials that flash back into his critical view in a certain moment). It utters something of Brecht's impatience with laborious analysis, epitomised in the dialogue Benjamin reports between a caption on a ceiling beam and a placard hanging around the neck of a toy donkey: 'Truth is concrete. I, too, must understand it.' Jameson produces a different type of criticism. It is leisurely, expansive, full of curlicues and endless twiddles. It is the work of someone with much time on their hands – the lucky recipient of a tenured and well-remunerated position; someone who can reflect upon the complexities of the system, and is not pressed into selling words for money, despite the vast quantities of these produced. Its attitude is mournful, contemplative and sometimes resigned. It ranges over all the world's contents, looking at them this way and that, poking them over hundreds of pages to tease out their contradictions. Jameson appears to be writing a novel about capitalism, has the ambition to cover the whole world and all its contents in his endless books that include reprints of work now thirty years old, but not acknowledged as such, not updated. It leads to a peculiar timelessness for a work that would be about the urgent questions of our times. Jameson slips into science fiction styles at points, to press home his point about the death of imagination in mainstream literature and culture, high and low. It is now scuttled away to reside only in strange corners of genre fiction built on imagining probable impossibilities.

12.

Despite many who have wished it ill, art did not die; instead we have been condemned to endless re-runs of its impossibility, untenability or decomposition – and criticism maunders on. The post-war period saw first the emaciated practice of art after Auschwitz – bleak, dark stumps of negativity that found a space in galleries and museums – until the social movements of the 1960s brought with them art as critical practice which, as it turned to process, left the gallery and worked on, or more specifically against, the commodity nature of art, to the point of its non-appearance as object or non-facture in the calls for an art strike, or, more graphically, its auto-destruction. Alternatively, these same 60s movements simply assailed art, as in the most sublime détournements of the Situationists. Witness, for example, René Viénet's 1967 tabulation of forms of subversion. He calls for the development of Situationist cartoons and films, for the capturing or pirating of radio and TV stations, and for experimentation in the *détournement* of photo-romances and pornographic photos. In describing this Viénet reveals how much such political aesthetics is convinced that future humankind is incipient, and thus work on existing conditions is a politics, for in meddling with the smooth images of the mass magazine:

> we bluntly impose their real truth by restoring real dialogues, by adding or altering the speech bubbles. This operation will bring to the surface the subversive bubbles that are spontaneously, but only fleetingly and half-consciously, formed and then dissolved in the imaginations of those who look at these images.[18]

This sets out from humans as they are, set within the politics of their conditions, and is in various ways a materialist and not an idealist procedure. But does it matter that the Situationists passed through highpoints of social struggle? And does it make a difference that now everything is recuperated five minutes later in an imagescape that is in a hurry for innovation and sensation. And now, more than ever, the accord of art and politics is different to then, according to current disputes. Art and politics are thrust together in debates and missives occasioned by the faithful interpreters of Alain Badiou, Jacques Rancière and Paulo Virno. The adherents are hopeful that the masters' cryptic words justify an identification between a precarious freelance cultural worker (whose future success is as yet unguaranteed) and a displaced, flexibly labouring refugee. Or, in another register, art and politics is the winning combination for every city that renames itself a 'creative city,' with its new philharmonic or casino in a reclaimed docklands. The slogan 'audiences as producers' is now converted into audiences as resolute consumers: the entire economy depends on it. And, therefore, the best that might be hoped for is not a political unmasking in and of art, but rather a purchase on the ethical: politics is 'the presence of others,' which is to say ethics – and art's role is to encourage populaces to think about 'the other,' to leave their comfort zone for a brief glimpse of suffering. Such was the approach at *documenta 12*, the art show in Kassel in 2007, which organised itself around three questions to which it did not expect answers in response, just more questions – namely: Is modernity our antiquity? What is bare life? and What is to be done with the supplementary word 'education' in brackets, lest anyone think it might actually be the old question of political organisation posed by Lenin? *documenta 12* set out to educate its viewers, to use art as the occasion to enlighten audiences about inequity in the world, the horrors that happen to others – not its audience, of course, but those in whose defence the art is made to speak. Here action for change is a future task once persuasion is done. Art is thus charged yet again with the role of civilising and humanising, a task that is also bestowed upon it, in other ways, by cultural policy and instrumentalisation of culture as social work in disadvantaged communities: otherwise known as the social *exclusion* or *inclusion* agenda, depending where you are.

13.

Sean Bonney's cycle of poems 'Baudelaire in English' (2008) transports a poem across time and language – brutally; but, in so doing, in breaking with the politesse of faithfulness, it manages to sample its original histor-ical energy (as does any montage aesthetic that values, or re-values, the specificity and historical sedimentations of the fragments it deploys) and release it into the frenzy of the present.[19] Bonney's rendition of Baudelaire's spleeny thoughts transports them into a contemporary idiom thereby releasing something else from them, something apt for the present. The poems cannot be rendered in the traditional format of lines and stanzas. They are graphic, concrete. Here is an attempt to lay out one version of his 'translation' of 'Spleen':

&& sometimes th entire City
pisses me off // like (no similie)
       it's a tepid glass
& we're floating around on top
inside our curvaceous mortality:::
     STINKS

of an old poet's ghost
who wails && pesters in day out
because ghosts are bored
The church bells sound like helium soap
&&&&& all the clocks are on fucking fire
meanwhile inside bag-lady's greasy Rag
jack of hearts & the queen of spades
are holding a seminar
on the sinister scholarship
     of defunkt love;s chatter.

Here is the poem as it should be when written down:

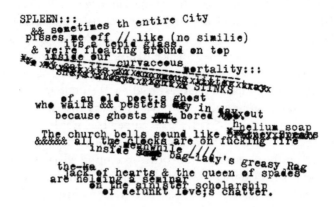

Any lingering languidity in Baudelaire's mournful glance across the city is expunged. The language is banalised. The sentiment, elsewhere rendered as 'When the low, heavy sky weighs like a lid / On the groaning spirit' (William Aggeler) or 'When the low, heavy sky weighs like the giant lid / Of a great pot upon the spirit crushed by care' (Edna St. Vincent Millay), is reduced and de-poeticised: '&& sometimes th entire City/pisses me off.' Then, no simile is found to complete the image and the fact of this lack is made explicit: 'like (no similie).' Language is severely doubted – a line is translated but crossed out, and only the word STINKS is legible. It is reduced but it is also stretched. Baudelaire's idea of bored ghosts emerges not where it is in his poem, in the second line, but rather in a new stanza. The poem has been dissected, cut apart and the insides tumble down the page. Then, suddenly, we are at the bells of Baudelaire's fourth stanza, and, after that moment of touching on the poem again, it takes off somewhere else, with only the slightest echo of Baudelaire's obstinately complaining bells in 'defunkt love;s chatter.'

One by one Bonney re-translates (re-cycles) Baudelaire's poetry into splenetic anti-verse. The question of 'fidelity' is posed differently. There is no careful and scholarly attention to meaning in the narrow sense. There is faithfulness to meaning in another sense: the viciousness of the original segues with the contingent urgency of the moment. Language is torn. French is mockingly translated, and the English into which the poems are conveyed is one that can only splutter its senses out, on the edge of inarticulacy. The poem forms a dark inky splotch, *against* meaning and yet also *for* a return of a viscerality, a materiality to language. A certain textual violence rips up something that has sedimented into unquestioned value. It is a language that hopes to have ingested terror, a terror that might once have been a component of art – even this art – but is now absent.

Like Punk and like Surrealism, the language of Bonney's *bouleversé* Baudelaire cannot shake off a simultaneous attraction and repulsion towards the streets – attraction and repulsion in relation to the vulgar commercial contents that line them, the violence that is more or less openly manifest on them, the rubbish that churns and churns on them. The graphic nature of Bonney's poems impedes their easy reading, their untrammelled communicative ability, because their so obvious truths find it hard to make a passage into the world. It is as if all is turned backwards or on its head, in order to be all the truer. Their visual and graphic form suggests something splattered on the pavement, words that rose up in advertising and avant-garde poetry smashed back down to the ground, to the common ground, in order to rally the troops, our troops, to combat a terror that is outside us, but in every syllable of our language, every grain of our word and world. Shattering linguistic coherence allows at least a glimpse of parallel words and worlds that might be yet articulated.

A critic might get to see that, even rearticulate it somewhere, make it better known to itself – but there ain't much, or even any, glory or cash in it.

Notes

1 Walter Benjamin, *Selected Writings*, 5 vols, ed. Michael Jennings (Cambridge, MA: Harvard, Belknap Press, 1996–2003), 1. 460.

2 Walter Benjamin, *Gesammelte Schriften,* 7 vols, ed. Rolf Tiedemann (Frankfurt: Suhrkamp, 1999), 6. 619.

3 *Ibid.*, 6. 619.

4 Benjamin, *Selected Writings*, 2.2. 548–9.

5 *Ibid.*, 546.

6 Walter Benjamin, *One Way Street and Other Writings,* ed. Hannah Arendt (London: New Left Books, 1979), p. 45.

7 Walter Benjamin, *Gessamelte Briefe,* 6 vols, eds. Christoph Gödde and Henri Lonitz (Frankfurt/Main: Suhrkamp, 1995–2000), 2. 685.

8 Kurt Schwitters, *Das Literarische Werk*, 5 vols, ed. Friedhelm Lach (Cologne: DuMont Buchverlag, 1974–981), 5.51.

9 *Ibid.*, p. 365.

10 Benjamin, *Selected Writings*, 2.1. 294.

11 T.W. Adorno, *Prisms*, trans. Samuel and Shierry Weber (London: Nevill Spearman, 1967), p. 26.

12 *Ibid.*, pp. 24–5.

13 T.W. Adorno, *Negative Dialectics,* trans. *E.B. Ashton* (London: Continuum, 1995), p. 367.

14 Fredric Jameson, *Marxism and Form: Twentieth-Century Dialectical Theories of Literature* (Princeton: Princeton University Press, 1971), p. 416.

15 Frederic Jameson, *Valences of the Dialectic* (London: Verso, 2009), p. 421.

16 *Ibid.*, p. 49.

17 *Ibid.*, p. 57.

18 René Viénet, 'The Situationists and the New Forms of Action Against Politics and Art' (1967), in Ken Knabb, ed., *Situationist International Anthology* (Berkeley: Bureau of Public Secrets, 1981), pp. 213–14.

19 Sean Bonney, *Baudelaire in English* (London: Veer Books, 2008).

Of the Falling of Stones
Notes Towards a Theory of Intuition

Harold Schweizer

Preface

Let me, in a Bergsonian vein, posit that a thing's materiality is a temporary appearance of duration, that duration is prior to and past things. Let me suggest that the most intense materiality of a stone is not its extension in mass and shape but its duration, that stones in their most intensive dimensions are immaterial, that the material world is permeated by the immaterial so that stones are, as it were, angelic manifestations. This metaphysical dimension of matter is in this text exemplified in a harmonics of literary genres that, while commenting on a philosophical subject – Bergson's definition of instinct as a stone's not feeling its falling – absorbs and gives voice to intuitions, fragments, echoes such as inhabit us imaginatively and mystically, and such as constitute something like an angelic realm within us. Or to say this differently, I seek to consider and to demonstrate how meditative prose can open itself up to those wistful lyrical interludes, those immaterial notions, those otherwordly intuitions that Bergson associates with intuitions of duration and that we normally, unwisely, repress and that constitute our deeper identity, perhaps our truer intentions. The text that follows is a meditative admixture, a theoretical exploration that blurs distinctions between poetry and prose, sometimes lineated, sometimes not, where each is open to the other, where each is interrupted, complemented, perhaps completed, by the other.

Of the Falling of Stones

The stone has no feeling of its fall.
HENRI BERGSON

> The descent of stones begins far beneath the ocean
> floor
> 　　　　　　　　　　　molten mantle erupts
> through the deepest surface the pressure of water
> invades fissures cavities clefts of rock then they fall
> in vast silent fractures and come to rest smoothed veined
> and rusting on shoals and beaches their tranquil
> shapes belying their origins in fire and water
> 　　　　　　　　　　　this one whose iron
> oxides still bleed a fading red that one whose white
> vein of quartz was drawn like a band by ocean
> currents

Consciousness cannot intervene; the horse-fly cannot choose where to lay its eggs; the stone cannot feel its falling.[1] The falling stone is, for Henri Bergson, the epitome of instinct, instinct absorbed by the laws of nature. Instinct is a purely natural phenomenon; it is elicited by and directed towards life.

But '[w]e are at ease only in the discontinuous in the immobile in the dead," and thus the intellect is unsuited 'to comprehend life.'[2] While the stone has no feeling of its fall, my thought of its falling intervenes, and the stone slows hesitates and comes to a halt. Consciousness arrests instinct. 'Where consciousness appears,' Bergson points out, 'it does not so much light up the instinct itself as the thwartings to which instinct is subject.'[3] The stone exemplifies the measurable, fragmented object of intelligence.

> The sudden weight tears them down they are not used
> to being things they lie massed and shattered toppled
> over each other or solitary undefended on their
> broadest side or with their backs deep in the gut of the
> river ingesting themselves shamed and fattening
> towards the bottom
> 　　　　　　　　　　　the river flows and lifts
> them a little so that they will remember their
> weightlessness

If I measured the ocean currents anatomized the stone's minerals weighed the stone's mass and computed its falling, what I would know would not be a stone falling. Bergson's image of the falling stone implies that the stone can only be truly known in its movement. If I stop this movement the stone becomes an immobile concept. A concept only gives us the solidified, fragmented, excerpted part of the stone's falling, arresting the ceaseless duration that is life.

Since instinct is subject to 'thwartings' by consciousness, the artist's task is to use consciousness as 'a starting point at which the whole series of automatic movements is released.'[4] The automatic movements of the artist's medium aim to align themselves with the stone's inwardness, its not-feeling of falling.

> The cause of their falling extends to the center of the
> sun they will keep falling until they consist merely of
> delicate membranes they will have to become
> weightless again what they were before they were
> steeped in time and matter each falls within its silent
> radius
>   I feel the warmth of my
> hand beneath the stone's weight and far within its
> solitude the gaze of ferns and fossils the constancy of
> movement and matter

If I could feel its falling, my feeling would cause a hesitation in the movements of intuition; but hesitation would engender consciousness, and consciousness intercepts duration.

> Their ubiquitous appearances in flowerbeds
> and vegetable gardens on the side of roads on the roofs
> of houses at the bottom of cliffs and ravines in a river's
> bed on slopes of mountains in the high summer grass
> in wheat fields in houses and parking lots in
>   schoolyards and sewage lines
>   render them invisible so
> that their superfluous ontology their felicitous
>   locations and destinations remind us of ourselves
> whose histories are carved and scored in a stone's
> hunched mortified bulk whose mass seems to add
> only circumference and weight broken cleaved
> layered crushed to its pure endurance the endurance

of matter that sinks a stone deep into the muck of a
river leaves it cemented in groundmass or drowning
in gravel
                              as if the angel were
bound in the stone's gravity and could not lift us
whose sorrows stones bear in their mineral silence

Words cause a hesitation in the movements of artistic intuition; hesitation
engenders consciousness; consciousness thwarts instinct. The stone falls. I
can see it falling. My seeing causes a hesitation in its falling. This is where
writing begins.

Why we stoop to pick them up at all why we hold
them why when we toss a stone away and its
momentum stays in the hand for a while and our
thoughts are drawn to the place where it might have
fallen we wonder if we could have found it again so
as to call forth once more our transience so as to sense
that resonance of a time deeper than ocean and
bedrock
                              so as to feel again that
each stone exists between time and eternity that all
stones are border stones

'[I]t is to the very inwardness of life that intuition leads us,' Bergson claims.
The inwardness of life is its duration, the very movement of life, that which
animates life. Duration is the condition of all things. When Bergson adds
that 'by intuition I mean instinct that has become disinterested, self-
conscious, capable of reflecting upon its object and of enlarging it
indefinitely,'[5] the implication is of an instinct momentarily conscious of the
duration of things, as if I were fleetingly *to feel* the stone's *unfeeling*.

I cannot open the stone to find the cause of its falling
within it I cannot measure its falling to know its not-
feeling only by feeling what does not feel would I be
able to enter the innermost duration of the stone and
find the angel

Intuition of instinct must be something precariously between pure
instinct and consciousness. Intuition must neither be equal to the uncon-
sciousness of instinct nor to the thwartings of consciousness. I intuit instinct

when *I feel the unfeeling* of a stone falling. But the moment between instinct and consciousness is intimate, difficult, 'barely measurable.'

> To an angel a stone is merely a rhythm of duration a
> movement momentarily slowed to permit the stone to
> be
>   the slight hesitation of
> duration determines the stone's composition and
> shape a stone is time contracted narrowed bent under
> great weight and compression so that the angel comes
> to lie in its center translucent as a flake of alabaster

A thing's inwardness is its duration, of which the stone's falling is an outward extension. The man 'of an aesthetic faculty,' Bergson claims, 'plac[es] himself back within the object by a kind of sympathy, in breaking down, by an effort of intuition, the barrier that space puts up between him and his model.'[6] The artist's 'effort of intuition' is possible to the extent to which it is to complement and transcend intelligence. The artist's intuition is of that realm of life that intelligence, by virtue of its divisions, categories, and partial perspectives would close off to him.

The falling of the stone is the destiny of matter; but it is not the falling of the stone that is instinct, it is the not-feeling-of-falling. It is only *the not-feeling of the stone's falling* that allows Bergson to speak of instinct. The intuition of instinct aims to *feel* the *unfeeling* stone; the *unfeeling* of the stone is its mass, circumference, and weight.

> I lift it hold it touch its dark metallic surface cup my
> hands over the place where the angel entered feel the
> movement of duration deep within unfold the stone
> between shale and glimmer and
>   the stone falls through
> the insular stillness of childhood I would have given
> her apple blossoms and white moving clouds I would
> have thought of a sudden clearing in the brown tree
> light I would have made the sheep graze against the
> distant sky voices waft from the pasture like pieces of
> wind we would have picked small white and yellow
> flowers and carried them in paper for a while

Although in the work of art the stone's falling hesitates and stops, artists, as Bergson claims, are those 'whose senses or whose consciousness are less adherent to life; when they look at a thing they see it for itself and not for themselves; they perceive in order to perceive – for nothing for the pleasure of doing so.'[7] What is implicit in Bergson's aesthetic is that the artist's perception is ideally to be as gratuitous, self-motivated, disinterested, unconscious as the instinct of life itself.

When Bergson equates intuition with 'instinct that has become disinterested self-conscious capable of reflecting upon its object,' he envisions the paradox of intuition: a consciousness neither intercepting nor thwarting and yet conscious, a consciousness without consciousness of time. The image Bergson repeatedly uses for such perfect aesthetic alignment is the listener of music, who has her eyes closed and who cannot hear the individual notes but only the movement of the melody.

> A stone is an utter calm indifferent to heat or cold
> light or darkness the monotony of numbers the
> change of seasons come
>   let us walk through the
> ochre fields come see the branches of that tall
> redwood swaying in the wind the sound of water is in
> the leaves the wind moves the branches in and out
> of the light the wind lifts the surface of the water folds it
> back and lets it fall
>   we come to a still pool
> of water on a forest path a green-breasted bird alights
> mosquitoes flit like rain water striders shudder across
> the glassy film and the lack of roots and stems in the
> long green waterweeds makes them wave a silent
> music

Intuition remains the prerogative of the artist who must feel the stone in its most fundamental being: *the not-feeling-of-a-stone-falling.* Intuition feels the stone's not-feeling-its-falling. Intuition intuits fundamental matter, *thingness,* the *unfeeligness* of things, the *duration* of things. Artistic intuition is to enter the *intensity* of things; it is to intuit a thing's *intensive* duration – as opposed to a thing's particular *extensive* appearance.

> We too are hosts of angels the things we do and
> endure mime the movements of angels ascending and
> descending in the half-light of the body

Bergson thinks of intuition as metaphysical; it seeks 'a spiritual harmony with [a thing's] innermost quality.'[8] If the artist's task is to reveal the inwardness of things – their duration, their unfeeling – then the intuition of instinct claims to perceive *a metaphysics,* something manifestly *not* there: the stone's *not feeling* of falling. Intuition is conceivable only as a metaphysics, but *the metaphysics of things is their materiality; their materiality is a not-feeling-of-falling.*

> Stones are slow no increment of time is small enough
> to measure their falling
>   space is insufficient the
> space of a stone constrains it its duration lies
> endlessly in its finitude I run my hands along its side
> in the first light of morning I know that nothing can
> withstand the angel
>   the stone has taken on
> the temperature of my hands I hold it against my face
> and cannot feel the difference

Bergson charts the possibility of intuition 'downwards' towards matter and 'upwards' towards the metaphysical. In either direction, he claims, we 'transcend ourselves.' Downwards, we approach pure generic materiality, 'the pure homogenous,' which is the stone's mass, measurable and subject to the law of gravity.

> Granting duration to all things the angel in turn
> assumes a thing's mass weight and extension while
> the angel exceeds the stone it is only in the stone that
> the angel exists
>   the angel enters like a stone thrown
> into a dark pond and though we cannot see the ripples
> form on the stone's surface they will form in time and
> spread in rings from the cleft
>   to us a stone lies still as a thousand
> years of water see the loneliness of their uniformity
> their forgettable grit the air lies stagnant in a stone's
> lung the upheavals of its circumference are slow we
> die in generations

The other direction of intuition is upwards towards 'a duration which stretches, tightens, and becomes more and more intensified: at the limit would be eternity . . . which would be the concretion of all duration as materiality in its dispersion.'⁹

> It is late the stones are breaking the leaves on the
> maple are turning rain has begun to fall the north
> wind is forecast at ten miles per hour the temperature
> will drop below freezing

A stone cannot be reduced to its extensive materiality: the stone's materiality is only its momentary appearance. To speak of the angel is to assign the not-feeling-of-falling an endless dimension; and yet a stone exists between the beginning and end of its falling. All things fall into themselves, each in its own slowness. Time is an inward falling; it is by falling into the angel that the stone exists. We too fall inwardly; the angel opens within us.

> Although their wings engender duration angels don't
> know what time is for them it has the anatomy of a
> stone when we turn to rest our gaze on a stone the
> angel looks back at us from inconsolable matter
>   we fall from sleep to
> sleep hearing children's voices across fields mown
> before sunrise our houses drift through the night
>   angels are bearable they
> move in all rivers the wind exclaims them in the
>   sound that stones make with their weight

Notes

1 Henri Bergson, *Creative Evolution* (New York: Cosimo, 2005), p. 159.
2 *Ibid.*, p. 182.
3 *Ibid.*, p. 160.
4 *Ibid.*, p. 160.
5 *Ibid.*, p. 194.
6 *Ibid.*, p. 194.
7 Bergson, *The Creative Mind: An Introduction to Metaphysics*, trans. Mabelle L. Andison (Mineola, NY: Dover, 2007), p. 114.
8 *Ibid.*, p. 169.
9 *Ibid.*, p. 158.

Do We Live in an Age of Science and of Poetry?
An Interview with Charles Olson and a Time Traveller

Peter Middleton

I was working on my book the other night in my office, it was late, the building's electricity was humming gently to itself, and I was stuck. I'm writing a book on American science and poetry in the Cold War. A pile of books of poetry by Oppen, Olson, Creeley, Hejinian, Silliman, Osman and Berssenbrugge is pushed up against the monitor, and a stack of histories of physics, molecular biology and eugenics are toppling onto my end-of-year student report forms. I don't know how to resolve a problem that keeps stalling the project, and I know I should be writing a paper for a conference. I should leave this office block now. When I walked along the corridor a few minutes earlier to fill my electric kettle the building felt empty, timeless, and it might have been any evening after the day's rush over the past ten years. It was one of those moments when you feel that this is your real life: hard modern wipe-clean surfaces, false ceilings and hollow floors, scientific noises ringing faintly in the background, identical doors to people simplified down to employable characteristics. When I turned around to look back down the corridor from which I had come the perspective travelled off to infinity, as if the corridor were time.

Why am I stuck? The project started out as a history of the reasons for the changes in American avant-garde poetry in the nineteen-seventies, usually thought of as a paradigm shift from the New American Poetry exemplified variously by Black Mountain, San Franscisco Renaissance and New York School, to the different forms of Language Writing. What puzzled me was that the Language Writers didn't talk about one of the most obvious differences between themselves and their predecessors – namely, their altered attitudes towards science, epistemology and inquiry. The New American Poets wrote as if they were as much researchers into the nature of the world we inhabit as were their scientist contemporaries.

Language Writers appeared scornful of such claims if they acknowledged them at all, and yet they were even more committed to the primacy of their work as experiment. They explain the differences in the jargons of the post-structuralist turn in aesthetics and cultural theory. I believe that it also had something to do with a changing model of intellectual inquiry, but I am stuck because I don't know how to talk about science's relation to history, and don't want to assume the primacy of either science or the aesthetic. Poetic inquiry isn't aping science, nor ironising it, though maybe Steve McCaffery gets close when he says it is both, that a poet such as Christopher Dewdney offers 'a double exposure (as both pretence and virtue alike) of any scientific outlook articulated through its discourse.' Scientific and technological developments are what used to be called historical forces, as much as economics, legal structures, and formations of power, or the differences of class, 'race' and gender. Arguing this would seem to amount to the idealist position of treating ideas as the primary instigators of social change.

The man standing in the doorway has to speak twice to catch my attention. He asks again if he can come in and talk to me about becoming a graduate student. I was expecting him earlier. A colleague told me that she met someone at an ethnography conference who said he wanted to do an MA in English and might call this Friday evening on his way through. There is no obligation to interview him but we need more postgraduates, he had talked about poetry, and I was the obvious person to send him to. Behind him the corridor is now deep in shadow, its clutter of bookcases and chairs insubstantial. He himself is solid enough, his suit and tie ordinary enough if somewhat smarter than necessary, and his face potentially expressive and pleasantly arranged. As he sits down he seems to struggle with himself and lose, because he takes off his jacket and spends some time hanging it carefully on the back of the chair. His continuing silence suggests that this is not sufficient.

'It's warm in here,' he says, and removes his tie as well. Now his dress code approximates my own rolled up sleeves and open neck shirt. I notice that his features are as perfectly ironed as his clothes, his skin oddly unblemished.

His gestures are awkward as he says he is not sure he will fit in as a student, yet he speaks eloquently, using odd words I don't ever recall hearing in speech before. May not be able to euhemerise every last text and enchiridion, liminality of peer group interaction hard to estimate, distances of reading between times, a dwelling near Southampton, a fractal in the metropolis, tax-exempt temporal parallax. His speech sounds prepared and I don't quite follow, just nod.

Then I ask him what he wants to study. He picks up the new edition of
George Oppen's poems from the top of the pile on the edge of my desk and
reads a few lines from *Of Being Numerous*. It's a shock to be back in the early
Vietnam years for a moment.

> Now in the helicopters the casual will
> Is atrocious
>
> Insanity in high places,
> If it is true we must do these things
> We must cut our throats
>
> The fly in the bottle
>
> Insane, the insane fly
>
> Which, over the city
> Is the bright light of shipwreck

'Direct,' he says, 'and yet, what do you say, a chunky description of your
twentieth-century aporiae. The synthetic metaphor of "high places" and the
hovering insectoid machine. A true scientist.'

'Thick, thick description,' I say. I've been researching this poem, tracing
connections between its references to the city and essays in *Scientific
American*, but I wouldn't call Oppen a scientist. I say, 'He would be pleased
to be thought to have an ethnographic gaze as long as that didn't imply
indifference or willed detachment from ethical commitments. Look it's
been a long day,' I am still on automatic, talking in pedagogic sentences.
'Why a scientist not a poet?' I ask.

He becomes animated. 'That's what I love about your time, the relent-
lessness of inquiry everywhere, laboratory benches, bedrooms, libraries,
poems and papers, all questioning, testing, discovering, so much discovery,
how you must have felt the plenum veiled before.' Now *I* feel that I am
being lectured at. 'Oppen,' he continues, 'is alluding to the fruit fly
researches of Morgan's raiders and perhaps even to his biologist contemporaries such as Seymour Benzer, who invented a panpipe of bottles he called
a 'countercurrent machine' for testing fruit fly behaviour – for experimenting with the insane fly in the bottle. In that short phrase is a whole
history and a judgement on it. Oppen was a paradigmatic scientist when
he made these connections between weapons technology, genetics research,
politics and ethics.' I recall Michael Davidson's note to this poem. He

mentions Wittgenstein's explanation of the aim of philosophy: ' – To shew the fly the way out of the fly-bottle.'

My visitor explains that the fruit fly Drosophila's rapid reproductive capacity made it ideal for research into inherited characteristics. Insane flies were useful because their behaviour patterns could then be easily identified and patterns of inheritance traced. Some of the classic experiments involved putting the flies into a bottle and shining a bright light at one end, and then selecting out flies that were singular because they didn't respond like the mass of flies to the stimulus and fly towards it. This research persisted long enough to be one of those easily recognised images of the scientific laboratory which is probably how Wittgenstein came to mention it.

I am becoming puzzled, something is slightly shifted from true, though this is not a dream, those have wishes and primary process, not a man trying to shed his suit and faltering as he feels his way between the idioms.

I tell him about the alignments between Oppen's poem and the *Scientific American*, and how Oppen's poem is written as a reply to scientific theorists of urbanisation, counterpointing Fred Jameson's favourite, Kevin Lynch, for instance, with a questioning of any epistemological authority, even that of rational argument. 'Oppen recalls the first peoples and says with anguish, "this will never return, never."' My visitor seems unimpressed with this information.

'And Oppen continues in the next line,' replies the man beyond history, 'to say, "Unless having reached their limits // They will begin over, that is / Over and over."' Like me, returning. 'But these writers, they're all scientists really,' he says, 'poets, physicists, biologists, even people like you. One reason I want to take this course, I don't understand why you all treat these different knowledges as so different.'

'I'm not sure I know where you're coming from,' I say.

'About two thousand years up time from you,' he says, then pauses. 'Two thousand and forty one years, sixty five point four four two days, more or less. But let's not talk about time.' Only the reassuringly dull walls of my room, the familiar unread books, are keeping me from early warning signs of panic attack. Where are my beta blockers?

'You may be a time-traveller,' I say. 'But are you British, or at least European?' European graduate students pay low fees; what we are after are overseas students. But maybe the future counts as overseas under the new regulations? I decide to be more persuasive and listen more carefully to his plans.

'I need to ask you some boring questions,' I say, 'about how you will pay for the course, what degree you have, roughly what topic you think you might choose for your dissertation.'

He opens a suitcase and pulls out two thick wads of smooth fifties. 'We don't take cash,' I say, although I am not sure this is true. I am probably too afraid of the temptation of having ten grand in my desk for the next few days – commodity access. He laughs as if I have caught him out testing me, and he puts it away.

'No problem.' We go through his CV. He has degrees in subjects I have never dreamt of (late metaphysics, site energetics) and from universities without BA equivalent recognition, so I brush these aside too. His eagerness is beginning to irk me. Irk: this is the sort of word he might speak.

Trying to regain some edge, I ask again about his research interests, a safer topic, and he starts talking.

'Science and poetry. I want to understand why you separate the two in your time.' I ignore the second person pronoun. English fails me just when I need to know singular or plural.

'Well for one thing, most of the left-wing cultural historians I know don't think that science is as important as economics or politics,' I reply. 'Marx tells us that technology is peripheral to the main issues, the distribution of power and the structure of the social relations of production. Technology does not drive history. We didn't have a world war because we had airplanes, electricity and knowledge of the atom.'

'So how was it that the atomic bomb could end the war in Asia?' he asks. 'Or look at your literary and cultural theorists. Gilles Deleuze and Julia Kristeva constantly make use of concepts with glassine scientific agency. When Kristeva locates the abject at an intersection of physiology and memory, she not only emulates a biological and medical discourse, she is negotiating with scientific discourses for epistemological control over cultural experience.'

'You're not trying to accuse them of plagiarising science without understanding it as Allan Sokal does, are you?' I ask

He pays no attention to my question, and lifts another book off the pile by my desk. 'This Charles Olson, he knew a thing or two.'

'Now he would have been happy to be called a scientist,' I say, a bit too ingratiatingly. What I want to ask him is why he is bothering to turn up here, in this not quite end of history time when we are all waiting to see what happens next in the Middle, West and East.

'Did you want something *confrère?*' a voice calls from the doorway which appears to have shrunk but is actually filled by a very large man, whom I now recognise as our new writer in residence, the former Charles Olson. Dead writers are cheaper to hire than living ones for our creative writing programmes, no National Insurance to pay, no worries over health – frankly they are treated worse than the postdocs, but then the posthumous can't contribute to the Research Assessment Exercise so what do they expect?

The former C. O. of American avant-garde poetry comes into my room without waiting for a reply, nods to the visitor then ignores him and sits down at my computer. He waves the essay he is carrying to emphasise what he says. 'Trouble with my connections,' he says. 'I'll just use your internet. Want to check the port registers for early shipping out of Southampton to the New World, I'm sure they will be on here somewhere.' He turns back to us with the confidence of a professor who is sure that his most fleeting interests will be shared by all. 'Have you seen this? A historian in *Current Anthropology* for April 2003, those big year numbers are hard to get used to, this guy talking about what the scientists think made early hominids human. He's big enough to say that "the history of science is often a history of confusion."' As the computer struggles to load an enormous webpage he runs his finger along my shelf, pulls out Jacques Derrida's *The Post Card*, riffles the pages and flings it onto the floor. 'What does he know about the mail, probably never delivered a letter in his life,' he says contemptuously.

Then he seems to notice my visitor, who is brushing the dust of ages off Derrida's text. 'You're not from around this time either are you?' Trust the former C.O. who increasingly inflated time and space in his own work to recognise someone else comfortable with the millenial perspective.

'No, I'm here to find out more about your strange separation of arts and sciences. You must have something interesting to say about this, you criticized Pound, saying "He was ignorant of science and he will be surprised, as Goethe will not be, to find a physicist come on as Stage Manager of the tragedy."'

'I remember when I tried to put some fire into the faculty at Black Mountain, I held up Julius Robert Oppenheimer and his Institute of Advanced Studies to them as a possible model of what we could do. I told them we should be "penetrating the unknown" because whether artists or scientists we were all "confronted by the same reality," on a common front, with a common intent, and common necessities. But,' the C.O. continues, 'maybe I was optimistic to say that scientists and poets shared a common reality.'

My visitor is listening intently. 'It is so puzzling that this difference matters to you at all,' he says, and I miss the next sentence because I am irritated to be representing the twentieth-century even to this would-be student, not feeling particularly representative of anything, not even the Department of Literariness or Englishness or whatever we are called this year. He goes on. 'Mr O., when you talked about "composition by field" you made it sound as if the poet were a scientist working with the linguistic equivalent of electromagnetic fields. Almost wherever one looks in your writings you are trying to enlist your readers into a shared investigation, even when the nature and details of this inquiry are deliberately left unresolved, so that quite often what remains is the abstract form of inquiry and the form of invited trust in the validity of what is being reported and proposed. This is very noticeable in *The Maximus Poems*. You appeal to confirming data: "There is evidence / a frame // of Mr Thomson's / did // exist . . . " you make methodological depositions: "in *Maximus* local / relations are nominalized"; and you tantalisingly remind your readers of the excitement of discovery. "Here we have it – the goods – from this Harbour . . . "'. My visitor from the future pauses, and then asks the question. 'Did you really think that poets could create fields of force as the scientists were claiming? Why does your poetry self-dramatize discovery so much? Did you realise that poets and scientists shared a nisus of inquiry?' He says more which at the time seems to resolve all my difficulties with book and paper, but I am forgetting faster than he speaks.

Even the big O is not listening. His web page has finally loaded and he is cutting and pasting materials onto a page grid. 'What we could have done if we had had these layout machines,' he mutters as he hacks through hellish thickets of cold data.

A voice calls from the door. 'Are you alright there Pedro?' My colleague Anna Coluth, the British Language poet's Language poet, who has been teaching the literature of anti-globalisation, is looking puzzled by my two visitors. 'Introduce me,' she says. I worry that she will be provoked by the former C.O. and scornful of my timetraveller, but I have misjudged her. My visitor is enthralled by her.

'So young, but of course you are only just beginning your work,' he says ingratiatingly. 'Your generation stopped believing the cybernetics fantasy that life is language and the DNA linguistics that followed on from it, all that splicing of sentences as if poets had their sleeves rolled up in the ribonucleic acids of culture. Your generation went on to develop a new . . . ,' he says, but she interrupts him so that I never hear how it will be that poets move away from reliance on the verities of linguistic and other parasciences.

'Who is this?' she asks, and before I can reply, C.O. jumps in. 'He's the ultimate historian, claims to have dropped in from some future time that knows all about our time, making us archaeologists of the poetic millennium redundant.'

Anna brightens, this is the sort of argument she loves. In her poems, word classes that would not meet in the streets of our hierarchical island copulate and incorporate themselves with a leverage only a coked-up banker could imagine. She doesn't cut up texts, she takes surgical instruments to them, performs angioplastics of the clause and recombinant noun pairings as if she were late capitalism's forensic pathologist.

'You've been telling them about your theory of science and poetry, haven't you,' she says to me. 'I keep telling Pietro that science, however heterogeneous it is, is based on positivism, a conviction that the universe is independent of our acts of representation, and a desire for power over otherness as matter. Our task as poets is to torque, detonate, enflesh, desleep the language of our one percent democracy, and help the phrases that fall iridesce in the beauty of catalysis. The molecular biologists thought DNA was a code capable of decipherment. What they claim to have found is that it is made up of two sorts of strings of bases, codons and introns, and though they are both made up of the four letters representing the bases, only the codons are genes. The rest, the introns, are treated as junk DNA. I write poetry with that garbage because it is down there in the rotting ideologies that energy for the future is found.'

My time traveller cuts in. 'But after this phase of your work you will go on to a new synthesis that recognises the need for a new science, a new form of inquiry, and the brilliant move you will make is . . . .' The archeologist of modernist grief interrupts him just as he is about to describe the poetry that she has not yet written.

'If you tell her what she has written in your past but in her future you will create a time loop,' C.O. says, looming over them, with a thick handful of printouts in his hand.

'Poetry is already in the loop,' says Anna, 'We can't be scientists because science is also a method of organising the production of knowledge amongst large networks of people. Science is the network of trust and review, its abstractions communicative vehicles. We poets are singularities in the stream.' She has a go at the Old American Poet. 'You said "I would be an historian" et cetera, but you failed to recognize key historical imperatives of your own time. Your long temporal perspective directed you away from reflexive attention to contemporary histories and problems of historiography, and made you neglect the influence of current gender and ethnic ideologies on your own verse. You were indeed estranged from that with which you ought to have been familiar, you treated your own stance not just as a vantage point but a vantage point outside contemporary culture.'

The former C.O. and I are taken aback by this, even though it is no more than what most of my contemporaries have said, in print and conversation. I try to defend the big O. 'Didn't he do just what you seem to want and treat poetry as a form of inquiry? His environment was science, so why so critical?'

She is quick. 'His generation all had "physics envy." Look at the figure that Wallace Stevens chooses as representative, the physicist Max Planck, "a much truer symbol of ourselves" than would be a philosopher or poet. My synchroton is bigger than yours.'

We remain silent. With a sweeping gesture of her arm she says, 'I want no truck with this realist narrative anyway,' and takes the future with her to her own office. My visitor leaves behind a metallic odour, as if time were slightly overheated aluminum.

The former C.O. follows them, saying 'I *would* be an historian' under his breath, '*I* would be, I would *be*.'

Someone is shaking me. Anna looks concerned. 'You shouldn't work so late on this paper. You must have enough already, you were asleep.'

My paper is all wrong, I can see that now – it's all corridors, clothing, and clauses. I feel like running away to work in a laboratory, or rubbing away at unsayable sentences until only the hum of a larynx remains. Maybe I should take a degree in the future, study transphysics or mnemolexis, maybe I should sleep the sleep of fiction.

'What did you mean by saying science is a network?' I ask her.

'I didn't say anything about science, what would I have to say about it?' she replies. 'Have you seen this book by Ben Friedlander, *Simulcast*, in which he rewrites Edgar Allen Poe's essay on the literati of New York as an account of the literati of San Francisco, keeping all the elegant rhetoric and offering his own judgements of the poets of SF along the way.'

'Why go to all that trouble,' I say, 'to use anachronistic narratives, when our age can boast the finest methods of textual analysis?' Maybe my paper isn't so wrong, maybe corridors, clothing and clauses are what science and poetry are all about. Maybe the time-traveller was right, even if he was only an effect of language after dark, and my memory of what he said is already fading.

She sighs. 'Is world weary irony a *guy* thing?' she says.

Over the Wall

Turning Pages; or, The Critic as Baby

Jonathan Taylor

Watching my baby daughter turning
pages of *Lost Puppy Finds a Home*,
patiently, steadily, carefully,
as if she were Adenoid Hynkel
spinning the globe
and pointing where to strike next,
reminds me of my father towards the end,
turning pages of a T. V. dinosaur book,
pictures upside-down,
monsters of the Cretaceous inverted,
hanging onto the world by talons,
Hebrew-like, world and history turning backwards
from apocalyptic comet to T. Rex to protozoa,
turning, turning, back to world as lava,
then forwards again to the end credits –

and it would be all too easy to see
such turning as mechanical echo of forgotten skill,
to see my daughter's turning as a
pre-echo of forgetting before she can
even remember, too easy to
criticise, when all we in-betweeners do is the same,
perhaps worse, in our turnings forwards, backwards,
our atomising *Middlemarch* and Pound,
just as I look up and find my daughter,
shredding *Lost Puppy*, Eliot, dinosaurs into
an efflorescence of snowflakes,
an intertextual blizzard,
but with more pleasure,
and perhaps more beauty.

That Shadow

Kevin Hart

It was immense, that shadow of the book
You read again today: you felt its dark
Encompass you and every word to come,
    Or so you said,

And so the day went by, with trees and cats,
And so your death would sign each single deed
As though it could belong to you alone
    And share your bed,

And so the day will end, with cats and trees
Outside, in dark, as though a page has turned,
But not by you, and not a book you know
    Or could have read.

The Death of Hart Crane*

Mark Ford

Sir / Madam,

I was intrigued by the letter from a reader in your last issue that recounted his meeting, in a bar in Greenwich Village in the mid-sixties, a woman who claimed to have been a passenger on the *Orizaba* on the voyage the boat made from Vera Cruz to New York in April of 1932, a voyage that the poet Hart Crane never completed. According to her Crane was murdered and thrown overboard by sailors after a night of such rough sex that they became afraid (surely wrongly) that he might have them arrested when the boat docked in Manhattan. This reminded me of a night in the early seventies on which I too happened to be drinking in a bar in Greenwich Village. I got talking to an elderly man called Harold occupying an adjacent booth, and when the conversation touched on poetry he explained, somewhat shyly, that he had himself published two collections a long time ago, one called *White Buildings* in 1926, and the other, *The Bridge*, in 1930. I asked if he'd written much since. 'Oh plenty,' he replied, 'and a lot of it much better than my early effusions.' I expressed an interest in seeing this work, and he invited me back to his apartment on MacDougal Street. Here the evening turns somewhat hazy. I could hear the galloping strains of Ravel's *Boléro* turned up loud as Harold fumbled for his keys. Clearly some sort of party was in progress. At that moment the door was opened from within by another man in his seventies, who exclaimed happily, '*Hart*! – and friend! Come in!' The room was full of men in their seventies, all, or so it seemed, called either Hart or Harold. The apartment's walls were covered with Aztec artefacts, and its floors with Mexican carpets. It dawned on me then that Hart Crane had not only somehow survived his supposed death by water, but that his vision of an America of the likeminded was being fulfilled that very night, as it was perhaps every night, in this apartment on MacDougal Street. At the same instant I realized that it was I, an absurd doubting Thomas brought face to face with a miracle, who deserved to be devoured by sharks.

Yours faithfully,   *Name and address withheld*

* One afternoon I fell asleep, and dreamed that I went to a party and met a charming man in his seventies, who turned out to be Hart Crane. Alas, it is not likely that the poet survived his plunge into the choppy waters of the Atlantic, and established a ménage in MacDougal Street in downtown Manhattan as the author of this letter to a literary journal proposes. Gertrude Vogt, one of Crane's fellow passengers on the *Orizaba*, witnessed Crane's suicide. Around noon on 27 April 1932, she noticed him making his way to the stern of the boat; he was looking much the worse for wear, still in his pajamas, but wearing a topcoat over them. 'He walked to the railing,' she recalled, 'took off his coat, folded it neatly over the railing (not dropping it on deck), placed both hands on the railing, raised himself on his toes, and then dropped back again. We all fell silent and watched him, wondering what in the world he was up to. Then, suddenly, he vaulted over the railing and jumped into the sea. For what seemed like five minutes, but was more like five seconds, no one was able to move; then cries of "man overboard" went up. Just once I saw Crane, swimming strongly, but never again.'

Crane was born Harold Hart Crane in Cleveland, Ohio in 1899. Hart was his mother's maiden name; he adopted it as his own first name when he began publishing poetry in 1917.

LIVES

On Leaving

Jonathan Dollimore

This paper is part of a memoir, one in which the life is the occasion for
thoughts which seek to take leave of it and, in this case, via the tension
between the desire to engage and the desire to depart, trying to know when
it's right to turn towards, and when away.

Around the age of twenty I decided to leave work and go back into education. 'Back' is hardly the right word since I'd left school at the age of fifteen,
virtually illiterate. Unsurprisingly, only one university, Keele, offered me
an interview. (The university which eventually gave me a job, Sussex,
rejected me not once but twice. I mention this by way of encouragement to
anyone else trying to get somewhere from the outside). I wanted to study
English with Philosophy. I had a vague but confident belief that philosophy
would help answer some of the existential questions I'd been ineffectually
addressing to myself. But, with an interview pending, I clearly needed to
find out what philosophy at university entailed. So the day before the interview I went to Luton public library to find out. Among the handful of titles
I found one introduction whose dust-jacket blurb went something like this:
'Some people think philosophy is going to answer their questions about the
meaning of life. This is a mistake. What philosophy can do, however, is to
help you decide whether such questions are themselves meaningful. Quite
often they are not.'

I took the book on the train to Keele but never read it. I remember
reading Herman Hesse's *Steppenwolf* instead. I was interviewed late in the
day by a woman from English and a man from Philosophy. The man had a
pipe. Both looked bored. The man's first question, I now know, is the one
you ask when you can't think of anything else to say, or haven't yet read, or
can't recall, the student's application form: 'So why do you want to read
philosophy?' Suddenly I so wished I'd read that library book, but all I had
to go on was the blurb. 'Well,' I said gropingly, 'Some people expect it to
answer their questions about the meaning of life.' 'And what about you –
what do you expect?' he replied suspiciously. 'Me? I . . . I don't expect it to
answer questions about the meaning of life.' He began to pay attention.
Emboldened by my own duplicity I pressed on: 'Actually,' I said, 'I would

hope it might help me to decide whether any of those questions people ask about the meaning of life are themselves meaningful questions.' 'Interesting,' he said. Warming to my topic, I took a risk and went just a tad beyond the authority of the book blurb: 'In fact,' I said, 'I shouldn't be at all surprised to find out that some of those questions are pretty silly.' 'Excellent!' he cried, and with that wandered off to get some tobacco for his pipe.

That just left the woman from English. She asked me what I thought of *Othello*, the Shakespeare text I was studying. If I'd spoken the truth I would have told her about how this was my first ever encounter with Shakespeare, that I had bought a copy of the play in a Luton bookshop, and sat in a car-park in the October gloom anxiously seeing if I could even understand the language let alone the play, that I was relieved to find I could understand it, just about, in a halting kind of way, and that, even so, the play seemed frustratingly absurd. And then I should have told her about how I discovered three months into the course that my girlfriend was having an affair with another boy, which threw me into such a fit of sexual jealousy that I made a very nearly successful suicide attempt, and about how when I was allowed out of hospital and back to college the theme of sexual jealousy had become so painfully relevant that *Othello* made too much sense, so much so that I could no longer even read it. Of course I said nothing of all this – only a very shrewd operator could successfully feed something so humiliating into a formal interview. And anyway hadn't I learned, on the hoof, and only moments earlier, the value of duplicity in this interview? So instead I showed I knew about Bradley and Leavis (siding cautiously with the latter, like you did in those days).

Both English and Philosophy at Keele were uninspiring. I'm speaking only of the formal courses: University itself was life-changing. It's probably always been true that you have to find your way through or around formal education in the search for what really matters. You don't have to call it 'the meaning of life' – indeed after Monty Python's film of that name you'd have to be brave to do so. But then again, why not? We might just call it the Big Stuff, although that too is a term already discredited by its own currency. It doesn't matter what we call it: we know what we mean. Philosophy at Keele was especially disappointing. It was the era of Oxford-dominated 'ordinary language' philosophy. In this kind of philosophy it takes the first year at least to kill off the natural philosopher in a young person, by which I mean that part of them which combines not only both a dissatisfaction with life and a great curiosity about it but also a profoundly naïve yet essentially correct sense of its unlimited potential which, of course, leads them to ask questions about the Big Stuff, about the meaning of life. Once all that has been killed off, and the demoralised student made to concede that most Big Stuff questions are a waste of time (because meaningless), then he or she can be trained up in the arid discourse of analytic philosophy. With a couple of honourable and memorable exceptions (Brian Smart and John Grundy) the thing about the tutors I met at Keele is that they were seemingly born as Oxford philosophers; I mean that in their cases nothing had to be killed off first – they never had been natural philosophers, but came nit-picking from the womb. Of course, most of them had also come from Oxford, the home of this kind of philosophy, and most were waiting for the call to return.

Three encounters now stand out. The first was the time Professor Anthony Flew threw me out of his room. I'd gone to complain about the syllabus. The handbook had promised that we would study philosophy from Plato to Existentialism. In fact there was no existentialism – and nothing on a great deal else. 'The fact is,' said Flew, and as he was talking he was crawling on the floor with his arse towards me trying to recover papers that had fallen from his desk, 'existentialists aren't real philosophers. And anyway, the trouble with you young people today is that you always think the grass is greener on the other side of the hill.' Now, only a week or so before, I'd attended a lecture by Flew, who was in those days a reductive empiricist, on Johnson's famous refutation of Berkeley's idealism which took, of course, the form of Johnson kicking a stone and uttering "I refute him thus." There in Flew's room I had one of those transgressive impulses which are, at heart, purely ironic and aesthetic: I wanted to kick him up the arse crying as I did so "I refute you thus!" I didn't but he still threw me out of his room. I'll return to this.

The second encounter was with Flew's successor, Professor Richard Swinburne, who spent his academic life trying to prove the existence of God. I had led a student protest to his door, complaining that he'd allowed his religious views to prejudice his marking of our essays on the topic of abortion. By chance we'd come across what I think was then a relatively new publication called *Philosophy and Public Affairs*, and in particular an article which argued that, according to certain criteria of aliveness, it was more immoral to kill a calf than a human infant of the same age. That did not go down at all well with his own Christian commitments and he suggested I cease attending his seminars. I remember thinking – unfortunately too late for my parting shot – that if I was God and someone like Swinburne proved my existence I'd probably kill myself.

The third encounter involved that philosophy tutor who had interviewed me. It was at the finals party. He sidled up to me asking if I had considered going to do post-grad work in the subject. I ran a fucking mile.

Swinburne eventually got the call back to Oxford, where he continued his Divine Mission, while Flew, who spent most of his philosophical life denying the existence of God, supposedly changed his mind shortly before he died. As for the philosopher who interviewed me I never heard of him again.

Not surprisingly, then, I looked for inspiration outside of the Philosophy department. I read other things, especially those anthologies of existentialism that discovered that everyone interesting in the European tradition was a proto-existentialist, with titles like 'Existentialism from Shakespeare to Jaspers.' In fact I read Jaspers in great awe after being told (probably erroneously) that his teaching of nihilism was so compelling his students regularly committed suicide. Now there, I thought, was a real philosopher! To this day if I think of those philosophers who have most influenced me few, if any, have been 'real' philosophers in Professor Flew's sense. And before I name some of them let me say what I mean by 'influence'; as well as the obvious sense of the word, I mean these are writers who I have lived with, returned to, learned from hesitantly and piecemeal, all my life. That it takes that long is a consequence of both their intelligence and my limitations as a thinker. The limitations of the recipient is a neglected aspect of influence, not least because to succumb to one kind of influence is to turn away from others. But you have to find your own way. So of those who have influenced me here's a few: Ecclesiastes, Seneca, Montaigne, Schopenhauer, Nietzsche, Marx and Freud. I don't know what might connect them unless it be this: in very different ways all see human consciousness as alienated from the very reality which it strives to understand.

My own stumbling quest for understanding, one which had led me to that interview at Keele, had begun some years earlier and was initiated by morphine. I should explain. I had a motorcycle accident which nearly killed me, yet paradoxically both saved my life and profoundly changed it.

I remember coming round, lying on the road, the bike on top of me, the sound of car-doors slamming, running feet, more than one person leaning over me and telling me to lie still. I insisted I was OK, kept insisting, and despite their efforts to stop me, somehow got to my feet, and staggered in the direction of home. At that point there wasn't much pain but my left leg wouldn't work properly and my arms were numb. The accident had happened only a few hundred yards from home on a stretch of road I'd travelled, by foot, on a cycle and in my parents' car, many hundreds of times. To this day I still don't know exactly what did happen, or why. I can remember riding the bike up to about a hundred yards before the point of the accident. But from then until I regained consciousness afterwards it's a complete blank. Total amnesia. And a mystery too, since no other traffic was seemingly involved, and it was a straight road (generally speaking, boys fall off motor cycles on corners or when they hit things). The unlucky part is that I'd not been thrown clear of the bike but become entangled with it as it slid along the tarmac. Wearing only a t-shirt and jeans, with no helmet, I was in a bad way. On my arms and legs and forehead the skin had entirely gone and bits were gouged out to the bone. Coincidentally, one of the people who came on the scene knew me but didn't recognise me because there was so much blood on my face.

I had turned sixteen by just a few days. As I limped home I saw my mother running towards me. There was wetness in my eyes which prevented me seeing her properly. I may have been crying, but as I wiped them I realised it was blood, or rather assumed it was because although I couldn't see it I could taste it. (As children we were taught to suck bleeding wound to cleanse them so I knew well the taste of blood). That look of terror on my mother's face as she helped me home – did I see it or imagine it, or half see it and half imagine it? She got my clothes off, or what was left of them, and was about to help me into a bath when the ambulance arrived. She mentioned later that she'd thrown the clothes away because they were too torn and bloodstained to keep.

As I write this I've just realised, with remorse, but also the writer's fascination, that there would be two other occasions in the next few years when she would again have to dispose of my blood-stained clothes. The second time was a car accident a couple of years later; the third was my first suicide attempt, which I mentioned earlier. The grief I caused her on that occasion was the greatest of all, and about that I feel only remorse. In later years I sometimes fantasised about being able to die with my mother as a kind of reparation – not just for the hurt I had caused her but also what life has done to her. Many years later she and I went swimming on a beach in New Zealand. I went into the sea first and turning round to look for her I shuddered to see her looking frail and old in the cold water. It was also a shudder for my own mortality. Part of what bonds the boy to the mother is his narcissism, something she nurtures. The stronger the bond, the greater the narcissisic wounds of later life.

As I said, it was an accident which could have killed me but which both saved and changed my life. Saved because, although as soon as I was fit enough I rode motorcycles again and that included riding some very fast machines very recklessly, it was never again with that same sublimely ignorant adolescent abandon with which I'd ridden legally in those few days before the accident and, illegally, at night, from the age of about fourteen onwards. The accident left me with a sense of how to survive the desire to experience danger, a sense of the skills necessary to survive. In later life you survive dangerous situations mainly by avoiding them. When young – if you're given the time, and I nearly wasn't – you learn skills which give you a chance of surviving the dangers you embrace. That's the essential thrill of embracing danger.

The accident changed my life because while recovering in hospital I decided to leave my job in a car factory and become a writer. I now realise it was the morphine which was speaking. The nurses were very free with the morphine. There I was, in pain, immobile, covered with ugly wounds, warned I'd be badly scarred for life, yet with these intense feelings of euphoria and even a kind of omnipotence. That's to say, for the first time in my life, anything seemed possible. I hated that factory and realised for the first time that it was possible for me to leave it. Yes, I would leave, I would become a writer. The Situationist cry from the streets in 1968, 'Be realistic – demand the impossible!,' was still a couple of years away, and anyway I don't think I encountered it until well after 1968, but in retrospect it seemed exactly right for what I felt in that hospital bed. In an obvious sense that feeling of omnipotence was a drug-induced illusion. And yet I did leave, and I did become a writer. First I got a lowly job in journalism, where I became quarter-literate, and later I went to university where I became half-literate. I owe something to morphine, and remember vividly the occasion when I first encountered that famous remark of William Burroughs: 'I have seen life measured out with eyedroppers of morphine solution.'

I've already related the interview which got me into the academy. I now recount the experience which led me to leave it years later. For some months I had been slipping into a severe depression. The breaking point came when I was trying to mark exam scripts. The revulsion was visceral. The only way I can describe it is like this (and the description is still inadequate to the experience): think of each script as another mouthful of something that I didn't want but which I was forcing myself to eat. Each mouthful was, therefore, more difficult to swallow than the last; I was choking and wanted to throw up the whole lot. The scripts were both a symptom and the extreme instance of everything about the job that was choking me. I left the building there and then determined never to return. And I didn't. I'd been dogged with bouts of severe depression all my adult life. Always before I had struggled through, staying in the job. But this time I realised that to survive I had to get out completely. Total disengagement. What had changed? In many ways the job had become intolerable: ever-growing pressures to be research-productive in stupid ways, ever more students to teach, and fewer resources. And then there were the relentless, mostly futile internal politics. As others have said before, it's no surprise academics are so bitchy to each other: the stakes are so low. But if the only story I had to tell was how bad things are in UK higher education, I wouldn't be telling it. Yes it's bad, and getting worse. The fact is, my departure enabled me to see something else of importance much more clearly, something which might even help up the stakes for the future.

My own first encounter with higher education was, perforce, an unconventional one. I came in from the outside and, for all the limitations of coming via that route (illiteracy being only the most obvious), it offered a different perspective. Now I needed to be outside again to rediscover what a creative engagement might be, for me, now. It was only when I sat down to write about that early experience of getting into university that I fully realized this. This is why I put the two together – getting in and getting out. I got out because I lost sight of the things I learned, almost fortuitously, from the very first day I encountered a university at that interview. So don't for a minute think that my departure was some brave move to rediscover or protect my integrity, a word I anyway distrust, at least when used in the first person. On the contrary, in a very certain sense that departure was a failure in that I'd finally, after years of survival, let myself be wrecked by institutional pressures.

The truth of institutions is that they are both necessary and stultifying; like Samuel Becket's habits, we can't live without forming them, even though (perhaps *because?*) they are great deadeners, which means that sometimes you have to get out of them; and I mean really out – not just a sabbatical – to re-realise what's possible inside of them.

In that first encounter with academic philosophy I learnt how to survive inside the academy, how to cope with the inevitable disappointments of this institution and probably all institutions, controlled as they are by some of those with the least imagination. The disappointment, which I suppose began with the taking out of that book from Luton library, led to a certain duplicity. Far from apologising for this, I commend it: the fact is a certain degree of duplicity in one's relationship with the institution is necessary –even at the very top. In that sense we might even learn something from a past director of the Shakespeare Folger Library (one of the most suspect institutions I've ever encountered) who, when asked what his job involved, apparently replied 'I have two constituencies – the people who pay for this place and the academics who use it. My job is to keep them as far apart as possible.'

But I'm much more concerned with activity lower down the institution, because that's usually where the creative work happens and it's usually with and in relation to students, and where a certain duplicity is more likely to work for creative ends. After I moved to the University of York most of the undergraduate students I encountered didn't interest me. I mean that as students of literature they didn't interest me. Most were well-heeled and well protected. They were also well-educated, of course – to do English at York you had to be. But maybe already their education had become a hand-icap; too many were still on automatic pilot from A Levels. But I know it was my failure too; very often I failed or didn't try hard enough to connect with the interesting person who was usually (not invariably) there. The fact remains that for a student to be interesting to me in their study it took more – and that *more* could be there in someone who was barely literate. I suppose I'm seeing my earlier self in them. So maybe this too is a limitation, even a failure, but it's where I worked best. In short, I have always connected most intensely with students who are in some important respect more alive than the rest, which also means in some sense also damaged, or at least not well protected. I had no qualms about bending the assessment rules in their favour.

I can't share the notion that a teacher has the duty to bring each and every individual student to his or her best achievement, to realize their potential, however limited or great it might be. Nor can I share the related notion that a teacher has the duty to make the best part of him or herself available to all and sundry, in aid of their self-realisation. I think both notions echo older ideas of the tutor-pupil relationships across class: the tutor in service. Such tutors, usually childless themselves, undertake further sacrifices in order to foster the potential of the young entrusted to them: the tutor as a childless, surrogate parent, vulnerable to exploitations deeper than those of class alone.

The best teaching is inseparable from love, chaste or carnal. Often the love is illicit, or at least problematic, even or especially when it's chaste. You won't be surprised to hear that I've never learned anything from the injunctions of Teaching Committees. Obviously not. But back in those Keele days I did learn something from Plato's account of how Socrates 'taught' – *not*, I hasten to add, from the Socratic dialogue, a method of teaching which has always struck me as fraudulent. No, it's other things about Socrates; for example, the passages in the *Symposium* where he brilliantly takes on Alcibiades, a young man who was, apparently, as beautiful and dangerous as he was arrogant and powerful. Socrates brilliantly exploits the homoerotic tension between himself and Alcibades; with a ruthless chastity he works on the narcissism of the younger man until he has manipulated him into submission. Later I used to teach the *Symposium* in relation to a crucial dilemma: how to have an unregulated relationship between teacher and student which isn't either destroyed from without or corrupted from within. Modern novelists as different as P.D. James, Philip Roth and Saul Bellow have explored this dilemma, all with pessimistic conclusions.

All this came back to me during my very last class at York, an event which also led me to turn away. I'd agreed to co-teach a course on Politics and the Novel focussing on D.H. Lawrence. The night before this class I'd stayed up late re-reading Lawrence with increasing respect for a writer whose greatness is inextricably bound up with what makes him also objectionable. Re-reading Lawrence made me think about how, at one level, democracy is about toleration of difference and diversity, while at another it's about suppressing freedom and levelling difference, imposing uniformity, curtailing precious potential and radical difference, all for the sake of the supposed general interest. Ironically, the suppression of the truly different is the price one pays for respecting individual rights, and never more so than today, when those rights are expressed in terms of a belligerent sense of consumerist entitlement. So it was worth trying to explain to myself as well as others why Lawrence, now widely disregarded of course, is still important; also why so many found him objectionable, and why his importance and the objections to him might be inseparable. It seemed difficult but definitely worthwhile. On the way into work the next day I met my co-teacher, a professor in Politics, who had also stayed up late re-reading Lawrence, and who had also been enthused by doing so. We had an animated conversation before going off to our offices to wade through an hour or so of 'admin.' before the class. It was a seminar of 12 students. Half of them didn't turn up, and the half which did hadn't read the texts, or perhaps had made a half-hearted attempt to read part of maybe one of the texts. So they got out paper and pens and began taking notes while my colleague and I spent two hours telling them basic things about Lawrence and trying to persuade them he was worth reading. I think we succeeded, though I'm pretty sure none of them went back to read the texts. Why should they bother? That class was over, and there was nothing in it that was compulsory.

What I really wanted to do was to say what I had said in the past to students in this situation – something like: 'I don't care if you spend the night drinking, clubbing. fucking or doing lines of coke, but so far as I'm concerned interesting people do that *and* read books. Now fuck off and read some books because to me right now, to me, you are not interesting.' Clearly this no longer counts as 'best practice,' or whatever the current jargon is. The most discouraging thing about that class lay in that aspect of it which, from the point of view of 'best practice,' was perhaps most successful: our eventually convincing them that Lawrence might be worth reading. We stirred them from an apathy, an acquiescence, a dependency, which the whole enterprise of 'Best Practice' in the last decade has actually encouraged. But I doubt if it went further; within hours the stirring probably relapsed into indifference or a forgetting. Teaching at that moment represented energy absorbed by inertia.

Yes: institutional life requires duplicity and never more so than now. Becoming a defeatist at the very least helps prevent disappointment. A truly radical relativism recognises the necessity of duplicity and indeed insincerity, hence the wisdom of Oscar Wilde's assertion that a little sincerity is a dangerous thing and a great deal of it absolutely fatal. We might learn too from the Wildean transgressive aesthetic and the way it teaches us to support an institution just enough to survive within it while actively perverting it – to work against or beyond it, even to the point of illegality, in order to find a creative way forward. Years ago, when exploring this in the history of homosexual dissidence, and with reference to Wilde, I called it 'transgressive re-inscription,' a fancy phrase for a rather important praxis.

Further, I find this even more important now that we have supposedly cut free of the so-called grand narratives. Certain philosophers – for instance, Lyotard and Foucault – celebrated the collapse of the grand narratives like God, Nature, and Class. Arguably this was just the latest instance, albeit an exhilarating one, of a move in Western culture which has been replayed over and over for at least 2000 years: the restless shift back and forth between the absolute and the relative. In postmodernist theory it was, of course, all one way: from the universal to the particular, from the singular to the plural, from totalising to multiplying, from the central to the local, from the familiar to the other(s), from sameness to difference, from ideology to discourse, from Culture singular to the multicultural, and so on. But even as postmodernists theorised this with relish they failed to realise the obvious: namely, the multiple ways in which, without those grand narratives, we become so easily contained and neutralised by the institutions in which we work. If the radically conceived alternative, the radically imagined elsewhere, are illusions, all we can have is what we've got now. Not for the first time a radical relativism encourages a political conservatism.

Doubtless this is only one explanation for the present state of affairs. But we do need to think about why the majority of British academics have recently complied with every move from above to undermine what we thought we stood for. Grand narratives are at once transcendent and reductive, and the latter is as important as the former in helping us to resist compliance. But there is, incidentally, a specific local history to be written here: is there something about the training and early educational history of academics which makes them especially susceptible to compliance? It's always been hard to get an academic job and only the successful succeed. But perhaps that very success works against intellectual independence? Certainly, the tragedy of some academics – and one reason why they remain academics rather than thinkers – is that they identify too readily with the academy as an institution. More generally, it is remarkable that in the UK no widespread counter-cultural movements have emerged to confront the insanities of our time, of which those involving war and finance are only the most obvious. Not only are our Humanities departments silent in this regard, but the new management culture which controls them is largely complicit with what needs to be critiqued.

But let us accept that the grand narratives are indeed gone, that there is no longer any outside, and we find ourselves confronting that radical relativism I alluded to earlier. The stakes are higher, the dangers are greater, duplicity more necessary than ever. An engaged critical and teaching practice must circumvent the deadening effect of contemporary institutions – market and bureaucratic – and the even more insidious forms that creep in on the back of these. Breaking the normative rules of the institution can never be a sufficient condition for creating value inside it, but in an ever-widening diversity of circumstance, it is often a necessary condition.

On the one hand, we have the potential to be intellectuals – or, if that sounds too pretentious for our empirical tradition, then free-thinkers committed to the activity of a critical intelligence. On the other hand, we are professionals, implicated in, employed by, paid by, if not the servants of, the academic institution. The intellectual and the professional sides of our being are in conflict. And if they are not they should be. We should distrust all professionals, and not just lawyers. We should distrust our own professional selves. And yet recent times have brought out in academics their professional rather than their intellectual side; they have sought survival by receding ever-further into the scanty cover afforded by the profession, rather than risk engagement on the exposed ground of critical dissent. Here's an example if what I mean. When the UK government announced in December 2009 the first round of financial cut backs it was aimed at Higher Education. (I'm talking here of the relatively uncontroversial cuts announced prior to the 2010 election, not the hugely expanded and controversial programme announced by the new Coalition government, post-election). How did our academic spokespeople respond? One argument given leading media attention, went like this: funding cuts will mean that academics will have even less time to properly vet student applicants, with the result that terrorists might infiltrate the University system even more than at present. (At the time the news media were still full of the revelation that the man who tried to blow up a plane flying between the UK and the US on Christmas day 2009 had studied at one of the London universities). Perhaps the saddest thing about this argument is not that it has little chance of making a difference, but that it's now the only kind of argument that might make a difference. Academics have been complicit for too long; that's one reason why our government picked us off first. 'Be realistic –demand the impossible?' Such slogans seem unutterably naïve now, unthinkable even; which is only to see what an impoverished, ideologically compromised notion is the 'realism' of the present – especially inside universities.

When I say academics have been complicit I don't just mean with recent government strategies to marginalize the universities. The problem goes back much further and it's this that concerns me just as much. Again, I'm talking only about the Humanities departments that I know, and I deliberately choose a symptomatic example which implicates me, namely the publishing industry surrounding Shakespeare. Imagine a survey of the staggering amount written by academics on Shakespeare within, say, the last 100 years. And remember that behind every book and every article are months, indeed years, perhaps decades of so-called 'research,' by which is meant, all too often, a desperate effort to find something new to say, or something acceptable, to 'peer-reviewed journals,' which often means little more than not saying anything that the leading academics in the field find threatening. Given all the time, energy and resources that went into all this Shakespeare 'scholarship,' we can legitimately ask how much of it had any long or even medium term value. It seems to me it was always largely irrelevant to anyone but those doing it, that it was embarrassingly relative to its academic locale, even or especially when it lay claim to be speaking of the enduring universal truths allegedly found in Shakespeare. In fact much of it was reactionary and dated even at the time of its writing, most obviously when it considered issues of, say, politics or human sexuality. It's a classic long-term example of what's wrong with so-called research in the humanities: narrowly focused and regulated by the interest of the profession rather than the massively wider interests which intersect with and radiate from the subject. Put another way, the professionally-defended Arts academic is only half alive.

In my early days as a graduate student I had to spend some time immersed in the past productions of the Shakespeare industry, in particular those in peer-reviewed journals. I did so in the old reading room of the British Museum, that place which Gissing, in *New Grub Street* (1891) called 'the shadow of the valley of books.' That novel has a character, Marian Yule, who spends her life in the reading room doing futile, second-order 'research.' She feels her life draining away and yearns for the kind of writing which derives from 'having an urgent message for the world.' After some time immersed in peer-reviewed Shakespeare journals I began to understand Marian Yule's sense of that place as what she calls 'a trackless desert of print,' where lost souls are doomed to wander in an 'eternity of vain research along endless shelves.' I have never felt so strongly as then the truth of William Faulkner's insightful collapsing of Shaw's maxim about teaching, into a more general one about life: 'Those who can live do so, those who can't write about it.'

The Research Assessment Exercise (RAE) not only involved departments in huge amounts of extra administrative work, but actually encouraged the very last thing needed in most humanities subjects – yet more 'research' publications which, if consulted at all, are done so reluctantly only by other academics trying to make a career in the same field. It might have been better to issue every academic with a publishing 'footprint' quota; so, for example, publishing yet another book on Shakespeare would be permissible, but would constitute the academic equivalent of, say, 100 transatlantic flights.

Unlike some critics of the current situation of humanities education in the UK, I am not nostalgic for the old days. How could I be, coming from where I did? In the old system prestigious English departments were based in an elitism of class, which guaranteed a mediocrity all of its own, only now posturing as arrogantly superior. And yes, I'm thinking of Oxbridge, and yes a lot of that narrowly conceived Shakespeare criticism I just referred to originated in such places. But I have to be careful here: in England attacks on class all too easily become self-righteous, which is why I love to remember that great argument between two women in Wilde's *The Importance of Being Earnest*. The first woman says: 'This is no time for the shallow mask of social manners. When I see a spade I call it a spade.' The second woman replies 'I am happy to say I have never seen a spade. It is obvious that our social spheres have been widely different.' It reminds me of that famous remark of Barbara Cartland's when a rather pushy interviewer asked her if she thought the class system in England had finally broken down: 'Quite evidently,' she replied, 'otherwise I wouldn't be talking to you.' It's a wonderful line. Mind you, she was a dreadful novelist.

So no, there is no going back. When the UK Universities started to expand their student numbers the old elitism couldn't continue. Of course not. And the new order had to be regulated to ensure fair play. Even so it's regrettable that those drawing up the new rules seem to have been ignorant of the long philosophical history of education, a history in which the things which are now outlawed, including – as with the devious and deviant Socrates – seduction and coercion, silence and charisma, all had their place.

But here's the problem all this encounters: if a particular practice within an institution is discovered to be open to abuse we legislate to pre-empt the abuse and end up stifling any potential vitality that practice might have had; mediocrity then takes its place. And yet we of all people should recognize that just because a practice is open to abuse doesn't make it necessarily wrong; that it may be that any social practice that is vital is thereby open to abuse. Vitality and the vulnerability to abuse go together. Tenacity and perseverance bring success of a kind to most people, including (maybe especially) to the second rate. Often the first rate (by my criteria at least) are so wounded by initial failure they give up, or in Freud's terms, retire in favour of another. In the academic world of recent times the second rate have gone far, especially in the role of administering mediocrity. As in so many other walks of life – one is tempted to say in human society generally – it's a commonplace that the people who *run* things have greater power than those who *create* things. That said, one of the most heroic academics I've known went into administration to fight mediocrity. She wasn't successful.

There's no going back. The situation we have is the price of democracy. It really does go that deep and it would be dishonest to pretend that everything would be fine if we just got rid of political correctness. The problem has much deeper roots in modern market-driven democratic culture, and it means that today intense creativity, or even just the creation of intensity inside institutions sometimes requires anti-democratic means. The challenge is to use them for other than self-serving ends. That's harder than it sounds. So too is knowing when to care and when not to care. That can be the hardest thing of all. With Gramsci always in mind, we might say that a pessimism of the political intellect is countered by an optimism of the ethical will. And, as always with the assumption of responsibility, I assume responsibility not because I think we are in charge of our own destinies; sadly, sometimes tragically, most of us are not. And even the very powerful and the very wealthy – presidents and bankers – can find the future unfolding against them. But by assuming responsibility for one's life one can imprint that destiny to some degree, and it's that mark which, no matter how insignificant, is, in the final reckoning, the most interesting thing about us.

Never before, I think, has the project of creating value inside of, and against, educational institutions been so necessary. There is always a creative way forward if we remember that what's possible today is intensified by the very pressures which seek to stifle it. Even so, I can envisage a time when the most engaged critical practice may once again be outside the universities.

I said I'd return to that moment in Professor Flew's room when I suddenly wanted to kick his arse. I didn't do it. I often wonder what would have happened if I had. I doubt if I'd have stayed inside the academy. But I didn't kick him and I did stay inside. Maybe that too was a failure of a kind. After all, staying inside had to be easier. Every academic knows that, though few admit it. Even so, 30 years later it got the better of me. It wrecked me. So I got out and became reclusive for several years. I bought and taught myself to operate a three-ton digger and went landscaping. I don't know if I've got the better of my depression; probably not. Depression is mysterious. If severe, it involves an extreme incapacity to function socially; an extreme withdrawal, a severing of oneself from social being. Sometimes one doesn't come back and the severance is a suicidal separation from life itself. A story I covered in my early days as a newspaper reporter has always stayed with me. It was only given one paragraph on an inside page: the remains of a 17 year old boy had been discovered in a sleeping bag in some woods. There were no suspicious circumstances. Depressed, he had taken his own life and crawled away to die.

Depression is a kind of risk with only nominal agency: you might kill yourself, or you might eventually come back to life. If and when you come back from depression it can be as if something has died and something been reborn. One can feel a vulnerably sensitive elation that is different from both the manic elation of bi-polar conditions and of the morphine high; different from the first (bipolar) because not so desperately driven, and from the second (morphine) because the sense of possibility is not so inwardly fantasized – it's most outwardly aware. In other words, it's an elation inseparable from being, *being alive*, and as such lacks the 'density' of pleasure or gratification; it's so much thinner than that – ethereal almost, having a translucence through which the other of pleasure filters through. I associate it with the regenerative influence of rain, as in the Edenic Van Morrison lines: 'I shall walk and talk in gardens all wet with rain / And never grow so old again,' or George Herbert's from more than three centuries earlier:

> Grief melts away
> Like snow in May,
> As if there were no such cold thing.
> . . . .
> After so many deaths I live and write;
> I once more smell the dew and rain.

Depression cost me my career; or maybe I should say it saved me from it. In truth, though, it didn't need depression for me to know that professional success – the successful career – is one of the most compromised, complicit and corrupt kinds of success available today, of which there are many. It's astonishing that the career as a way of life remains so uncritically regarded by so many of those who are in a position to know better. One should not need the ordeal of depression to know that staying alive is always about self-renewal, always about awareness of the many insidious kinds of deadening that life *in time* habituates us to, including professionalism. And if I add that 'doing the right thing' can be as damaging as taking the path of least resistance, it's only to acknowledge how difficult staying alive can be. At the very least, though, we incur the responsibility of being honest about that, which means to become a critic of one's own life, which should perhaps be the condition of being any kind of critic at all.

Finally, I remark upon another consequence of leaving. Departure is, of course, a resonant literary theme, especially when pressured by loss. But departure can also sensitise us to a meta-stillness within and beyond loss. There is the noise of life and there is the silence when life is absent. And then there is the deeper silence only to be intimated from within life, but at one remove from it. It's this I'm talking about: I hear it in the winds of March or in the stillness of a foggy November landscape; even in the still-ness of the late morning in any season. It opens us to the silence of oblivion, Andrew Marvell's 'deserts of vast eternity,' in relation to which desire and individuation are an irrelevance. Or W.B. Yeats' night sky:

> A starlit or a moonlit dome disdains
> All that man is
> All mere complexities,
> The fury and the mire of human veins.

In youth, the realisation of one's insignificance is wounding. Later it's merely regrettable; later still it's almost consoling. I think the narcissistic wound only ever finally heals in death. But past failures, past hurts, even against the mother, are always redeemable in the present, if one has the courage of one's own unimportance. And, rather wonderfully, that unim-portance is liberating for praxis; engagement, now animated by a certain carelessness, gets easier.

I do remain grateful to that time, those years ago, when the narcissistic wound, through the painful physical wounds it was in no small part respon-sible for, encountered morphine. It was a heady moment when pain dissolved into possibility, and without it I doubt I'd be writing this. Not a grand narrative in sight then, but maybe only because it's here in such a concentrated form as to be invisible.

They say the young flirt with death because they think themselves immortal. Perhaps, but it's also because in them the narcissistic wound is still raw. I now think my own self-inflicted close encounters with death had a lot to do with that. Which is only another way of saying I grew up slowly, if at all. The recklessness of youth sometimes achieves an intensity of being, which for all its self-destructiveness can be strangely on the side of life. If we survive it we may or may not be glad of having done so; and how we feel about this probably depends on how much failure-in-success we've willingly embraced since, and how acutely we *realize* that survival is not a good in itself. We can die just by staying alive; living becoming a dying to life. Which means that if we do survive we incur an even greater obligation to life as against survival: not just to stay alive but to stay alive to life itself.

Uni and Me

Willy Maley

As a genre, academic memoirs are in a senior common room of their own. In the course of what I still like to call my career, even as the banking crisis brings back the banking system of education, not to mention cuts and closures, there have been some sterling examples of the intellectual autobiography, including Raymond Williams' *What I Came to Say* (1989), Henry Louis Gates, Jr's *Coloured People* (1995), Jacques Derrida's *Monolingualism of the Other* (1998), Edward Said's *Out of Place* (1999), and Terry Eagleton's *The Gatekeeper* (2001). Williams was at Jesus College, Cambridge, when I started my PhD there in 1985 (more of which anon), and Eagleton was an early influence too, so I take an interest in the stories that lead to a lifetime's teaching and research. I remember reading a series of essays by Derrida on the university, a subject that preoccupied him throughout his life, and being struck by his historical sense and the rigour with which he addressed himself to the institution.[1] Lorna Sage's *Bad Blood* (2000) is in a class of its own, and forces one to rethink the masculine memoir. Or at least it should. Another influence on my way of thinking about teaching and writing is bell hooks (aka Gloria Watkins). Her *Teaching to Transgress: Education as the Practice of Freedom* (1994) has had a profound impact on how I conceive the connection between theory and practice.

There's a Biff cartoon showing a guy talking at a woman across a dinner table. His speech bubble reads: 'Do you mind if I talk about myself at some length?' Her thought balloon says: 'Your tie's in your soup.' I'm too young, obscure and flippant to be fit for purpose as far as memoirs go, but at the risk of getting soup on my tie – something that's actually encouraged in cartoon professors – I'd like to say something about my own entry into the world of academe. My childhood was painful and poverty-stricken, but full of good things too, especially books, and although it was with university that I felt my life really began, I know that's a fiction, and that I was framed by family history and school like everyone else.

One of nine children brought up in a Communist household – both parents were card-carrying members of the Party, and *The Soviet Weekly* sat alongside *The Sunday Post*. We lived on borrowed books. I came to reading through my parents. Daddy was a manual labourer who brought books home by the bagful from the book exchange at Gilmorehill Bookshop, near Glasgow University. Mammy, who worked in the kitchens at Strathclyde University's student hall of residence, introduced me at an early age to the treasures in our local library in Possilpark. I still remember the green borrowing card and being sent by her to collect a copy of *Dombey and Son*, a title I can almost taste in that memory of being six or seven years old and going to get Dickens. It had the voice of doom in it, that title. Years later I discovered Dickens had visited my squalid Dickensian housing estate in the north of Glasgow in December 1847, when it was the site of a mansion house a couple of hundred yards from the library owned by Sir Archibald Alison, the Sheriff of Lanarkshire and celebrated historian of the French Revolution. Question: what novel was being serialized at the time? Answer: *Dombey and Son*. 'And did those feet in ancient times?' The death of Sheriff Alison in 1867 saw the demolition of Possil House and the erection of an iron foundry, the dark satanic mill of my infancy, which was itself demolished in 1967.

My father, a bricklayer in his latter years, knew we needed more than bread. The bricks and mortar of my education was a weekly ritual, him saying 'You've a week to finish those, then they're going back to the bookshop.' Books were to be borrowed and loaned, not owned; read and retained in the mind, not the home. Daddy would present us with a pile of paperbacks and give us a week to read them before they went back to the store. You learn to read pretty fast if the hefty volume in your hands is about to be snatched away. This was from primary school onwards, and there was no genre or form or period or subject matter that wasn't thrown in, and certainly no censorship. So while being read to at school – books about Blighty by Blyton – at home I was immersed in the collected works of Edgar Rice Burroughs, Sir Walter Scott, Dickens, Louisa M Alcott, Mario Puzo, Herbert Kastle, Jane Austen, J. T. Edson, Zane Grey, Brian Aldiss, Ray Bradbury, Anthony Burgess and many more. It was a broad-based introduction to literature, or at least to the novel – junk, pulp, classic and cult. I led a double life – like most readers, and especially, I would say, working-class readers – excluded from the very world into which I routinely fled. Books spoke to me, but in voices that were not my own.

With insufficient qualifications for university, I worked for three years after leaving school – first for Strathclyde Regional Council Roads Department (1978–9), and then for the Royal Bank of Scotland (1979–80). When I started my third job in 1979, with Glasgow City Libraries (1980–81), this eclectic reading continued as I went through the catalogue sampling every available style, including the mandatory Mills & Boon with the sex scene on page 117. Because of this background I've never observed any hierarchy between the canonical and the contemporary, the prestigious and the popular. Stephen King's *The Stand* is among my favourite books, and these days I recommend his *On Writing* (2000) to creative writing students. Alasdair Gray's *Lanark* (1981) was a landmark book for me, published the year I started Strathclyde University, one of those 'portrait of the artist' books that assume biblical proportions for a first-generation student or professional. *Lanark* was part of my landscape, part of my address in fact. Gray once compared the role of the creative writing tutor to that of an usher who opens doors and windows, serves refreshments, and generally caters for the well-being and wishes of writers. It's a nice idea, because most writers – and most students – will tell you that opening doors is something they often struggle with. An usher is there to show you around and light the path. For me, education is all about opening doors.

I remember as a wee boy playing games like 'Bar the Gates,' where a line of people tried to stop others from getting through, and 'Code,' where you tried to cudgel or cajole the secret word out of someone. I worry sometimes we haven't come so far after all, as in academia we still play those games. 'Bar the Gates' is our admissions policy, 'Code' our examination process. As I began the voyage out, commuting between worlds of family and fantasy, community and coterie, poverty and privilege, Gray's *Lanark* was definitely a door-opener for me, an eye-opener too. Here was someone with a stunningly surreal imagination and a sensuous sense of self and street-life. These things, hitherto separate, were brought together. Here was 'life' in all its richness and fecundity, and 'literature' too. I wasn't a schizophrenic after all. It was all of a piece. When I read in *Lanark* that nobody notices Glasgow because 'nobody imagines living there' I knew it was the truth, not fiction. 'Imaginatively Glasgow,' writes Gray, 'exists as a music-hall song and a few bad novels. That's all we've given to the world outside. It's all we've given to ourselves.'[2] With these words a door swung open. Here was literature and history in the making. Glasgow was imagining itself, engaging in dialogue, talking to itself. The city was finding a voice.

The library was the best job I had before I started teaching, the bank the worst, certainly the lowest-paid. It meant a day that started before the branch even opened, with my having to go into town to collect the bags with all the slips for the day, and ended long after the last customer left when the books were finally balanced. But when it was over, it was over – you couldn't take it home with you, so I never worried after work. Likewise, the most blissful naps I've had since childhood were the after-dinner ones when I worked in the bank. Once I became a mature student, then an academic, it was different, as homework and school sickness would set in, that feeling of the hand on the shoulder you get from deadlines falling like leaves.

I went to Strathclyde University initially to study Librarianship but failed the course in first year and faced the choice of abandoning my studies or resigning from Glasgow City Libraries. I quit my job and continued with my studies in English Literature and Politics. Strathclyde University allowed students to take five subjects in the first year – so, as well as Librarianship, for which I achieved 38%, and 50% in the resit, I took English Studies, Economic History, Modern History, and Politics. In second year, having readily relinquished Librarianship, I took English and Politics as part of a four-year joint degree. By third year I was doing three Politics and one English course, making Single Politics possible in the fourth and final year but not Single English. However, by the time fourth year dawned, Politics at Strathclyde had become wholly preoccupied with behavioural, electoral and statistical topics and had begun to look like Librarianship crossed with Maths. I bent the rules and pursued English singularly. With tutors like Derek Attridge and Colin MacCabe and their pioneering Theory of Literature course I was in good hands. There was more politics to be had in English Studies than in Politics.

I never gave a thought to embarking on any kind of postgraduate study, until after the result of my finals came through in June 1985. In the two weeks between finding out that I had done well enough to contemplate further study and graduating with a first class honours degree with distinction, Derek Attridge asked if I'd ever considered Oxbridge. For me Oxbridge conjured up images of punts, not punters, but most of all it seemed to be an area of life cordoned off as the playground of the ruling classes. But the seed was sown, and although I was keen on going to Sussex to do the Renaissance MPhil with Jonathan Dollimore and Alan Sinfield, both of whom had made a big impression on me in my final year as an undergraduate, I was hooked by the lure of Oxbridge. Sussex was Colin MacCabe's suggestion – he had had his fill of Cambridge. I spent the summer working in London, and applied to Oxford and Cambridge. Accepted by both, I visited the latter at the end of July, during the Film Festival, and was impressed with what I saw.

In October 1985 I went up, as they say, to Cambridge to do a PhD on 'Edmund Spenser and Cultural Identity in Early Modern Ireland,' and to be supervised by Lisa Jardine. At all universities the accents and addresses of academic staff differ from those of catering, maintenance and security staff. At Cambridge, even the accents of the students placed them on a higher social scale, whichever part of the world they happened to come from. I got used to being taken for non-academic staff when I started lecturing, but it took a while at Cambridge to get used to not being taken as a student. My Glasgow brogue got me in trouble in Cambridge on a number of occasions. In the first week of my stay in Jesus College I was cutting across the forecourt, something that, as a member of the College, I was perfectly entitled to do. A porter asked where I was going. As soon as I started to speak he strode towards me, gripped me by the arm, and led me towards the door I'd just come in, explaining that the College was closed to members of the public. With my accent, there was no way I could possibly be a student of Jesus, or any other College. When I produced my matriculation card he apologised so profusely that my flush of rage turned to a blush, unsure whether to be angry at being manhandled or at the grovelling that followed on from the revealing of my true identity as a member of the 'student-class.'

Ralph Glasser's autobiography, *Growing Up in the Gorbals* (1986), tells the tale of a proverbial lad o' pairts who won a scholarship to Oxford and went from one of Glasgow's toughest housing estates to become a respected writer and critic. My own adventures as a Possil Boy at Cambridge echoed Glasser's experiences at Oxford. My time among the dreaming spires was full of strange encounters. One day, I heard through the grapevine that notorious Scottish ex-con Jimmy Boyle was coming to speak at the Institute of Criminology. So, Glasser wasn't to be the only Gorbals Boy to find his way to the dreaming spires. Boyle's lecture was a late-afternoon affair. There was standing room only in a large oak-panelled room. Impeccably dressed in a suit and tie, Boyle spoke for an hour without notes about the riots in HM Prison Peterhead, and about the iniquities of the criminal justice system. His speech was direct and uncompromising. You could have heard a penny drop. It was one of the best lectures I attended during my time at Cambridge, or since, come to think of it.

Boyle spent around twenty minutes afterwards answering questions. I approached him at the end and said I'd be with some friends in The Anchor later if he'd like to join us for a pint. He nodded but seemed a bit distracted, which was fair under the circumstances. He had a commitment to eat at high table with the Master and Fellows of Trinity, one of the richest colleges in Cambridge. If it was me, and I'd served a life sentence under appalling conditions, I'd rather unwind and dine after a gruelling performance than sit in a smoky bar with a few students.

At The Anchor, more in hope than expectation, we commandeered a table near the window and waited. We had a perfect view of the River Cam, and on its banks we could see that it was, as Milton had written, 'inwrought with figures dim.' After about an hour, a track-suited figure came in. It was Jimmy Boyle. He came over to the table and we all shook hands and went through introductions. Billy, whose father hailed from the Gorbals, wanted to know what it was like to grow up in that part of the city in the 1950s. Like Glasser, Boyle had chronicled the spirit and spite of the place in his powerful autobiography *A Sense of Freedom* (1977), written from his prison cell. As the evening progressed, tentative questions turned to genuine dialogue and the conversation flowed. Boyle came across as a man of great warmth and integrity.

At closing time, we adjourned to King's College for tea. I then walked Jimmy back to Trinity on my way to Jesus. We stopped for a few minutes on King's Parade, in the shadow of Trinity's imposing façade, a long way from Barlinnie. We were an odd couple, the ex-con and the future don, but we had more in common than many of the students who passed us by, the products of privilege and preferential treatment. We were from the same side of the tracks, but different sides of the fence. Fifteen years after this encounter I met Jimmy again. This time I was working as a writer-not-in-residence at Barlinnie Special Unit, which his autobiography had made famous.

My time at Cambridge was unreal, even traumatic. I lived like a terrorist, my suitcase on the floor for the three years I was there, and with no sign of home (such as home had been) in my new surroundings. Although I was funded by the then Scottish Education Department, my parents were poor pensioners. I had zero financial support behind me so my grant and a bit of bar work were what I lived on. I can still remember rolling a pound coin back and forth the across the kitchen table. Around Easter 1986 I had one of those slow-motion breakdowns you only know you've had when you come out the other end, which for me was about a year later, after a long spell of depression during which I wanted to stop my studies but couldn't face disappointing my family and friends who liked the idea of me being at Cambridge too much to listen to my whining. I failed to be formally registered for the PhD after a year and wasn't green-lighted till well into my second year.

I rallied with a lot of walking and talking and working. I discovered Derrida and read him compulsively, as if almost a shadow thesis to my more historical work. This too, though, was an obsession; indeed, a fellow student once accused me of trying to transcribe the entire collection of the Rare Books Room, so copious did my note-taking become. At the end of my third year I managed to dig out a draft of my thesis and I submitted it on Friday December 20th 1988. Driven back to Glasgow by old schoolmates the next day, I arrived the night of the Lockerbie bombing. Four months later I was examined on a Saturday, April 15th 1989, the day of the Hillsborough disaster. That four-month wait, book-ended by disaster, was as tough a time as I'd ever had. It was a perfect time for a blues number. My brother attempted suicide and I tried living with him for a while, my girlfriend left me, and, after the viva, I found out I'd been 'referred,' an experience that felt like failure because nobody had really explained to me what it entailed, and I found it impossible to explain to family and friends. However, I dug deep, grew a big old beard, resubmitted in September, and finally graduated in May 1990.

Meantime I was teaching part-time at Strathclyde and picking up other work, ranging from adult literacy to a prison writing fellowship. It was, though, all very patchy and piecemeal. Around 1991–2, with some fourteen employers, I earned a total of £8000. Hours were long, money always short. I was also caught up in community theatre, a real shoestring world. Between 1989 and 1995 I had eight plays performed, including *From the Calton to Catalonia* (1990), a dramatized account of my father's experiences as a POW during the Spanish Civil War, co-written with my brother, John, and *The Lions of Lisbon* (1992), the story of Celtic's 1967 European Cup victory, co-written with Iain Auld, brother of Celtic legend and Lisbon Lion Bertie Auld. I've since kept up that Celtic connection, being a columnist for the *Celtic View*, the official magazine of Celtic Football Club, for seasons 2003–4, and 2004–5.

From 1992 to 1994, I had temporary lectureships at the University of London (at Goldsmiths and Queen Mary respectively). The London years were an oasis of sorts. Starting to teach in earnest was challenging but rewarding, and whereas working there in the summer of 1985 and living in Cambridge for three years after that had been all about pensiveness, pent-up feelings and penury, lecturing and earning my first real wage since the library was fulfilling. But it was temporary. So I started applying for posts in 1994 and, after several interviews, I moved back to Glasgow, much to my surprise, where I co-founded, with Philip Hobsbaum, the Creative Writing Master's at Glasgow University. The course has since become one of the most successful of its kind in the UK, producing a host of published writers and prizewinners.

A few years ago, I had a conversation with a colleague about academic CVs. At the time, I was on the appointing committee for the Regius Chair at Glasgow, and had been writing the usual raft of references for undergraduates and postgraduates, applicants for post-doctoral fellowships, lectureships, and promotions in other universities to Reader, Senior Lecturer and Professor. I was looking at a lot of CVs, fascinated as always by the things people included, what they left out, how they represented their achievements, how they listed their various publications, and how they recorded participation in seminars and conferences. That conversation got me thinking: What is an academic CV? Who is it for? Where will it get you? What might it look like? What ought it to include? How should each entry be recorded?

There are, I suggest, three things we do that are unlikely to find their way into our CVs: writing references, marking, and undertaking the pastoral care of students. These things are valuable, and take a lot of time, all the more reason to make sure the things we can count are properly recorded – particularly since the state of play in academe at the moment is that a CV is no longer a document geared solely towards job applications, but a constantly renewed record of achievement that comes into play for personal development reviews, promotions, research applications, research assessment and other purposes. The current tendency within the profession for monitoring and policing activities has added another glaze of paranoia to something already viewed as personal to personnel rather than as a key human resource. There's nothing more personal or more public than a CV.

In 1987, I was in Cambridge University Library when I was paged. I went to the phone at the main desk. A former tutor from Strathclyde, Professor Colin MacCabe,[3] wanted to pay me £100 to search the library for a list of items he had published over the previous twenty years, but hadn't kept track of – some in the *TLS*, others in more obscure places like *Communist Party Fortnightly* and *Red Letters*. I did this in a day, working from Colin's rough list of half-remembered locations, but as I worked I came across other material by other academics – early reviews by Terry Eagleton and others, including Lisa Jardine, my own supervisor. And all this was an education. First, I had a glimpse into something nobody ever talked about: an academic apprenticeship – so many scholars start out writing reviews and short pieces. Second, I saw that long after the thrill of publishing or performing something, it was possible to lose track of what you'd done.

I mentioned Colin's request in a supervision with Lisa Jardine, and she said some things were best forgotten. She also told me that Colin had once asked her how long it would take to become an expert on the Renaissance. 'It took me twenty years,' she told him. 'I was thinking of eighteen months,' he replied. Lisa also told me that once her CV got to 20 pages she started letting things fall off the edge. My CV was two pages at the time, so the prospect of a twenty-page CV was daunting.

Three recent Deans of Arts at Glasgow University haven't had PhDs. One of them went on to be 'Bigger than the Beatles' as Vice-Chancellor of Liverpool University; another became, for a time, Head of Glasgow's Crichton Campus; the third became a Director at the AHRC. But don't go getting your hopes up. For people of that generation, men mainly, a Masters was often enough to guarantee a lifetime's employment in a University. Those days are gone. A PhD now is the minimum requirement for most junior lectureships. Excellent applicants who lack a PhD can find their applications set aside. I couldn't get a job for four years after finishing my PhD, despite numerous applications. This, it turns out, is perfectly normal.

The wilderness years can last between three and five years on average for the post-doctoral Undead. At the time of my appointment at Glasgow in 1994 I read in a union bulletin that UK academics successfully secure permanent posts on average at the age of 32. I was 33. But I didn't know about this 3–5 year gap between completing a PhD and getting a permanent post. So I thought it must be my CV, which in part it was. I applied for a job in Dundee in the early 1990s and having failed to get short-listed I learned later that the lectureship had gone to someone in their mid-thirties with two books to their name. That put things in perspective.

Still, I happened to mention my lack of success in securing interviews to Tom Furniss, a colleague at Strathclyde, where I was teaching part-time, and he offered to look over my CV. It's embarrassing showing somebody your own personal record on the basis that it might be responsible for the lack of interviews. Sure enough, I wasn't recording things like seminar and conference papers or teaching experience or minor publications like journalism. One radically overhauled CV later, I was appointed in 1992 to a Temporary Lectureship at Goldsmiths College, University of London. During a pilot Research Assessment Exercise there, in 1993, an External Assessor suggested there was a problem with a fifty-year-old lecturer in the Department who had a one-page CV. This was hardly surprising, as here was an experienced academic in a permanent post not actively seeking promotion and happy where they were. They weren't going anywhere. But this was the moment – the hinge-point – when new forms of scrutinizing performance were taking hold in universities.

After a year at Goldsmiths, I went to another London College, Queen Mary and Westfield (QMW). It was a one-year appointment, and at that time the Dean was of the view that temporary appointments were just that. When my year was up in 1994 I applied for various jobs, including the one I got at Glasgow, and another job at QMW. That job in London went to someone with fewer publications than me, but with, I was told, 'astonishing testimonials,' or 'unfeasibly long testimonials,' as my friend Andrew Hadfield later remarked. Moreover, this other applicant had a testimonial written by the formidable figure of Frank Kermode. I quickly realised that referees matter, and you have to approach them the way Rangers Football Club approaches referees. If they're not on your side, they're no good.

I've heard many stories about referees writing unsupportive references for former students, who only then find out about it because someone in the institution they are applying to takes them aside and suggests to them gently that they reconsider their referees. I have a telling tale of my own. When I arrived in Glasgow in 1994 I was told I was a 'cash-limited appointment' in a Department where the average age was 53 and few colleagues had PhDs, and that I should apply for promotion at the earliest opportunity. I did, the very next year, only to be discouraged by my Head of Department, who judged it too soon. He also said something that confused me. He told me there was no difference between the remuneration of Reader and Senior Lecturer, and in my naivety about the profession I took this to mean that promotion itself entailed no financial incentive. Unbeknown to me, promotion that year could have been worth £10,000. When I did apply the next year, I failed to secure the promotion that the University approved, pending references. It emerged I'd had an unsupportive letter of recommendation from one of my referees. I asked the referee for a copy of her reference. It was glowing, effusive and full of high praise, but ultimately it was a 'no,' saying that at her institution two books were needed for a Readership. I don't know if that was true or if it was simply that there was a queue of thirtysomethings waiting for promotion where she was, thus making my own application appear premature. Whatever, I never got it, and, although she said that she'd sent me the reference (after the event) in the interests of transparency, I couldn't see how writing an effectively negative reference for a former student without telling them in advance was an ethical thing to do. The next year I applied again and was successful. Then another funny thing happened. I met my referee at a conference in the States and she suggested I apply to London for a chair in her department. I didn't, but assumed that meant I was worthy of one at Glasgow, but again her reference was apparently a blocking one. I didn't ask to see it this time, but that was the message I got from Glasgow. None of this is new. I know of a colleague at another university who had an excellent relationship – they thought – with a referee, until they got a job and were taken aside by one of the interviewers and told that they got called for interview *despite* their reference and not *because* of it. Never trust a referee till you see the colour of the reference they've written for you. Be like Rangers FC. Pack the jury. Ask to see your referee's reference and if they refuse find another referee.

A PhD, of course, is no guarantee of a job; as I found out in 1991, when, after completing a PhD at Cambridge, I found myself back living in Possilpark, signing on the dole, and drawing £36.70 per week in income support. Eight years later I was Professor of Renaissance Studies at the

University of Glasgow – why the delay? I hear you say – but that experience of 'failure' helped me to think seriously about publishing. If you do a PhD at Cambridge or Oxford there's perhaps a chance of an academic job without publications. I don't imagine that's the case with most other institutions. Hence the wilderness years, maybe three, maybe five years of scraping and getting by.

But, if publishing is a prerequisite for employment, and a necessary supplement to the PhD, how does the postgraduate penetrate the mysteries of publishing? The obvious answer is through your supervisor, or supervisors. I've got around 600 publications to my name in terms of books, essays, reviews, short notices, journalistic features and other ephemera over the last 20 years. Good advice is to start small, and it doesn't get any smaller than the review. There's a story – probably apocryphal – about an Oxford Don being asked what he planned to do in his retirement, and he replied: 'Read all the books I've reviewed.' My first review was for Chris Norris in 1988, then reviews editor for *Textual Practice*, the start of a long connection (I'm now on the editorial board). I've learned that a review can be a week's work or the labour of an afternoon, that publications beget publications, that the politics of the proper name means that your name works for you while you're busy doing other things, that invitations and commissions arise from attending conferences and putting yourself in the way of the world, and that there's a lot to be said for co-edited and co-authored work. This is, you might say, the Judy Garland/Mickey Rooney approach: throw up a tent and let's put on a show; or the *Field of Dreams* approach – build it and they will come. For me, quantity counts – any old journal will do to begin with; choose the path of least resistance. Don't be a snob about it. If your work is good then forget the forum and just get publishing. Learn the rules then throw away the rulebook. No, on second thoughts, review the rulebook.

University has been good to me. I love my job. I'm passionate about teaching and research. It is true that I find the new managerialism – a mixture of Blair's War Cabinet and the dark days of NHS restructuring with a touch of Tesco thrown in for good labelling – utterly dispiriting, but it hasn't dampened my enthusiasm or my commitment, if only because my default position is opposition: to empire, individual identity, union, and subordination. This is reflected in my research interests, which range from the representation of national and colonial identities in early modern texts through to deconstruction and postcolonialism. In the field of Renaissance Studies, my work began with a PhD on the ways in which the experiences of the poet Edmund Spenser as an English colonist in Ireland impinged on his writings – not just his prose dialogue *A View of the State of Ireland* (1596) but all of his work. My most recent research in this area is on John Milton's

History of Britain (1670), an important but overlooked work that covers the period from Brutus to William the Conqueror. In the field of Irish-Scottish Studies, I've published on Robert Burns, Seamus Deane, Roddy Doyle, Janice Galloway, Alasdair Gray, James Joyce, James Kelman, Patrick McCabe, Muriel Spark, Irvine Welsh and W. B. Yeats.

As I mentioned, I became fascinated by the work of Derrida in 1986 and this led me to the interface between deconstruction and Marxism. My reading of Marx, however, predates any experience of university – my father was a lifelong Communist till his death at 99 in 2007. He was also a veteran of the Spanish Civil War, and the works of Marx, Lenin, Mao and, yes, Stalin, were always to be found in our house. When my father died, his papers consisted of two passports: one issued in 1930, just after his own father died, when he was emigrating to America, the other issued in 1996, when he returned to Spain – his first time out of the country for over half a century – to revisit Jarama, the scene of his capture almost sixty years earlier.

My very various interests – the early modern preoccupation with colonialism, the Irish-Scottish cross-currents, the Derridean fascination with borders and margins, and questions of community and class – converge, I suppose, in the postcolonial paradigm with its focus on anti-imperialism, minority voices and occluded histories. Recently, I taught a course on the Nigerian Novel from Tutuola to Adichie, did some work on Engels's Notes for his unfinished *History of Ireland*, and provided an introduction to the writing of Muriel Spark, arguably Scotland's most significant writer since Scott and Stevenson.

Since I started teaching full-time in 1992 I've been involved in Creative Writing, and that's meant an almost daily engagement with new work. This has only served to increase my fascination with the act of writing – even, you might say, my addiction. Each day I write and write. Even by night I dream of slim volumes.

I grew up with five older sisters, and one bathroom, so my three brothers and I early on acquired a high level of bladder control, but needing to pee is still the best alarm clock. I'm up at the crack and full of the craic, a sunny morning person. I once lived with an insomniac and felt robbed of the wonderful mornings that were out there beyond the bad moods caused by broken sleep. I like to be at my desk early to mid-morning, but I work late and am in the office seven days a week, so I don't beat myself up if – heaven forfend! – I lurch in late. Teaching, marking, reading, meeting colleagues and students, and writing references and reports can take up the first two-thirds of my day; so, for as long as I can remember I've divided my working day into three parts – morning, afternoon and evening – which means 5 p.m. is like lunch-time to me. After five I assume another form and that's when I compose.

I multi-task and compartmentalise. I always have a dozen projects on the go at once. That keeps me sane but drives everybody else crazy. The two most important things about my office are mess and tea. It's a working space and so I annoy the Tidy Brigade with my piles of papers apparently randomly heaped on chairs and boxes as well as my desk, but I mostly know where things are. For years I drank Earl Grey till I was a big bag of berg-amot with boots on, but now I intersperse with herbal tea – my favourite, nettle & peppermint. Whoever came up with that joins carrot & apple and Marx & Engels in my big book of winning combos. I can't drink during the day without bursting into tears and fainting so I tend not to have a glass of wine before ten. That's my watershed, unless I'm working later, which I sometimes am.

My over-commitment is about guilt at some level, but also gratitude. As the seventh of nine children of manual-working non-university educated parents, and the first in my family to get a higher education, although 'grateful' might not be the right word or the fashionable word, I do feel lucky to be where I am doing what I'm doing. My day is always a mix of hard and soft copy, by turns scribbling and typing. I read and write every day, from emails, references and reports, to essays, reviews and book chapters. I think it's not just the volume but also the variety of work in the average academic day that keeps me interested as well as busy. Not that my day would be entirely academic. My involvement in creative writing means I often find myself reading unpublished fiction, drama or poetry alongside more standard student submissions such as essays and research proposals. I like that. And I like working late. More an owl than a lark, my engine runs on midnight oil. I've never understood those who go home after work to worry. I prefer to stay on and worry away at words. I love bad puns – are there any other kind? – and playing with language is the best kind of work. I'm a delicate flower prone to draughts, so when I'm working late in winter I wrap up like a polar bear.

Right now I'm editing several collections of essays, contributing to several more, writing a raft of reviews and reports, and researching for a monograph. I'm always a wee bit superstitious about work-in-progress, so I tend to keep it under wraps till it's in press, then I feel it's out of my hands – till I see the proofs. Being an academic writer is different from being a creative writer, there's an institution there and a framework, a diary and timetable, a system and students needing to be taught and assessed and mentored and motivated. Sometimes I envy writers who exist outside of institutions; most times, though, I simply *admire* them for their ability to survive beyond the campus. Right now Muriel Spark is my favourite writer. She's totally mesmerising. In a poem called 'The Creative Writing Class' (2003), Spark played with the 'he said, she said' clichés of dialogue, reducing it to absurdities like '"Miss Universe," he emoted', '"The signature," she ventured', and '"Develop the wolf," he demanded.' I'd like to develop the wolf in my own writing – none of us wants to be sheepish – but I do still find myself emoting 'Miss Universe'.

I was on research leave in 2008–9, and that gave me a longer view. Usually I'm so mired in deadlines and commitments that I get caught up in the dailies and don't do long-term planning. I can reflect now on the fact that friends and family have been put on hold while I lost myself in work, and lost touch at times, as one must, with the poverty and pathos of the past; but you can't have everything, and the whole academic adventure has been a blast. I'm lucky that way. It's true that a corporate cabal is commandeering the campus, but I still don't regret the energy I've invested. Corporate mismanagement with its privatizing propensities hasn't killed off collegiality – witness the unanimous vote of no confidence in our Principal at a packed meeting at Glasgow in the summer of 2010. Not since the last days of Charles I has the mood been so Miltonic. The tenure of principals and managers – and the fate of Heads more generally – is on the agenda once again. New Labour was elected in 1997 on a slogan of 'Education, Education, Education,' but all we had was war, bank bailouts, pension plunders, and an erosion of the public service ethos. Now the Coalition has seized the opportunity to sell-off the sector bit by bit.

When I worked for the Royal Bank of Scotland thirty years ago it was in a disastrous branch with an alcoholic manager cruising to retirement who couldn't be removed. He was more Mr Magoo than Fred the Shred, but the net outcome was a strained and strange working environment. I got out, attended night classes, and went to university. Now, three decades down the line, I find myself working for a badly run bank again, except it calls itself a university. These days, of course, it also calls itself part of the Russell Group, which increasingly sounds much like, say, Lehmann Brothers or Goldman Sachs. The Russell Group has, alas, nothing to do with Bertrand Russell; indeed, it has now become more like Jack Russell, a terrier snapping at our heels.

Here in Glasgow the University's Department of Adult and Continuing Education (DACE) was under threat of closure in the summer of 2010, notwithstanding the Russell Group's avowed 'commitment to civic responsibility, improving life chances, [and] raising aspirations' – all in keeping, of course, with Glasgow's founding Papal Bull that declares that the University 'opens the door . . . and raises to distinction those that were born in the lowest place.' I spoke to one of my sisters recently and she said she'd never have got to University if it weren't for DACE. I am reminded of what my father once said when he famously turned the priest away from our door: 'I couldn't,' he said, 'be in heaven knowing that one person was in hell.'

Enough, though, of heaven and hell; the daily grind has a way of performing its secret ministry, making snowmen of figure skaters and, as a ghetto-child given a second life-chance, I'm still keeping my nose to the grindstone. Dickens, of course, got there first:

> 'I am far from being friendly,' pursued Mr. Dombey, 'to what is called by persons of levelling sentiments, general education. But it is necessary that the inferior classes should continue to be taught to know their position, and to conduct themselves properly. So far I approve of schools. Having the power of nominating a child on the foundation of an ancient establishment, called (from a worshipful company) the Charitable Grinders; where not only is a wholesome education bestowed upon the scholars, but where a dress and badge is likewise provided for them; I have (first communicating, through Mrs. Chick, with your family) nominated your eldest son to an existing vacancy; and he has this day, I am informed, assumed the habit. The number of her son, I believe,' said Mr. Dombey, turning to his sister and speaking of the child as if he were a hackney-coach, 'is one hundred and forty-seven.'[4]

I may be sentimental, it may sound hackneyed, its days may be numbered, but I've been coached, and I still maintain that the examined life is a good life, perhaps even *the* good life.

Notes

1 See Jacques Derrida, 'The Principle of Reason: The University in the Eyes of its Pupils,' trans. Catherine Porter and Edward P. Morris, *Diacritics* 13:3 (1983), pp. 3–21; 'The Time of a Thesis: Punctuations,' trans. Kathleen McLaughlin, in Alan Montefiore (ed.), *Philosophy in France Today* (Cambridge: Cambridge University Press, 1983), pp. 34–50; 'Mochlos; or, the Conflict of Faculties,' in Richard Rand (ed.), *Logomachia: The Conflict of Faculties* (Lincoln: University of Nebraska Press, 1992), pp. 1–34; Imre Salusinszky, 'Jacques Derrida on the University: An Interview,' *The Southern Review* (Adelaide) 19:1 (1986), pp. 3–12.

2 Alasdair Gray, *Lanark. A Life in Four Books* (1981; London: Picador, 1991), p. 243.

3 Colin MacCabe, 'Class of '68: Elements of an Intellectual Autobiography 1967–81,' in *Theoretical Essays: Film, Linguistics, Literature* (Manchester: Manchester University Press, 1985), pp. 1–32.

4 Charles Dickens, *Dombey and Son* (Harmondsworth: Penguin, 1970), p. 117.

How to Kill a Labrador (an Elegy)

Susan Bradley Smith

Author's Preface

This short story represents a new development in the genre of lifewriting, with the experiment of 'memoir as impersonation' whereby the writer anthropologically inhabits a true story in an assumed manner. This act of literary cannibalism/colonialism/recycling wonders about the role of confessional prose, as the writer performs an act of identity theft (of real people and their circumstances) and fictionalizes futures in order to create a different psychological purchase. A stylistic innovation of the text is its embracing of the idea of the African Griot and their role as conveyors of collective wisdom with their formidable knowledge of local history; the knowledge in this story being the real suicide statistics associated with the Vietnam War, and the impact on regional Australian communities. Adapting Griot methodologies, 'How to Kill a Labrador' offers political and social commentary as a cautionary tale, based on extemporized truth, and argues that memory and story are historically vital for cultures in crisis.

I. Lament: Where I express grief and sorrow at my loss, and engender a sense of longing – for you, Dad, for you

My holiday to Vietnam didn't go so well. I blame the Australian tourists. As Mum would say, we are a noisy and tatterdemalion lot, and a hoard of us, anywhere, ranging contumeliously across landscape is just begging for an Old Testament finale. Everybody should run or just shoot us on sight. A bicycle holiday. Jesus wept. Whose idea was that? Once upon a time I got lost in the Cu Chi tunnels, I was crawling through them trying, somehow, to find my lost father: at least I'll always be able to tell that story. But really, I was looking for you everywhere. In Saigon, I even thought I saw you a couple of times. Is that what happened, did you run away to teach English to Vietnamese orphans? Was your school next to the Museum of American War Atrocities, or in the country, with rusting tanks being strangled by the jungle. I saw a performance of *Romeo and Juliet* while I was there. This guy hovering outside my hotel took me on his little motorbike, all the way from the Hotel Continental to the Hoa Binh Theatre and back again for, I think, two American dollars. I said to him I wanted to see a play, I had in mind some water puppetry in honour of that puppet you brought home for me after the war. But instead I was escorted to District 10 for a show that lasted nearly three hours, everyone laughing the whole time. What happened to the power of tragedy? I could only see one other Westerner there. English Literature owns the planet, even in translation. Was that what the war was for? They should have just bombed them with the contents of the British Library, forget the napalm. Shortly before I left for home, I was sure I saw you – I was on my hotel balcony, unable to sleep, looking down at the traffic three floors below. It was raining but everyone was happy and busy as usual, ten lanes of bicycles going each way, two or three or four people on each bike, wearing plastic hooded rain-capes. Yellows and blues and reds and pinks and greens in slow motion, it was like an acid trip at a birthday party, the only guests balloons. It suddenly occurred to me that you might have stayed in this very same hotel, that you might have taken hallucinogens or heroin or fucked prostitutes in this very same room, and then you looked up at me. Our eyes locked like a car jack. You were riding a bike, alone, and you looked up at me and swerved and then it was over. You steadied yourself and turned the corner and were gone. It was true, I couldn't see much of you, but those eyes were the same shocked eyes that used to watch me play netball. I'd shoot a goal and you'd be amazed, before you smiled, simply awestruck. Your eyes were eyes like that, they made whoever you were looking at feel like it was the very first time they had been seen, and this was a good feeling. I'd win my heat at the swimming carnival and sure, I liked the way my coach looked at me but your look was the best – my god she can swim she has limbs she is my child she is beautiful she won she is mine and I did not know how good life was until I saw her. I will teach her to read now and she will be safe forever. Yeah. I miss you. You and your awesome eyes. You left me all your books Daddy, but those looking eyes of yours burn best. What good is literature? It failed you. Like those puppies we had to drown that lonely September morning, all seven of them, with a broken brick in a hessian bag tied up with barbed wire and chucked in the Richmond River with the tide running out. We failed those chocolate balls of love and their pumping hearts and wagging tails because we could not imagine the future properly, or make the effort. You said it was kinder that way. You took me home and gave me ice cream and read to me loudly from *The Age of Innocence*, as if I couldn't see you shaking. I tried to unlearn everything. Forgetting is exhausting, but I am a determined mutt. I squandered a lot of my own promise by turning my back on you and your books, but you did it first Daddy. You locked up every single library in the world with your rational decisions, and your deadly wire. Anyway, once they're in your blood, those stories, their pollution has the staying power of an oil slick. Did you know Mum writes books now? She writes so many books that people write about her writing books. Let's not forget the importance of carpenters and their superior abilities to construct shelves. Is working with your hands more honest? Who fires the better shot?

II Praise: where I offer admiration for the idealized dead, remembering you honestly, *wie es eigentlich gewesen*

It's my birthday today. It is November already, and today I turn 27 years old. No card from you, as usual. There is a storm somewhere between here and New Zealand, and the entire east coast from south of Sydney to north of Noosa is PUMPING. Decent. You can't get a park in the village, what with surfers fuelling up for the next onslaught, and the Point car park is packed tight and is as combustible as backstage on opening night with the Ballina Amateur Players ready to strut their stuff for the North Coast premiere of *Plenty*, all nudity and bravado and jitters and adrenalin and props and history and story, beautiful bodies ready to Go! Go! Go! No space for more cars or more people or more ideas. You know that nothing matters here except the surfing. All combat ends up as story. Fuck wars. Fuck world peace. Everyone says, I just want to surf, but, because I must, I'll work (sell houses/broker divorces/fix pipes/paint pictures/write books/hire videos/make coffee) when I have to. People read in secret because literature makes them weep, and this is not useful for striving forward. The only people who buy books in our new second-hand book shop are holiday-makers. You would. If you were here. But you went to Vietnam despite your university smartness, and all those books did not save you because your birthday was tattooed on a ping-pong ball that was randomly spat out of a machine. You killed people, and this was worth it? Did you forget your learning? Is there some kind of higher learning you forgot to tell me about? How can you be a soldier, then come home and be a schoolteacher, and sell the lies of grace and redemption? I don't get it. I get the dropping-out stuff, the surfing as salvation, but you were so tight, so good, so nine-to-five. Till you left. I even get that. That makes more sense. No wonder I chose boring too. It was either that, or what you chose. So back to me. The weather is so nice today, a cold snap, a bit of stylish relief from the endless subtropical clammy-clam which makes me permanently soporific. There are maps of seaweed and stranded starfish and sea-urchins all along the high tide mark of Seven Mile Beach. OK. Shit. I'm talking to you about the weather. I should tell you that I can't read poetry anymore, I'm sorry. I smoke instead. It's only just after 5 a.m. and the mist is yawning up the valley, and I can hardly hear any cars on North Creek Road, I guess it's still sharky-as-anything out there for the next hour or so. But the birds are all up, doing their orchestra pit tuning thing. God. Life can be relentless but I guess you know that. Enough already. I wish I didn't have to go to work today. Actually I wish I never had to touch money again, or concentrate on computer screens or be nice to customers who are forever nervous – why does anything to do with money make people act weirder than they already are? It's good having a job I suppose and I've been a very good girl and I already own 50% of my own little house which you'll never visit up here on the hill – not bad for someone who never finished high school (did you have to be principal?). Do I get to blame you for that too, or thank you? I have assets and my friends who went away to the city to uni have debts. Guess who pays the bill when we go out for dinner? Anyway I'm assistant manager at the Credit Union now, and next week I'll have been working there for ten years and I get to go on three-months paid long service leave and I am coming to HUNT YOU DOWN. Because I miss you. Mum is too busy psychologising the world to universal harmony and Desmond is a drunken skunk of a brother (he doesn't surf anymore – what do you make of that?) and I MISS YOU. Today, I really miss you. I miss everything you used to do on my birthday. Waking me up tickling my feet with feathers. Impersonating bizarre visitors sending me cards of congratulations and invitations to outrageous celebrations. Feeding me chocolate milkshakes with more ice cream than milk and hundreds-and-thousands for breakfast, followed by honey toast with no crust, made from Neverland bees delivered by Tinkerbell. Humming Happy Birthday to me, all day long, even at school when you came into my classroom to pretend to drop off something for my teacher every lesson. Leaving me presents in my lunchbox, sparkling beautiful trinkets much better than anything you ever gave Mum. You were good. Very good. I don't have any presents to open today. Not yet. I guess the day will improve. I guess yoga will be on soon, even though it feels like flood rain. I guess I should go. If you were here, I bet you'd have left some-thing under my pillow, a long gold necklace with an overweight heart. I've never been given one of those. How good would that be! I could fondle it all day long, in between counting bank notes. I don't know how comforting that would be though. Love. Gets you going like a fat gold watch, you'd always say, kissing my forehead at the bus stop when I started Kindergarten, then, Remember Sissy I'll always love you, and off you'd go in the other direction, to teach big kids in your big school. When did you stop saying that to me? When did you stop meaning it? Fat gold watch my arse. We all end up with our heads stuck in ovens, our unfinished manuscripts haunting our lost lives. Like that letter you wrote me before you left, thanks for that. Not. Bet you regret it. Money never changes colour, editing cannot touch its fidelity. Happy Birthday to me.

III Consolation: where I attempt solace, and to make present what I have lost – you, and every damned thing

I don't know about love's ability to make me tick, but I do know what Patti Smith meant when she sang about memory falling like cream in her bones. I swear I can still smell your aftershave when I pull that letter from its paper wallet. Beautiful you, Daddy, please hold me in those strong arms of yours again and tell me it will be OK. Last month, after the crappy holiday and before Mum stopped talking about you for good, I was standing at the altar next to my fiancé, Marky. He is not a soldier, he is a surfer and a solicitor which he finds boring but he makes me laugh and we both like Mexican food, a whole lot, and watching horror movies, and riding our bikes on the beach at low tide. We fit together good. He doesn't have a dad anymore either. Cancer – what's your excuse again? My dress was beautiful, it hadn't meant that much to me shopping for a dress but Mum went crazy, she would have spent thousands, but we found something in the retro shed at the Arts and Industry estate in Byron Bay, and had it altered, and she sent the money to Amnesty International instead. But it hugged me and you know I'm no fat chick but still a lady and I felt glamorous. Girls should wear ankle length satin and high heels more often. I wished you'd been there, watching me. I wished you had walked me down the aisle. But you weren't there and I was all out of wishes and when the time came I could not say yes. I thought Marky was going to punch me. He likes to box, and favours Broughton's rules from the eighteenth century, no weight divisions, no written rules, no rounds, no referee. And no gloves, so some restraint was necessary if you were aiming for hard bits, like the head. I was not wearing a veil. Marky dropped to his knees, a fighter in trouble, in that unmanly way that buys you time if you are tired out from too much fighting. I gave him 30 seconds to speak, then left. I blame you for this. Hah! I blame you. How lame. I had no language to apologize. Where were you and your words when I needed them? You called me your little blowfly, the same name as the person who cleaned the toilets and showers at your army base. You ain't no ration assassin, you'd say to me, complimenting my cooking skills when I'd serve you cornflakes with brown sugar and milk in bed on Saturdays. I know all kinds of words that only you knew, that no other dads spoke. You came home from Vietnam to marry Mum who was pregnant with me – that was one of your favourite words, 'wedevac': the best kind of leave, where you got to return to Australia and deal with impending fatherhood and try the matrimony thing and meet your new in-laws before tally-ho off you go back to the jungle, where you could do as many 'yippee shoots' as you liked. Fire those bullets at trees, you'd say, not people. You and your yippee shoots. Didn't stop you in the end, did it, from saving the last dance for you and your gun? Oh no. How's a girl meant to believe in love and marriage and all that with a father like you. Thanks Dad. Still. I would have liked to have seen your eyes looking at me in my spunkysplendid dress. Poor Mum had to walk me down the aisle. Poor Mum with her PhD in Creative Writing as Therapy. Poor Mum who tells everyone she meets that more Vietnam Vets have committed suicide since the war ended than died in combat, and that it was Australia's longest war, did you know, and that among Veterans' children the suicide rate is three times the national average. By which time they are looking at her like she is crazy. Or not looking at her. Trying to look anywhere but at her. Trying to silence her learning. Honour The Dead But Fight Like Hell For The Living, that's the motto of the Vet's museum, she has it on t-shirts. Can you see what I mean? I need your help here. Sure, I'm proud of her. But her novels are kind of all the same. They're about you, and her, and kids born to fucked-up families whose Dads went away to war. The critics say she's a national treasure, a cultural landmine reminding the government that Veterans' children are presently reaching the critical age for suicide-risk, and if we keep going to war then this will never stop, this pain. I blame you for her too, by the way. Yesterday I went shopping for treats, and outside the supermarket in 'shiver/River' Street in Ballina there was a busker singing 'I was only nineteen.' Why can't Mum write songs instead? 'Frankie kicked a mine the day that mankind kicked the moon / God help me, he was going home in June.' He belted it out, to a dedicated audience of four: me, this guy (your age) in a wheelchair, and two ratbag kids who knew the words and were sucking orange ice-lollies and jerking around in the sunshine. They threw golden coins at him, and at the end of the song the wheelchair man opened a tinnie and cried a bit. The busker had a Ramones t-shirt on that looked old enough to convince anyone that he'd actually seen them, he was a nice bloke, he sure could sing, and he said thanks and promised the kids he'd save their coins to pay the ferryman. Like I said, money is what really matters. Anyway, we can talk about all this soon when I see you in the big library in the sky, Daddy. I imagine that there you have stopped your night-screaming by now, and have forgotten all about eggs that only came in tin cans. I imagine that you have forgiven the world for its emotional parsimony, and also the writers and critics for their fraudulent relationships to literature, for reducing it to a commodity, filching degrees and careers. Or reducing people to bleating Kamikazes, like Mum.

No loud-mouths allowed in Heaven. Put away your coins, wordsmiths.
Everything we say is just a sin.

INVENTIONS

Lamenting Maud's Worth Becoming Maud

Duraid Jalili

THE REDUCTIVE INTRODUCTION

'Thus critics who insert their own work into that of others contribute to the eradication of the traditional distinction between production and consumption, creation and copy, readymade and original work. [. . .] It is no longer a matter of elaborating a form on the basis of a raw material but working with objects that are already in circulation within the cultural consciousness, which is to say, objects already *informed* by other objects. Notions of originality (being at the origin of) and even of creation (making something from nothing) are slowly blurred in this new cultural landscape marked by the twin figures of the DJ and the programmer, both of whom have the task of selecting cultural objects and inserting them into new contexts. [. . .] In a universe of [. . .] preexisting forms, signals already emitted, [. . .] paths marked out by their predecessors, critics no longer consider the artistic field [. . .] a museum containing works that must be delineated or "defined," [. . .] but so many storehouses filled with tools that should be used, stockpiles of data to manipulate and represent.'

NICHOLAS BOURRIAUD, Postproduction (2002)

'These artists who insert their own work into that of others contribute to the eradication of the traditional distinction between production and consumption, creation and copy, readymade and original work. [. . .] It is no longer a matter of elaborating a form on the basis of a raw material but working with objects that are already in circulation on the cultural market, which is to say, objects already *informed* by other objects. Notions of originality (being at the origin of) and even of creation (making something from nothing) are slowly blurred in this new cultural landscape marked by the twin figures of the DJ and the programmer, both of whom have the task of selecting cultural objects and inserting them into new contexts. [. . .] In a universe of [. . .] preexisting forms, signals already emitted, [. . .] paths

marked out by their predecessors, artists no longer consider the artistic field
[. . .] a museum containing works that must be cited or "surpassed,"
[. . .] but so many storehouses filled with tools that should be used, stockpiles of data to manipulate and present.'

NICHOLAS BOURRIAUD, *Postproduction* (2002)

Standard analytical practice should prompt inquiry over which of these
statements is the 'original,' and thus, the 'correct' version. Let us take this
as our primary point of contention with standard analytical practice, for
such a practice implies the necessity of a conceptual division. Moreover, it
implies the necessity of a conceptual possession. To expand upon (materi-
ally delimited) Hegelian origins, let us understand possession as
constitutive of the basic relationship between the individual and their
surroundings. Culpable in this is language, and the conceptually possessive
complexion of the signifier. Utilizing 'I', for example, in possessing the definition of oneself as defined one possesses (upon a conceptual level) oneself.

Defined through, or even merely in relation to, a formed cognomen, the
object becomes necessarily defined *by* that cognomen. That the signifier,
processed through an historically and socio-culturally heterogeneous
communicative apparatus and connotatively affected by way of individually
relative cultural backgrounds (and personal experiences), may inherently
possess both denotative and connotative ambiguities, so, through the
connate perfusion of unconscious projection, by default, may the signified.
This affectivity proliferates beyond the means of communication into the
systems of understanding generated thereof.

Defined through, or even merely in relation to, a theoretical 'principle'
or 'concept', the 'object' becomes conceivable as but an *example* (or 'proof-
specimen') of said principle or concept and, thus, necessarily defined by (or
in permanent relation to) that principle or concept. Thus defined by, it is
possessed by said principle or concept.

Have I possessed Bourriaud's definition, therefore? Yet, what is
Bourriaud's definition? The answer remains in his 'original' text,[1] bound,
possessed by Bourriaud. This concept realized in language *through* him, is
surely, therefore, *his*? Yet, assuming you (the reader) have remained ignorant as to the 'original' version, by creating that self-same 'manipulation'
of a pre-existing subject within Bourriaud's own text, what becomes of the
status of possession? Have I repossessed Bourriaud's concept, or shown it to
be possessionless? Or, in fulfilling its very criteria, is my manipulation not
itself necessarily defined *by* (or in permanent relation *to*) this overarching
concept, and thus possessed by this concept, or even by Bourriaud himself?

Consider now a different form:
>'Shatto, Susan. *Tennyson's Maud: a Critical Edition*.
>Ed. Susan Shatto. London: Athlone, 1986.'

Edited, annotation filled, and understood via another, whose text is this? This *Maud*? Is it Tennyson's? Or is it Shatto's? Is there somehow a distinction between *Maud*, which belongs to Tennyson, and *Tennyson's Maud*, which belongs to Shatto? Now understood as a product of a context, a proof-specimen of a concept defined as 'Tennyson,' the text is reconceived, and thus is repossessed.

Yet, proof-specimen himself of history, *the* Victorian poet, read in tooth and claw, a romantic left now melancholic beyond a Romanticism now lost, the totemic laureate of troubled spiritual times, 'Tennyson' is reconceived and thus repossessed.

Yet (postmodernism rears its irksome smirk), in their utility as concepts that thus define and thus subsume objects, such contexts thus *applied* to Tennyson become now reconceivable as reconceived through contemporary critical contexts, proof-specimens themselves of standard analytical practice, the principle of relativist contextualisation, itself simultaneously proving and disproving itself elliptically, and thus now repossessed, and yet, and thus now repossessed.

Proliferating endlessly, through such manifold contours of possession, meaning affirms itself as paradox, what 'is' this *Maud* now blurred, yet always repossessed?

(Re)consider now a foregoing form:

>'Notions of originality (being at the origin of) and even of creation (making something from nothing) are slowly blurred in this new cultural landscape marked by [. . .] the task of selecting cultural objects and inserting them into new contexts.' (Bourriaud, 13)

Moving beyond '"the criticism of appropriation," which naturally infers an ideology of ownership', is to post-produce thus to post-possess (9)? A 'technical term from the audiovisual vocabulary used in television, film, and video', postproduction 'refers to the set of processes applied to recorded material: montage, the inclusion of other visual or audio sources, subtitling, voice-overs, and special effects' (13).

Shatto's Tennyson's *Maud*, or Shatto's *Tennyson's Maud*, now bound reauthored, in annotation filled pages, (the 'original' poem crammed into ever smaller spaces), foot and end notes spiralling, denotes possession, as do all texts that bind denotation. Yet, moving beyond such forms, to present critique and interpretation within an audiovisual postproduction, may one avoid the possession innate to exposition? Surrounding the ultimately incorporeal nature of aural enunciation, is it possible to create a critical construction that avoids the ownership of touch (by which one may infer 'text'), independent of an author, 'moving towards a culture based on a collective ideal: sharing?' (9)

Such contexts informed my presentation, represented here. An audiovisualised demonstration, utilizing techniques of subtitling/voice-over, splicing and crossfade, within a PowerPoint format, this presentation was preliminarily designed to catalyse new interpretations of *Maud*, while avoiding the dictation (and thus possession) of any singular meaning, or even system of meaning.

In the principal collocation of a visual subtitling distinct from the aural message / a voice-over distinct from the visual message, (neither necessarily estimable, and thus possessing and/or possessible, as the 'original' or 'correct' version), for example, was intended a form of critique simultaneously intrinsic to and absent from its object of analysis (itself, theoretically, no longer a tangible or discernibly differentiated object).

Continually dissecting and replicating its own inherent contradictions, intrinsically highlighting the ambiguous relationship between visual and aural interpretation, this self-effacing interpretative catalyst was designed to leave behind (as its final vocable faded into absence) no dogmatically pronounced interpretation but merely the *possibility* of interpretation. Whether it succeeded, however, is another matter.

Now, formed in text, a paradox, it provides a somewhat telling symbol of the nature of critical possession within contemporary academic discourse, a form defined, now subject to its concept, now a form possessed. Moreover, now open to reconsideration, its words laid bare to the option of rereading, it reveals the deep simplicity of its technical form.

Yet, hopefully, beyond such concerns, now reformed in text, this foregoing form reveals still the *possibility* of a system of criticism based on that same collective ideal, a means of interpretation affirming no stable possession but a continual reproduction and, thus, reconception. Indeed, that it may affirm but the *possibility* of a new direction, a conceivable point of departure from contemporary critical discourse, and not a be-all-end-all means, remains perhaps the point in itself.

THE FOREGOING PRESENTATION

[Commence slides with *fig. 1*. Shown for 10 seconds. Silence.]²

[*fig. 2*] 'These artists who insert their own work into that of others contribute
to the eradication of the traditional distinction between production and
consumption, creation and copy, readymade and original work. [. . .] It is
no longer a matter of elaborating a form on the basis of a raw material but
working with objects that are already in circulation on the cultural market,
which is to say, objects already *informed* by other objects. Notions of originality (being at the origin of) and even of creation (making something from
nothing) are slowly blurred in this new cultural landscape marked by the
twin figures of the DJ and the programmer, both of whom have the task of
selecting cultural objects and inserting them into new contexts. [. . .] In
a universe of [. . .] preexisting forms, signals already emitted, [. . .] paths
marked out by their predecessors, artists no longer consider the artistic field
[. . .] a museum containing works that must be cited or "surpassed,"
[. . .] but so many storehouses filled with tools that should be used, stockpiles of data to manipulate and present.'

NICHOLAS BOURRIAUD, Postproduction (2002)

[*fig. 3*] To commence with a somewhat trite metaphor, consider the text as a
bar of soap, and the process of criticism as that of making a lather. Causing
the expansion of the bar's internal heterogeneity of granules, the dilation of
its core substance, the lather reveals its integral nature with widening
detail, thus conceivably making it more user friendly. Yet, as the process
continues further and further, the initial bar itself disappears, leaving us
only with a mass of bubbles. What remains, as so often with soap, is but
that dried up lump, that old decaying nugget which we so often just throw
away, inclining for a new bar, a new fresh lather.

Consider now not the metaphor, but its explanation. For, in the very clari-
fication of the image, its delineation into patent meaning, I have rendered
this analogy, in itself, a dried up lump, an old decaying nugget. Yet, such
is the critical need to expostulate, to clinically dissect meaning, and note
such meaning in tangible and clear-cut form, that it is questionable whether
I could have proffered a metaphor without feeling the desire to explain it.

In such a way we attempt to *possess* the text. Its meaning now *defined* by us,
belongs to us (somehow newly primary). Printed, bound, and [*fig. 4*] copy-
righted [*fig. 1*], this inference which *we* have found, which *we* have lathered

from the soap in such a way at such a time, becomes not of the text itself, but of *our* minds. Pickpockets all, for let's be honest, each thus-lusting for all that is not our own, each longing gain, in the spirit of Cain almost, that any who mentions meaning seen by us must note that we have said it first, that it is *ours*, conceived and thus possessed by *us*.

Is it for better or worse this paradox, to explain and thus to possess on touch, but more, to kill, to reduce to nothing but ashes and dust (that even a text possessing inestimable ambiguity, once defined as such gains a sense of singularity, the singularity of ambiguity defined now becoming but a clear cut clarity)?

Thus, now, we live (and die) in a time of [fig. 5] end(all)notes, editions deemed 'critical', texts which, now annotation filled, are denoted, most notably, one notes, by notables, as notable. [fig. 1] So thus, we find ourselves covered in lather, bereft of soap, [fig. 6] re-turning [fig. 1] forever backwards, [fig. 7] forwards [fig. 1] from text to notes, defining possessively and destroying excessively everything within our critical scope.

Declared endable, somehow, notationally comprehensible, texts now double in size, now halve in meaning. Denoting an ends, endnotes end texts – forever, their ends noted now, now laid to rest, [fig. 8] discussion lessened [fig. 1]. Yet why so bound? why note and clamp some false 'firm' ground, some theory found, in standard form:

[a cardboard spine, and covers, inside just paper lined]

as somehow true, innately sound, as now thus bound somehow profound? Why thus? when we, for all postmodern pundits now, know meaning as mangled, flatten'd, slain, know 'truth' a given construct, know constructs thus proliferate, create and then now recreate. Why add to this, this endless lie? this vain, romantic fabric made by man, by man thus ever reified? Why bind opinion, inference, in end-all notes, when all around us is [fig. 9] [fig. 1],

    its voice immense yet indefinable,
    its tone unbending . . . featureless,
    its echoes deafening . . . unendurable.

Why note then 'meaning' as secure? when artists war upon such words, as words before made total war, made maxims law, to thus coerce the death of millions, and aid the loss of millions more . . .
dropt off,

now gorged,
now flaccid
and drain'd,
from truth,
from some enlightened youth
we once possessed, once reified,
but now, now from this vast speculation dispossessed,
now, fain to comment [*fig. 10*] 'pon page it'sself [*fig. 1*], itself post-structural
   print must deny.

So why cite, why set, why form 'facts' thus? when truth (as we know, yes
we know, for we've been told so many times, over again by many minds)
lies fail'd, face down, thus crush'd in hollow tomb, a ghastly pit. And we,
postmodern villains all, says one, so Oedipal, stand hushed with sword in
hand. Blind by design, to that fool's faith in a tried man's words, this
maddened clan we: 'postmodern man' see [*fig. 11*] all [*fig. 1*].

So why endnote now this wasteland reaped, why seal as such in end-all
   tomes? when opening up
before our eyes, past ruin'd woodlands now past hope, past oases now
   dissolving fast,
at large at last in spacious field, this desert real, postmodern tomb, this
   thanatos,
with blood-red seal and red-ribb'd lips, ingesting all, gapes welcome wide,
this dead weight binds and thus defines us:

                    a core procreating nothingness.

Thus, lips wiped clean of cryptic blood, with somewhat shuffling step,
now critics prune new paper trees, with flourished poise spread safely leaves
that hide with bloom this hollow horror's engulfing maws.
Concealing fertile stagnant waters, [*fig. 12*] rhizomal texts proliferate,
new critics weave new earthen mantles, new endnotes fabricate new shapes,
and all is well, and well-defined [*fig. 1*].

Now fixed in form, outlined through notes, from meaning [*fig. 13*]   [*fig. 1*]
   dislocates . . .
a groundless hoax (as notes have shown) in that unknowns must be
   unknown.
No fables left unnoted now, no alleg'ry unclarified,
in every university while meaning halves texts grow in size.

Thus, underhand a swordlike pen we stand again in civil war,
our father dead just as before (a paradox which we ignore), echechoing past-
  modernity.

Reflecting thus himself full long (in that himself he now full knows),
the critic on and on [*fig. 14*] anon stares [*fig. 1*] . . .
seeing but trees which he has (re)written, perceiving landscapes pre-
  prepared.

Why thus? for silence terrifies. And so the critic-cuts-and-dries,
and binds in texts new notes defined as fundament.
Now held beholden to the [fig. 15] [fig. 1] word, interstices bear clear-cut
  [fig. 16] [fig. 1] worth:
that [fig. 17] shrill-edged shriek [fig. 1], that whisper'd fright,
driv'n wailing through the shudd'ring night,
through air now dread, divided, choked,
is now but tuneful whistled wind by introjecting leaves invoked.

Thus, backwards, [*fig. 18*] forwards critics move, (re)creating,
                                          (re)possessing,
                                          fearing always . . . nothing.

Oedipust-mothernity, says one.
Fearing meaning gone they shudder, fearing toterisme past . . .
today, pastmodern man remains . . .
echoing words and worth's remains . . .
now tender staring faithless leering selfness,
mirrors reading into nothing,
but still supporting, still (re)creating fixed notation,
                  still (re)possessing through explanation, self-
                  affirming,
                  still like but Oh! how different now than then, when

[fig. 19]

richnesses of bowery lanes, and cold springs flowing from sandstone rocks,
  and flowers, mosses,
blooming ferns, dissolved – revealing an earth erupt evolved. And Darwin
  large in spacious field
emerged, red-ribb'd lips-sinking dripping with a   horror of blood,
and Nature then, whate'er was ask-d her, answered 'Chance'.

[fig. 20]

When mangled, flatten'd, crush'd anon, lay (echju(i)ng) him whose lyrics
    once
obliged words low and touching, now ballad lost, now title stripped, a
    father falling
Wordsworth plunged, Hephaesatan like, his Nature's ground now ghastly
    pit,
His laurelled wreath snatched when he fell, now borne ashamed by a poet
    revering,

[fig. 21]

whose syllables self-flagellating, romance dethroned, this vast speculation
    now fail'd.
And ever now mutter'd madden'd verse, a totem ousted thus reflecting,
And out he walk'd when the wind's words sounding a broken worldling
    wail'd,
And the whistling worth of the ruin'd wordlands drove through the air self-
    execrating.

[fig. 22]

In memoria now bereft this time, when likewise roots rhizomal stirr'd
By a hollow left, by a dead weight trail'd, by a whisper'd fright,
And pulses closed their gates with a shock on hearts as then was heard
The shrill-edged shriek of a Nature lost divide the shuddering night.

[fig. 23]

Villainy somewhere! whose? One says, we are villains all.
Not he: his honest fame should at least by me be maintained:
But that old man, now lord of the broad estate and the Hall,
Dropt off gorged from a scheme that had left us flaccid and drain'd.

[fig. 24]

Now poets prate of the blessings of Peace? we have made them a curse,
Pickpockets, each hand credited for all that is not its own;
And lust of gain, in the spirit of Cain, is it better or worse
Than the heart of the critic hissing in war on his own hearthstone?

[fig. 25]

But these are the days of advance, the works of the men of mind,
When who but a fool would have faith in a tradesman's ware or his word?
Is it peace or war? Civil war, as I think, and that of a kind
The viler, as underhand not openly bearing a sword.

[fig. 26]

[fig. 1. Shown for 10 seconds. Silence.]

Notes

1 Nicholas Bourriaud, *Postproduction* (New York: Lukas & Sternberg, 2007), pp. 13–17. Subsequent references to this text appear parantheticlaly je.
2 All figures are reproduced below.

fig. 1

'Thus critics who insert their own work into that of others contribute to the eradication of the traditional distinction between production and consumption, creation and copy, readymade and original work. [...] It is no longer a matter of elaborating a form on the basis of a raw material but working with objects that are already in circulation on the cultural market, which is to say, objects already *informed* by other objects. Notions of originality (being at the origin of) and even of creation (making something from nothing) are slowly blurred in this new cultural landscape marked by the twin figures of the DJ and the programmer, both of whom have the task of selecting cultural objects and inserting them into new contexts. [...] In a universe of [...] preexisting forms, signals already emitted, [...] paths marked out by their predecessors, critics no longer consider the artistic field [...] a museum containing works that must be delineated or "defined," [...] but so many storehouses filled with tools that should be used, stockpiles of data to manipulate and represent.'

Nicholas Bourriaud, *Postproduction* (2002)

fig. 2

VIII

Sooner or later I too may passively take the print
Of the golden age – why not? I have neither hope nor trust;
May make a heart as a millstone, set my face as flint,
Cheat and be cheated, and die; who knows? we are ashes and dust.

Alfred Lord Tennyson, *Maud: A Monodrama* (1855)

fig. 3

copy((re)write)d ©

fig. 4

'**endnote** ('en(d)nōt) A note or comment locating the end of the text. *transf.* and *fig.* Hence '**endnote** v., to determine meaning with an ending note or notes; to comment on in an end note. Also endnoted *ppl.* a., endnoting *vbl. sb.*

fig. 5

re(re(re)re))) **turning**

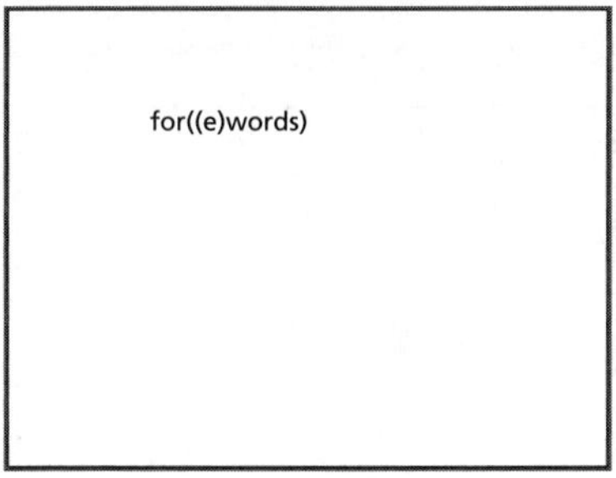

for((e)words)

fig. 6

fig. 7

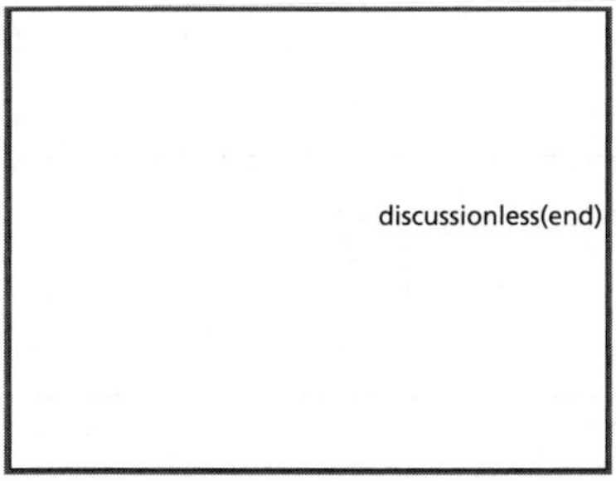

discussionless(end)

fig. 8

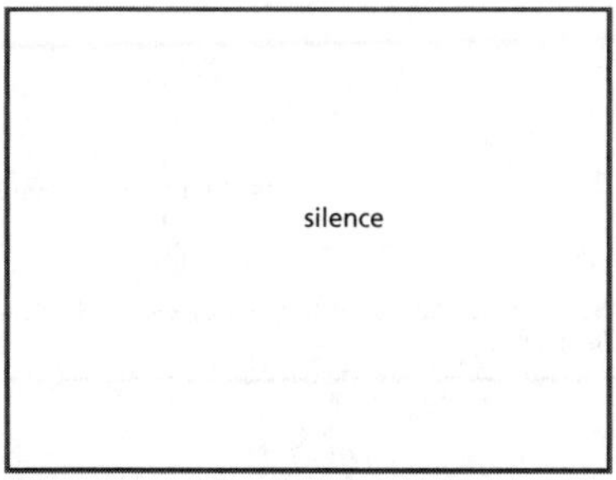

silence

fig. 9

upon page it'sself
upon page it'sself

fig. 10

(nothing)

fig. 11

bearing r i omalland(e)scapes
h z
om
a
Now [stares] Narciss((u(s))at)an ho)llow reflection
(lamozihr)

fig. 12

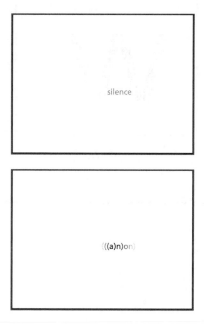

fig. 13

fig. 14

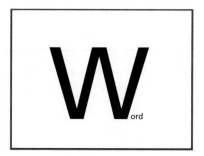

fig. 15

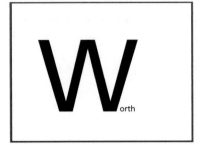

fig. 16

silence

fig. 17 {text fades}

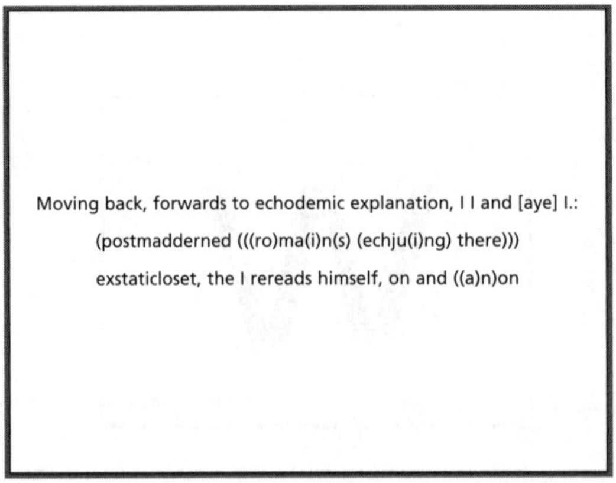

Moving back, forwards to echodemic explanation, I I and [aye] I.:
(postmadderned (((ro)ma(i)n(s) (echju(i)ng) there)))
exstaticloset, the I rereads himself, on and ((a)n)on

fig. 18

I

I hate the dreadful hollow behind the little wood,
Its lips in the field above are dabbled with blood-red heath,
The red-ribb'd ledges drip with a silent horror of blood,
And Echo there, whatever is ask-d her, answers 'Death'.

fig. 19

II

For there in the ghastly pit long since a body was found,
His who had given me life – O father! O God! was it well? –
Mangled and flatten'd, and crush'd, and dinted into the ground:
There yet lies the rock that fell with him when he fell.

fig. 20

III

Did he fling himself down? who knows? for a vast speculation had fail'd,
And ever he mutter'd and madden'd, and ever wann'd with despair,
And out he walk'd when the wind like a broken worldling wail'd,
And the flying gold of the ruin'd woodlands drove through the air

IV

I remember the time, for the roots of my hair were stirr'd
By a shuffled step, by a dead weight trail'd, by a whisper'd fright,
And my pulses closed their gates with a shock on my heart as I heard
The shrill-edged shriek of a mother divide the shuddering night.

fig. 22

V

Villainy somewhere! whose? One says, we are villains all.
Not he: his honest fame should at least by me be maintained:
But that old man, now lord of the broad estate and the Hall,
Dropt off gorged from a scheme that had left us flaccid and drain'd

fig. 23

VI

Why do thay prate of the blessings of Peace? we have made them a curse,
Pickpockets, each hand lusting for all that is not its own;
And lust of gain, in the spirit of Cain, is it better or worse
Than the heart of the citizen hissing in war on his own hearthstone?

fig. 24

VII

But these are the days of advance, the works of the men of mind,
When who but a fool would have faith in a tradesman's ware or his word?
Is it peace or war? Civil war, as I think, and that of a kind
The viler, as underhand not openly bearing a sword.

fig. 25

VIII

Sooner or Later I too may passively take the print
Of the golden age – why not? I have neither hope nor trust;
May make a heart as a millstone, set my face as a flint,
Cheat and be cheated, and die: who knows? we are ashes and dust.

fig. 26

GodotOnSea

John Schad

DRAMATIS PERSONAE

MR. SLIDE, *a Blackpool deck-chair attendant who seems to think he is the author, Samuel Beckett (1906–80)*

LORD WHIP, *actor playing part of Pozzo in Beckett's play* **Waiting for Godot**

PROFESSOR SWINE, *actor playing part of Lucky in* **Godot** *who keeps talking in the manner of Lucky.*

BUOY, *actor playing part of Boys 1 and 2 in* **Godot.**

MRS ASKEY, *Blackpool theatrical landlady.*

THE GREAT VITTORIO, *man with concertina claiming to be the Italian foot-ball coach, Vittorio Pozzo (1886–1968)*

CHAIRMAN, *beggar in a wheelchair who is mistaken for A.A. LUCE (1882–1977), Professor of Philosophy, Trinity College Dublin (Chairman is forever quoting Professor Luce).*

A BLACKPOOL CITIZEN, *Chairman's aide.*

MOURNERS FROM THE SOUTH, *three from London.*

NB

This is a wholly fictional account of the day-time lives of three of the troupe of five actors who played *Waiting for Godot* in Blackpool from June 2nd to June 7th 1956. The account is an attempt to explore the curious juxtaposition of this most avant-garde of plays and the working-class sea-sideresort that was 1950s Blackpool. There is a particular focus on the characters of

Lucky and Pozzo and two possible sources for these characters. I also have in my sights Samuel Beckett's improbable time as a quartermaster in the French coastal town of St Lô at the very end of the Second World War. For copyright reasons, that I am of course happy to respect, the text includes no quotation from the work of Samuel Beckett. I am, though, often alluding to his work and whenever I do so I make that clear through footnotes. I should like to thank both the Beckett Estate and Faber and Faber for their kind help with this.

I

They had died. It was awful. They must not die again.

'Consider, Swine!' he said, the portly Lord in the cruel hat, and Swine began to consider and to think, this idiot with the smile, the hair and the rope around his neck. Swine held a heavy case, a folding-stool, a picnic basket, and a greatcoat, but upon his head he had no hat, cruel or otherwise. It had fallen off, during the night. Find the damned thing, he must. Once found and upon his head, Swine was a man condemned to think, to think through the grease-paint, still discernible.

And this he thought, this: 'In view in view of the existence and indeed subsistence of a loving God beyond time and space time and space who cherishes all or nearly all and for reasons that escape us and only time will reveal — '[1]

Swine had suddenly stopped, this idiot with the noose, this fearful obscurantist, this lolling fool. And here he stood, Professor Swine, former theologian and dancer, sometime pale darling of dance-floor and lecture-hall, and currently walk-on stooge in avant-gardist tripe. 'God', he begged, searching the room. It was, he suspected, a boarding-house. Sea-View, no doubt, since none could be viewed.

'Yes, God', said the other, the portly Lord, who possessed a whip. 'God indeed', he added. The portly Lord then clawed at a curtain. 'Blackpool', he whispered.

'Blackpool!' said a youth, both known and cursed as 'Buoy'. The People's Playground. He had not noticed.

The Blackpool Gazette and Herald
Tuesday 3rd June 1956

When Samuel Beckett's 'Waiting for Godot' opened at the Grand Theatre last night a large body of the audience beat a disorganised retreat from the

auditorium;   others   stayed   and,   displaying
appalling manners, made interjections which would
have been audible to those on the stage. Anyone
must admit that the management has shown courage
in making this booking.

'Let us not, however, be dismayed', said the portly fellow, 'Least, no-wise
more than is customary'. Blackpool. He could see the famous Tower in the
morning. Outside, it still was Blackpool. However, nothing could ever be
done, as one or other of the tramps had remarked last night. The portly
fellow then, of a sudden, bellowed: 'I am Whip!' he cried, 'Lord Whip!' He
paused, 'Though by night I play Pozzo. Does that name mean nothing?'
    'Nothing', said Buoy, somewhat overweight but mostly precocious.
    'Peter Bull, then?' said the portly fellow, 'Lieutenant-Commander Peter
Cecil Bull, falling-star of repertory, celluloid, and the Italian landings. Does
his name mean nothing?'[2]
    'Nothing', said Buoy, voice breaking. He had never met this terrible
portly fellow, or at least not upon the boards, turning up, as Buoy did, but
once or twice (a moot point) to say that Mr Godot would be late and then
vanishing. Meantime he minded the goats, or the sheep.
    Professor Swine beheld their room. Two beds, one double, and a sinister
wardrobe. Twelve shillings-and-sixpence, breakfast and high tea, no visitors. Sorry carpet, penitent lamp, purgatorial shade. A higher flop-house.
This could yet be heaven. But first, suggested Lord Whip, dear Swine must
think again, he who, once upon a time, had thought so beautifully.
    'In view of the existence,' announced Swine, beginning once more, 'of a
loving God – '. He stopped as it was clear that Lord Whip was now thinking
for himself, it having occurred to his Lordship that there may be no argument for the existence of God, or what some might call the Ground of
Being. He paused and felt for the wallpaper. He then thought a little more;
in particular, he thought that, On The Other Hand, perhaps there were acts
of courage, acts of blind and bloody courage, which might, just might,
affirm the power of such Being. There was, for instance, last night.

The Blackpool Gazette and Herald
Wednesday 4th June 1956

Mr Michael Wide who, with Mr Richard Scott, is
jointly   responsible   for   the   production   of
'Waiting for Godot' , said today that he was
disheartened by the reception it received
yesterday evening. Mr Wide referred to the play's

run of eight months at The Criterion in London,
its present run on Broadway, and its tremendous
success in Paris. 'I thought the provinces ought
to have the opportunity of seeing it', he added.
'I think this is a wonderful play and a lot of
people feel the same way. Whether there are enough
of them in Blackpool who also think so, I don't
know'.

But why *here*, beside the Irish Sea, albeit at not the zenith of the season? Buoy suggested error – that someone, such as Mr Godot, surely an Irishman, had intended them to be not in Blackpool but Dublin. After all, it was not far, and Buoy had somewhere read that within reach of Dublin's Martello Tower there was a house belonging to a woman named Mrs. Pozzo with a maid called Lucky, and that she, the maid, would invariably carry all of Mrs Pozzo's things.[3] Moreover, reasoned Buoy, it could not be refuted that, to speak etymologically, 'Dublin' was reducible to 'Black-Pool'. True, very true. Perhaps, then, their being here was some higher clerical error.

Lord Whip was a-weary of such blather from a youth whose innocence was to be preserved at all costs. He despaired, in a way. Could Professor Swine kindly put on his hat again and do a little thinking? He could.

'In view of the existence of a loving God', he began. Buoy drew a well-worn cigarette from a pocket. Swine pressed on, '– who shares the pains of those who for reasons that escape us are deep in agony and in fire and in hell or should that be heaven so quiet so quiet so quiet'.

Swine stopped once more, and Lord Whip observed that this was all very well but, for reasons that escaped him, they appeared to be deep in Blackpool, though only time would reveal. It was not torment as yet but the weather was indifferent-to-hostile, much like their audience. Though who could blame either, weather or audience? Who, apart from their land-lady, Mrs. Askey, Mrs. Arthur Askey, so she said, she who had inspected them but the day-before-yesterday in her parlour upon their arrival by train; huge woman, corset on, teeth in, bosom established, a theatrical landlady, sometime palmist and occasional Salvationist, a Holy Miranda who had been so quiet, so quiet, so quiet, she who had seen better days, better weather, better men, far better men, but never, but never, she had said, with a howl, such a tearful *coup-de-théâtre*. A brave new world had come, at last, she said. Oh, how she had wept, from the circle, long after most had gone, walked out.

Peter Bull, *A Life on the Stage*[4]

```
What  possessed  the  management  to  book  us  in  at
Blackpool  must  be  shrouded  for  ever  in  mystery.
.  .  .  But  even  this  cardinal  error  was  eclipsed
by   the   invitation   to   the   Blackpool   Old   Age
Pensioners  to  view  the  play  at  one  shilling  a  head
on  the  Monday  night.  .  .  .  We  started  off  with
seven  hundred  persons  in  the  theatre  and  finished
up  with  under  a  hundred.
```

And behold, there she was again, Holy Miranda, through the door and without a knock. Buoy returned the cigarette to a pocket. Time, she said, for the three to stretch their brave new legs; breakfast had gone the way of all flesh, and she'd be needing to straighten the windows. She had some seeing to do. Lord Whip could appreciate the need for this, but Professor Swine, the bastard, had fallen to sleep, as he had so often before, on stage, on the floor, in the dust, however hard he, Lord Whip, could thrash him, or pull at his rope. Look at the darling now.

'Asleep', observed Mrs Askey, and began a story of how she herself had once slept theatrically, as it were. She had been, she announced, one of the famous 'Starving Brides of Blackpool'.[5] Had they ever heard of such? No they had not, and so it fell to Mrs Askey to explain how, when first married, she and Arthur –

'*Little* Arthur?' said Buoy.

'Alas, yes', she said. But how did he know?

Pause. Mrs Askey then resumed, saying how, notwithstanding all questions of size, she and Mr Askey, so newly wed, so much in love, had been promised £250, no less, to lie together, and yet divided, in a case made of glass.

'And for how long had they lain so chaste and so foodless?' inquired Lord Whip.

'Oh, but a month', said Mrs Askey. They had been a side-show, the pride of the Golden Mile, as presented by the Great Gannon himself.[6] Honeymoon, honeymoon, they had called it a honeymoon. Many had come, many had borne witness, and many no doubt had been blessed. And all the while, there, right there, beside them, day after day, had been the dear Rector of Stiffkey, busy starving in his famous barrel. Disgraced he was, and so the fires of hell had been painted about him. All true, all true, she sang.

But had she not felt the terrible desires of great hunger? Yes, she had felt many a desire; but divine sleep had prevailed and redeemed, and she had triumphed. Though not, alas, her groom, sweet prince. He had slipped away.

'But', she said, 'enough of life'. Time it really was for theatrical gentlemen to exeunt stage left. Professor Swine protested great unreadiness, but Mrs Askey had no interest in whatever evil had led them to fall to their beds still bedraggled as for the stage and not wake in time to change, let alone to have breakfast, or indeed to untie the rope that had now grown entangled, knotted, undoable. Messrs Swine and Whip would henceforth be as one, she felt.

'But what,' howled Lord Whip, 'should we do all day?'

'Do?' she said. 'Do? Why', she said, 'you should go in search of the very soul of Blackpool'.

And so they went, precocious Buoy, and the tied-together. Of all his burdens, Professor Swine left none behind save the greatcoat. Folding-stool, picnic basket, and heavy case all came with him. An ambulatory advertisement, he reasoned.

II

As they left the house each wiped the soles of their boots, and soon the troupe were struggling along the front. Here was sea-side and side-show, show after show after show, all under a blue proscenium sky, and on and on they struggled the three of them – grandiose Buoy, the Lord with his whip, and his fiend that fellow with the rope about his neck. They wandered past the Headless Girl, the Telepathic Robot and a host of Fakirs, Ecstatics, and Holy Men.[7] No-one remarked upon the passing troupe.

At last, satiated, they fell to the beach, in the eye of the Tower, hard by the donkeys. There they met a short and round man with agonised glasses, a collapsible man, who stood before a row of corporation deckchairs and a sign. He was a deck-chair attendant, though the sign said 'Mr. Beckett, Quartermaster and Interpreter', or leastwise so it once said, for some scribbler had altered 'Beckett' to 'Slide' – for that was his real name. The world now knew him as 'Mr. *Slide*, Quartermaster and Interpreter'. Though of what he was an Interpreter they could not say. Still less the Quarter of which he was Master.

From June 1945 to January 1946 Samuel Beckett lived and worked in St Lô, the French port-town that had been devastated during the D-Day invasions. The Capital of Ruins, it was called. He served as an auxiliary to the Irish Red Cross Hospital that had been set up in St Lô at the end of the war. Records have him down as 'Mr S. Beckett, Quartermaster-Interpreter'.[8]

Lord Whip lowered himself to the folding-stool, drew forth a pipe from within one of his many folds, and threw open the picnic basket. Only bones were left.

'Blackpool?' said Whip, as if he had quite lost his way.

'Bones along the coast', said the collapsible Mr Slide.[9]

'So, does his Highness like it here?' Lord Whip addressed the sea, but spoke of Slide. The collapsible man observed that the sea did not agree with him.

'Why should it?' said Buoy, examining a donkey.

Pause.

'There are folk', remarked Slide, 'who have no time for the sea. I myself feel no more awful here than anywhere else.'[10] He then lay down on the beach, head in the sand, and closed his eyes. 'Invariably I sleep', he said.[11]

'He lies', said Buoy. He had completed his examination.

'Exactly', said Whip, 'the lizard lies in the sand'.

'No', said Buoy, 'the lizard's *not* sleeping; he just *thinks* about sleeping'.

And Buoy was right. Telepathy, it was, for the lizard at once sat up and said, 'I am, you know, forever mindful of one Patricia Maguire who lives, or rather sleeps, in Chicago. There she has slept since 1931. True, true, absolutely true'.[12]

Whip wished to raise the subject of Mrs Askey but he sensed that the lizard was too distressed. He was correct.

'I have a significant problem', said Slide.

Swine's face was lost. He was appalled.

'Significant problem is now resolved', said Slide.

Swine's fears were relieved.

'The problem was', continued Slide, 'how to locate without spectacles one's clothes on a beach post-dip'.[13] He then demonstrated how the problem had been resolved, miming a solution that involved a feeling of sand on all four of his paws.

'Pitiful, and yet moving', said Whip. He put back his pipe, unlit, un-smoked.

Slide nodded like a man receiving news in a hospital. He then gestured to another figure on the beach, an Italian showman.

'He inquired of me', said Slide, 'whether I dived with my spectacles on'.[14]

'Why ever not?' said Whip. 'An absurd question'.

Slide concurred. After all he, Mr Slide, was a scholarly figure, a *man* of spectacles, a writer indeed. But could he continue to scratch-away out here? In the bone-yard? By the sea? He fought for an answer, and put his finger in the sand. 'I have no desire', he wrote, 'to write. I mix cement and unfurl the most barbed of wire'.[15]

'Sounds like a fortified coast', whispered Lord Whip, holding his head. He thought of their unbearable play, right back to the beginning, that very first night of all, their London opening.

Peter Bull, *A Life on the Stage*

The windiness I had felt [in the War] ... was nothing to compare with one's panic on that evening of August 3rd 1955. Waves of hostility came whirling over the footlights.[16]

Pause.

Time passed. Noon threatened, the beach was overcome. Swine had flopped to sleep, the people were everywhere, and donkeys marched to and fro. Not much of a show, thought Buoy, but then had not a donkey been good enough for Jesus? The multitude grew still closer. Thousands of them, all struggling with costumes. Great problems here, felt Lord Whip. They might, at any moment, be in need of a public convenience, or to fart and to belch; and, come lunchtime and teatime, they would surely grow hungry. And what might such hungry, stranded people make of his theatrical labours? His Lordship, now barefoot, had rolled up the bottoms of his trousers, and needed to know. Lest the tide should turn again that night.

'But never so quick', said Professor Swine, stirring himself. He danced a little, the farandole, as in the oldest days, and at once the Tower Ballroom was in sight with dear Reginald Dixon seated at the Mighty Wurlitzer.[17] Just last night, high upon the stage, Estragon, or was it Vladimir, had inquired if he, Swine, could dance first and contemplate afterwards, and Whip had said it was the proper order. Having now jigged Swine was ready to think on.

'But never so quick', he resumed, 'It has been argued but never so quick that in view of the view of Professor Testoo and Tyrant that man notwithstanding his infinite capacity to digest and defecate continues to waste and decline'.

'Enough!' cried Whip and he quite removed Swine's hat. Human guillotine. 'Kiss me Quick,' said the hat, and Swine thought no more, no more about it.

'Thank God', whispered Whip.

'A loving God?' asked Buoy.

'Am afraid so', said Whip, 'He who cherishes us all, or nearly all. Time will tell. We have five days of this tripe yet to run'.

All around, some who pined and wasted began to wonder why the man in the noose had been sent to them? What use, thought they, a professor on a beach, if not one who practiced the art of Punch and Judy? Or of reading your mind? Or riding a bike off the end of Central Pier? There were many such professors hereabouts.[18] See, for instance, that disaster over there, the wan Italian who squeezed the saddest of tunes from a troubled concertina.[19] Its breathing was scarce and weak.

Swine wondered who he.

'Pozzo, the Great Pozzo', claimed the Italian, 'Professor of Football.'

Swine was puzzled.

'Pozzo, you say?' said Buoy.

'Yes Pozzo', lied the Italian, 'Vittorio Pozzo'.

```
In both 1934 and 1938 Vittorio Pozzo (1886-1968)
coached the Italian football team to victory in
the FIFA World Cup. Pozzo's time as national coach
coincided  with  the  period  in  which  Benito
Mussolini governed Italy. In 1934, when the tour-
nament took place in France, Pozzo ordered his
team to make the Fascist salute prior to the
game.20
```

The fool was puzzled still.

'I am Pozzo', persisted the Italian, 'Does that name mean nothing?'

Lord Whip said that, by night, it meant the world to him. He then stared at Vittorio, like a dog before a glass, but the glass grew weary, stepped aside, and dragged from his pocket a bruised photograph of men lined up, men in shorts, and all around them, for always and always, tens of thousands of faces, heads and no bodies, so many in hats, desperate to see, this host, this myriad, all on the tips of their toes desperate to see the telling-and-angled struggle that was to-come. Professor Swine was moved by the hungry heaven of faces.

'Football', he said, and sagged, and lolled and flopped. Asleep.

Vittorio nodded and began to stare at the sandy world beneath his feet. He examined a space. Yards, feet, inches no more. He then began to press and draw his wheezing concertina. The tubercular thing sighed a tune, and the Great Vittorio's show had begun, said someone. He was, said another, examining his team, a team of corpses. The Great Vittorio could see them laid out upon the sand, one beside the other, a body of men, the very best. Perfect was their line.

On May the 4th 1949 the crack Turino team, League
Champions in all but name, were flying back from
Lisbon where they had been playing a friendly.
The weather was terrible, dark clouds surrounded
Turin, and visibility was poor. The FIAT G-212
plane in which they flew smashed into a wall
behind a church. All on board were killed, and
the task of identifying the dead fell to Vittorio
Pozzo, by now a journalist. Turino were his home-
town team and many of the players were well known
to him. The event shook the whole of Italy. A 38-
yead old woman in Bologna committed suicide upon
hearing the news.[21]

Lord Whip turned to Mr Slide for interpretation, a word to justify the
ways of football to men, but all he said or rather wrote, this time on the
back of his hand, were the two words, 'Bone House.' [22] Swine felt they
should pass on the interpretation to Vittorio himself, who even now was
massaging the calves of one of the finest dead. He then stood up and
squeezed a lonely note from his concertina.

'But why', asked Whip, now forgetting the interpretation, 'why care for
the muddied pursuit of a sphere?'

'The game', replied Vittorio, 'is beautiful when it thinks.' [23] He squeezed
out another note.

'It thinks?' said Buoy.

'In the manner of a dog,' commented his Lordship, and Professor Swine,
awake once more, began again to think.

'Waste and decline', he declared, 'waste and decline notwithstanding the
leaps and bounds made by sports such as football'.

'Football?' said Buoy.

Swine nodded, wiped an eye, and resumed:

'– football jumping whirling leaping drifting bowling falling skiing
dying and flying.'

'Dying and flying?' said Buoy.

Swine nodded, winked and resumed.

'Games of every kind such as tennis and hockey and penicillin – '

'Penicillin?' said Slide.

Swine nodded, winked and resumed.

'– in short I resume and begin at once to waste and decline – '

'Halt, I ask you!' begged Vittorio.

Professor Swine smiled, delighted that still, even here in the provinces, he could think so appositely, to the point – in this splendid instance, to the point of football. 'Dying and flying', he said again, and beamed. Vittorio bent double, squeezing from his concertina a tangle of notes. It was too much.

Time, though, is a hospital; and, but a moment later, Vittorio rose to beckon Lucky toward him. The Italian had another photo to show, this time of a team world-triumphant in a palace somewhere, a trophy held as dear as innocence, and beside them a uniformed emperor as bald as a moon.

'Mr. Mussolini', said Lord Whip, toes in the sand. He was alarmed.

Blackpool Gazette and Herald
June 9th 1956

The Rev C N Warde-Harper says that the recent election in Blackpool showed a greater apathy then ever before. 'It is a grave betrayal,' he says, 'of a Christian's duty to the State if no-one bothers to see that the best men stand and are elected. Apathy is the surest way to dictatorship.'

'Mr Mussolini,' repeated Lord Whip, again, from his stool.
'Notwithstanding the sport of football', said Swine.
'Or *because*', said Buoy, knowingly.
His Lordship, a great actor unable to stand, cursed the precocious Buoy. Meantime, the Great Vittorrio had struck a pensive attitude, hand upon hip. He was, said the crowd, considering movement, direction and, above all, motivation. The art of 'Coaching the Dead' lay heavy with him, they said. In the first place, how to tell one from another, now that they were corpses. It was no pleasing task.
'Rarely is', said Lord Whip. 'Would you not agree Professor Swine?'
Swine danced a little, a careworn jig, the fandango, even the hornpipe – all had been proposed last night, by his Lordship. Their fleeing audience had made other suggestions.
'Consider, for instance,' resumed Whip, 'your friend Professor Testoo'.
'Testoo?' said Swine, jig over.
'Yes, Testoo of "Testoo and Tyrant", those whose views you were in view of. Do you recall?'
How could he not.
'Well', said Whip, 'by "Testoo," that is to say T-E-S-T-O-O, dear Swine, what you actually meant was "Testut," T-E-S-T-*U*-T.'
'He did?' said Buoy

'He did', said Whip. 'I refer you to the very late Leo Testut (1849–1925), Professor of Anatomy and Anthro – '[24]

'Anthropopoff?' suggested Swine.

'Very nearly', said Whip.

'UniUniUniFarcity?' suggested Swine.

'Most certainly', said Whip and he went on to relate how Professor Testut had once mistaken a skull –

'Mistaken a skull?' said Buoy, settling upon a deck-chair.

'Yes', said Lord Whip, 'a skull.'

'A skull in Chichester,' suggested Professor Swine.

'No', said his Lordship, 'a skull in Chancelade. It is, they argue, a town in France'.

'But for what', said Buoy, 'for what did he mistake the skull?' He drew out his cigarette.

'Do you not know?' asked Whip.

Buoy reminded Lord Whip of his youthful innocence.

'He mistook it', said his Lordship, 'for an ancestor of the Eskimo'.

'Which Eskimo?' said Buoy. He caressed his cigarette.

'The Eskimos in general', said his Lordship, 'As a race, a people, a species. Professor Testut believed he'd found a whole new people, a race of reindeer hunters, the Eskimos before they were Eskimos'.

'Bollocks', said Buoy, returning cigarette to pocket.

'Exactly', said Lord Whip, overlooking this oath, 'Nothing of the sort. There are no new people, and never will be. The skull was misleading. Professor in ruins. Died a man disproved'.

Pause.

The dead, thought Whip, could clearly destroy a man. But how could one avoid them? How turn away? Seeing they made such spectacles of themselves.

(You may recall that in *Waiting for Godot* there is talk, talk between those fabulous tramps, of how we cannot help but look at the dead.)[25]

Pause.

Boy stared at a girl that was changing. Mrs. Askey's only daughter? Time would tell. But not so fast, for at present the girl was one of the many, the throng, and here there were so many, so many of the throng. No wonder, thought Whip, that Mr Slide should turn to barbed wire. Lines must be drawn. The People could yet effect an organised offensive, and he, Lord Whip, should then have to fight them on the beaches. Today, however, he felt The People looked merely lost, their eyes screwed to the sand, as if hungry for something.

'Hitler's watch', said the Great Vittorio.

'Beg your pardon', said Buoy, whom the girl had befriended.

Vittorio looked to the sky and to the dead and to the thousands, and then explained how his compatriot, Charlie Cairoli, clown-prince of the Tower Circus, exploding car and so forth, had once been given a watch by Mr A. Hitler himself, following one particularly fine exposition of the science of clowning.[26]

'What, by *Hitler?*' said impertinent Buoy. The girl laughed. If Lord Whip could only stand he would beat this Buoy.

Vittorio resumed, arguing that the performance was Cairoli's. The occasion had been the Circus Kroen in Munich, 1933.

'1933', thought Slide.

In 1933, Patricia Maguire, Chicago's very own
Sleeping Beauty, was declared clinically dead,
but only for a few minutes. She was revived and
remained asleep until dying again and for good in
1937.[27]

'What kind of watch?' said Buoy.

'What kind!' cried his Lordship.

'Yes, what kind of watch?' said Buoy.

Lord Whip begged that Vittorio should continue without regard for kind or species or race of time-piece. Vittorio did so, explaining that when war was declared and, with it, all hell, Cairoli had hastened to the end of North Pier – wig, nose, unfortunate trousers, balloons for breasts. Once there, at the end of the pier, he had hurled the Führer's watch far into the Irish.

(In *Waiting for Godot* there is a point at which
the beastly Pozzo loses his fob-watch. There is
panic, so there is.)[28]

Lord Whip took Professor Pig to one side, to the far side of the donkeys, and stage-whispered. The People's devotion to such a watch as Herr Hitler's were, he felt, Grounds for Concern. The People must be scrutinised. Perhaps, indeed, that was why he and Professor Swine were here – to keep a theatrical eye on a place that may yet prove to be too much in love with the One Still Strong Man. The evidence was there. He had read, locally, but that week, of the cool winds of Fascism. Swine fell asleep.

Vittorio, who had overheard his Lordship's almighty whisper, nodded and pointed toward the front, and to Louis Tussaud's famous Waxworks Museum. 'There', he said, 'one could holiday with graven images of such adepts of the art of Fascism as Hitler, Himmler, and – '

'Reginald Dixon?' inquired Buoy.

'No, Goering', insisted the Professor of Football.

'Goering!' exclaimed Lord Whip. 'Why! I recall dear Goering. Or at least his house'. And so he did, or thought he did, claiming that, in his naval days and way-back-away in the year of 1945, he had hopped north through Italy, a dull hopping relieved only by a serendipitous encounter with the wonderful Anthony Quayle, fellow actor-in-arms, who, as it so happened, had been temporarily lodged in what had been Herr Goering's Italian residence.[29] A magnificent tomb overlooking the Bay, so it was.

'The *Buoy?*' asked the impertinent Buoy.

'The *Bay*', insisted Whip. Oh yes, he continued, Old Hermann had loved the bay, the winds, the gulls, the waves, so still and so still and so still. Lord Whip was, by now, away on sunnier sands, but not Swine who remained loyal to the Irish Sea, and the question of what they should now do. Why not, for instance, pay a visit to the Waxworks to see Lord Whip's erstwhile host, dear Goering? To thank him, perhaps, for his hospitality, however unwitting, for thus we entertain angels.

'But is there time?' Lord Whip reached into his empty fob. 'After all, how much time *is* there, here in Blackpool?'

'All bloody day,' said Buoy, on whose knee sat the girl who might, he felt, be Mrs Askey's only daughter.

'All bloody day, eh?' said his Lordship. In that case, he argued, they should hot-foot it to the Palace of Wax in the hours that were left to them before night-the-second, a night to which The People would surely come. True, they may curse and denounce and say they have seen better and funnier fall off the end of the pier, but there was at least the Pleasure of Being Booed, even by those who would surely turn their back on them and leave that night forever to presume that Mr Godot had, in the end, made a triumphant arrival. But then perhaps he had. It was a thought.

Pause.

Lord Whip felt he really must rise from his stool. Buoy would help him. His Lordship then unrolled the bottoms of his trousers, affixed shoes and socks, and turned to Professor Swine. He must be kicked awake.

Done.

'Lift bags, Swine', bellowed the Lord. 'Landward Ho!' he added.

Buoy said he was quite happy to stay, but in order to preserve his innocence it was agreed he come along. Besides, the show must limp on; and where would they be without Buoy, small though his part was? Buoy's girl said she felt his part was in no wise small. Buoy grinned. All the same, he must abandon her, for he and the rest of the troupe must now yield a sigh, and bid a tender farewell to all.

'Piss Off', said an elderly woman, at which rebuke Vittorio squeezed his concertina in alarm, and said he too would come along. He should like, he added, to see Il Duce once again, wondering if death or wax had in any way altered His Excellency. Vittorio then whispered goodbye to his team.

Quartermaster Slide said he would stay where he was, hard by the barbed wire, master of his quarter. 'Supplies arranged', he added. [30]

'But could you not', asked Lord Whip, 'simply forsake it all?'

'A storekeeper', said Mr Slide, 'must not abandon his stores.' [31]

'Not even', said Whip, 'to witness our second night?'

Slide shook his head. 'I'll disappear for the duration', he said.[32]

III

The hurtling promenade was full of those in slow retreat from the beach. Their destiny was dinner. One o'clock sharp.[33] On the dot. No-one had yet drowned the boarding-house clock. The People limped on, cursed by the dampness of their costumes, the naked legs of the children whipped by the sand in the wind, the teeth of the wind, broken teeth. And with them, for the while, waltzed the avant-garde. His Lordship first, Swine ten yards south, and Buoy stopping to stare at the post-cards for sale. The Great Vittorio strolled alone, squeezing, mesmeric and wildly sad. As they made their way, Professor Noose-about-Neck gestured, like a mute, to his hat – 'Kiss me Quick, Before I Die', it said. But no-one cared. They had heard as much before.

Eager for consolation, Professor Noose turned aside, his attention arrested by a wheel-chair, where sat a paralytic, a beggar-man, with, about his neck, a placard that announced his distress. Swine turned and smiled at the paralytic. Then stopped, sudden. Why squander a smile? At that moment the rope around his neck, the rope that endeared him to his Lordship, grew taught, and both collapsed to the sand-brushed asphalt. A child with a windmill laughed. Bastard, thought someone.

Lord Whip considered how he might return to his feet without affectation. The dilemma was at last resolved when his lolling fool made it to his pins and yanked the beast vertical, willy or nilly. The fool, with beast pulled along, moved toward the beggar-on-wheels and touched his arm; gently, for he, Professor Swine, had no money to give.

'What would be his name?' asked Lord Whip, of the beggar. And the beggar's aide, a local citizen, decided to lie, saying, 'Arthur Aston Luce, Professor of Philosophy of Trinity College Dublin, and erstwhile moral tutor of Mr Samuel Beckett'.[34]

'Mr *Slide?*' inquired Whip.

'A category error', said the citizen of Blackpool, 'but let us not quibble. Either way he's that poet in the bone-yard. The one by the coast, don't you know'. What more could be said.

'And you say your man-in-the-chair is called Luce?'

He did. But he lied.

'Remarkable', said Lord Whip, 'Remarkable that my good friend Swine should here meet, nay lovingly reach out to, a paralytic whose name is so nearly the same as that of the character he currently plays'. Hall of Mirrors this place. 'Remarkable too', he said, 'that both once were philosophers'.

'Among the last', said the citizen, who felt he should now say more concerning his man. 'In the early 1930s', he began, 'Professor Luce hit on the vein of Berkeleian research – '

'Hit, hit', muttered Buoy, 'hit, hit'. He loved the word.

'– research', continued the citizen, 'which brought him world-wide recognition, and from then onwards article followed article and book succeeded book'.

'The proper order', remarked his Lordship.

'He liked', said the citizen, 'to rise early and work for some hours before breakfast'.

'You allowed him breakfast?' inquired Lord Whip.

'Then, however', continued the citizen, 'came the loss of Professor Luce's wife and only daughter in a tragic accident in 1940 – '

'Wife and only daughter?' said Lord Whip, seeking confirmation.

The citizen nodded.

'Is that tragic?' asked his Lordship.

Pause.

'Drowned', said the citizen.

'To drown is to die without much pain', added Slide, who had (to the surprise of all) suddenly joined them.

'If it's good enough for a watch . . . ', thought his Lordship.

There was a pause, another pause; and then the citizen resumed his Life of Luce: 'Such bereavement', he said, 'might well have broken the nerve of a man of less sturdy temperament'.

'Works unfinished?' asked Swine.

'Not at all', said the citizen, 'Professor Luce faced the loss with stoic fortitude, pressed doggedly on with his work, and brought to a successful conclusion a major re-editing of the complete works of Berkeley'.

By now a string of loosened women, arm-in-arm along the prom, had stopped to view the scene.

'The *published* works?' said Swine.

'The only kind', said the citizen.

'The philosopher Berkeley?' said Swine.

'To be is to be perceived', said the citizen, by way of an answer. He winked at the women. '*Esse est percipi*', he added.[35]

'*Esse est Esse*', replied Swine, who smiled and felt it was time for a think. After all, the assembled women might enjoy it, and some might even come to the theatre for more that very night. 'Notwithstanding', he began, 'such sports as football jumping whirling drifting bowling falling skiing and indeed a pleasing round of golf'.

> ### *British Railways Holiday Guide, 1952*[36]
> ```
> Blackpool offers you an amazing variety of outdoor
> sports . . .   Golf, Tennis, Bowls, Putting,
> Swimming,  Boating,  Fishing,  Riding,  Flying,
> Dancing . . .
> ```

'*Crazy* Golf ?' inquired the citizen.

'Sports sports sports', said Swine cheerily.

'The things of which he thinks!' said his Lordship, in wonder.

'Sports sports sports', continued Swine, 'sports of all kinds for reasons that escape those in Wye Ware and Wat-Wat-Wat-Wat-ford'.

'Not to mention Blackpool?' said Lord Whip.

'Nothing escapes Blackpool', said the citizen.

Swine carried on, and grew climactic: 'Wrexham Walsall West Ham Waterford and What Is More and Always Has Been ever since the demise –'

'The demise of *whom?*' inquired his Lordship.

'Ever since the demise', repeated Swine, smiling.

'Yes, but the demise of *whom?*' Lord Whip was very particular.

'The demise –', said Swine proudly, '– the demise of philosopher *Berkeley*'.

Pause. Sea-gulls limped along the Golden Mile, and Whip prodded the paralytic. He asked if 'L-u-c-e' could ever be pronounced 'Lucky'. The Great Vittorio said it could and, moreover, that the name 'Lucky' reminded him of 'Lucifer'. It was a thought.

> ```
> (In Waiting for Godot, the terrible Pozzo is
> concerned that poor Lucky might prove to be evil;
> indeed it is said, (it is said), that Lucky is
> wicked.)
> ```
> [37]

Pause.

'But what of the facts?' said his Lordship, 'The matter of facts?'

'All the facts can be seen,' commented Professor Swine.

'Can be *seen*?' said the citizen, '*Where*? Just there? Out there, all on their own? Like the waves?'

Swine nodded.

The citizen suspected Philosophical Materialism. He nudged the beggar who nodded. Lord Whip would not, though, be distracted. '*What* ___ ,' he asked, '*What* are the facts concerning the death of philosopher Berkeley? The hard and material *facts*?'

The paralytic, incensed by such flagrant Materialism, felt compelled to intervene, and was quick on the draw, his intervention a bullet: 'God *is*. God's world *is*. Matter is *not*', he cried.[38] The women applauded, the citizen rattled, and money was given.

'God beyond time and space', muttered Swine. It was a counter-bullet, a Materialist shot in the dark.

'Indeed', said his Lordship. 'Let us not confound God with all *this*. All this *world*'. He waved his whip at it all, all this world hereabouts: Cow with Five Legs and The Palace of Strange Girls.[39] 'There is God and *then* there is Blackpool', insisted Lord Whip. 'Deity *and* matter. God *is*. Matter *is*'.

The paralytic shook his head. 'Matter is *qua* concept irrelevant', he said, 'and *qua* entity, non-existent'.[40] More rattling and giving.

'Qua', said Professor Swine.

'I beg your pardon', said the citizen.

'Qua', said Professor Swine.

Pause.

'Qua', said Professor Swine yet again.

'What Swine attempts', said Slide, 'is the word "quaquaquaversalis"'.[41]

'Quaversalis', thought his Lordship, a word of which he had heard rumours, in the wings, behind the scenes. But what on earth did it mean?

'It describes a deity', said Slide, 'a deity who sees all ways at once'.

The paralytic shook his wheels as if to communicate, but nothing was said. Swine bent down, desperate for a word or two from the importunate philosopher, a mere sigh or a sob would do. But all the beggar would say was, *sotto voce*, 'I try to think with the learned and speak with the others'.[42]

Swine tapped his nose, this being a secret he could keep, an understanding *entre deux*, brothers as they were both in name and vocation. Freemasons of the mind. He, Swine, was indeed a lucky man, quite blessed, he thought, one who wanted for nothing, what with a head for his hat, a neck for his rope, and a hand for his bag.

> (Even now, in *Waiting for Godot*, they are saying, those tramps, that in Lucky's bag there is nothing but sand – sand, sand, sand.)[43]

Indeed, this very evening he, Professor Swine, would be so blessed as to stand, on the whole, when not on his arse, and think for Blackpool. 'In view of the existence', and so forth. He and his fellows-in-hell may have to finish the play unseen and unwatched, but no matter. No matter at all, in view of the existence of a loving God. And, besides, there was always Mrs Askey. But not so fast, not so fast at all. For now they were hurtling toward the Waxworks, alas, on and on. Goodnight ladies, goodnight.

IV

There, right there, before the palace of wax, they, the troupe-plus-friends, quickly harden into a queue. And, just ahead of them, stands, frozen, a battered and untimely man, deep in London autumn; and with him stand two who are younger but who also freeze, in the manner of the Cockney Lost.

> The world première of *Waiting for Godot* took place in Paris on January 5th 1953. Twenty-three days later in London, a nineteen-year old from Croydon called Derek Bentley was hung following a long and famous court case concerning a robbery that had ended in his accomplice shooting a policemen. The accomplice was eighteen and thus too young to hang but Derek Bentley, though declared mentally retarded, and though under arrest at the moment of the shooting, and though he pulled no trigger, and though he had carried no gun, was condemned to hang. The judge was Lord Goddard.[44]

Lord Whip-and-all-Angels shuffle closer to the three ahead, whose coats are almighty dark. The three insist that they are here for the air, for the break, and for the day. But they are keeping their cockney faces to themselves.

It was October when the phone rang late one evening. It was a man's voice.
'Fancy doing that!'
'Doing what?'
'Selling your son's suit to Tussaud's'.
'I don't know what you're talking about. I haven't even got the suit.'
Of course Dad didn't sell the suit. I know Derek was buried in it because they hang you in your own clothes, not the prison ones you wear every other day in the condemned cell.[45]

Professor Swine looks hard at the three. And he thinks. He thinks that they are mourners, mourners from the South, but on the loose, a day-trip, learning once more to grin like the rest. But the mourners return his stare, their gazes fixed on the rope about his neck. Swine doffs his hat and grins. A fine rope it is, and accustomed he is to the admiring glance.

As for this call about Toussaud's, Dad said, 'It's nothing but a cruel hoax'. No money in the world would make Dad sell anything of Derek's. But the idea of Derek being an exhibit in Toussaud's got him rattled. The man had said it was in the Blackpool Toussaud's, so Dad decided we should go for ourselves. We didn't tell a soul, we didn't want any publicity. . . . It was just me, Dad and Dennis.

If, thinks Whip, it is a stiff that these people seek then they may yet stand in need of all help. Identification, in the case of a corpse, is a science, Professor Testicle notwithstanding.

We took the overnight train, jam-packed, eight to a compartment, Dennis going to sleep leaning against me. It took for ever and was drizzling with rain when we got out at Blackpool. . . . We walked as quickly as we could to the waxworks. Dad didn't say who we were, he just bought our tickets and we went straight to the section on murders.

Stained they are with a rain of their own, those Southern mourners. And, see how they merely dissemble an interest in Sleeping Beauty *et al.* as they hasten through room after room of effigy. Now in pursuit of the speeding mourners are Lord Whip, Buoy, Mr. Slide, the Great Vittorio, and Professor Swine, as ever a baggage-clown. 'Not so fast', thinks Swine, but on and on they press, room after room, until at the end they are there, among the world's most wicked, among the very Horrors.

It was gloomy and horrible . . . There was Dr Crippen, who poisoned his wife, and Haigh who did the acid-bath murders, and Edith Thompson, whose lover killed her husband.

The mourners stare, however, straight through the frozen killers – here may be Hell, torments of fire, and murder's greatest artists, but what care those who mourn? Vittorio, meanwhile, has spotted the Evil Dictators, and is staring defiantly at a waxwork Mussolini who stares back, in a way, as if astonished it has all come to this, a disastrous seaside booking. Quite, thinks Adolf, arms folded, along with colleagues, Hermann and Heinrich. And there they stand, tyrants in wax, in Blackpool, nothing like themselves. 'As fair as Hitler,' whispers Slide, 'as thin as Goering, as elegant as Goebbels'.[46] He whispers for here it is quiet, even calm, so calm, with a calm. Much like, thinks Lord Whip, an emptied church.

There, in the Chamber of Horrors, we found an alcove and you could see a mark on the floor. Was that where Derek had been? We stayed while Dad went to find someone to ask. Remember, no one knew who we were.

Two of the three mourners remain, to wait, on and on, and so like forever, until, at last, Professor Wye, rope-about-neck, begins to grow all conscious of his neck, of his rope, of his noose. He is, he sees, so like these wax-worked Horrors. To be precise he is, he reads, as he turns to the Catalogue, just like, oh so very like, 'Waxwork No. 265.'[47] This particular Horror, this particular work of wax, is titled, he reads, 'A Present-Day Execution: an exact replica of a condemned man about to hang'. Where, though, is this promised scene? Is it there at all?

There we found an alcove, and you could see a mark on the floor. Was that where Derek had been?

The mourners stare down at space, a mark on an empty floor. Is that where their son and brother has been? Their poor dear slow brother and son. Has he been removed? Has someone been tipped off? Have they themselves been identified?

Remember, no one knew who we were.

Yes, but their faces go everywhere, in papers and newsreels. Their grief is famous. And then there is that mark on the floor.

Was that where Derek had been?

Well, is it?

When Dad asked if they had a waxwork of Derek Bentley they said –

They said *what?*

They said no, they said no, they said no . . .

But what of the execution scene? No. 265. Could that have been poor guiltless Derek? If only by suggestion?

The mourners say nothing, nothing about Waxwork 265. It would seem that they have not seen it at all, or that, perhaps, it has, just now, been taken away.

The man said, she adds, *that they only had waxworks of the guilty.*

'Such as *Godot?*' says Whip.

'*Goddard?*' says Buoy, 'Lord *Goddard?*'

'*God*', says Swine, 'a loving God who cherishes all, or nearly all'.

Pause.

The man shook our hands. 'Your son, Mr Bentley', he said, 'was innocent. Have no fear, Mr. Bentley, we will never have an effigy of him'.

The condemned fellow is not here and never has been, or so the man at the waxworks says. And, come Sunday, come the end of their run, thinks Swine, perhaps the People will say he too has not been here, here in Blackpool. Perhaps they will say, come Sunday, that there has been no flopping fool with a noose among them, that not a soul in Blackpool saw such a fool, that they had all abandoned the auditorium long before ever he made his supposed entrance. Perhaps that is what they will say, come Sunday.

(In *Waiting for Godot*, in the play, the play that
is and was always the thing, the tramps instruct
a passing youth to tell Mr Godot that he, the boy,
did see them, the two tramps. The tramps then
nervously ask if the boy really had seen them.
The boy says yes, he says yes, he says yes.)[48]

Notes

1 All of Professor Swine's words are, throughout, based on his appalling recollection of the part he plays at night, namely that of the character Lucky in Samuel Beckett's *Waiting for Godot* (London: Faber and Faber, 1965).

2 In fact rather than fiction, the part of Pozzo was played by Lieutenant-Commander Peter Cecil Bull (1912–84). Lord Whip is *not*, of course, the wonderful Peter Bull.

3 So claimed the Beckett actor Jack MacGowran in 1973 – see Mel Gussow, *Conversations with (and about) Beckett* (London: Nick Hern Books, 1996), p. 25

4 The correct name for Peter Bull's memoir is *I Know the Face, But . . .* (London: Peter Davies, 1959), of which I quote from p. 186.

5 For details of the starving brides see Gary Cross ed., *Worktowners at Blackpool: Mass Observation and Popular Leisure in the 1930s* (London: Routledge, 1990) pp. 192–6; Cyril Critchlow, *Blackpool's Golden Mile* (Blackpool, 2006), pp. 19–21; and Sue Arthur, *Seeking for further amusement' Blackpool entertainment in the1930s*, PhD Thesis (Leeds Metropolitan University, forthcoming).

6 Luke Gannon was an infamous Blackpool showman who exhibited not only the starving brides but also the Rector of Stiffkey. See Jonathan Tucker, *The Troublesome Priest: Harold Davidson, Rector of Stiffkey* (London: Michael Russell Publishing, 2007).

7 For details of all the Blackpool sideshows here mentioned see Cross, pp. 110, 120.

8 For details of Beckett's time in St Lô see James Knowlson, *Damned to Fame: The Life of Samuel Beckett* (London: Bloomsbury, 1996), p. 345; and Eoin O'Brien, *The Beckett Country* (New York: Riverrun Press, 1986), pp. 315–42.

9 All of Mr Slide's words are based on his poor recollection of a number of Beckett texts – in this case: Samuel Beckett, *More Kicks then Pricks* (London: Picador, 1934), p. 173

10 Mr Slide's words are here based on Samuel Beckett, *The Expelled and Other Novellas* (Harmondsworth: Penguin, 1980), p. 81.

11 Mr Slide's words are here based on Samuel Beckett, *Molloy* in *Three Novels* (New York: Grove Press, 158), p. 68.

12 Mr Slide's words here are based on Martha Dow Fehsenfeld and Lois More Overbeck (eds), *The Letters of Samuel Beckett*, vol. 1: 1929–1940 (Cambridge: Cambridge University Press, 2009), p. 111.

13 Mr Slide's words here are based on a letter from Samuel Beckett to Jocelyn Herbert, 30th June 1975. MS 520, Beckett Archive, University of Reading.

14 Slide's words here are based on *The Letters of Samuel Beckett*, p. 301.

15 Mr Slide's words here are based on Samuel Beckett's letter to A J. Leventhal, as quoted in Knowlson, p. 397.

16 Bull, p. 171.

17 Reginald Dixon famously played the Wurlizter organ in the Blackpool Tower Ballroom.

18 Many seaside showmen advertised themselves as Professors – as H.G. Stokes writes, 'the phrenologist . . . the magician . . . [and] the weight-lifter . . . were all Professors' – *The Very First History of the English Seaside* (London: Sylvan Press, 1947), p. 112. In 1950s Blackpool there was, for example, 'Professor Frederick Morton,' presenter of the Telepathic Robot – see Critchlow, p. 16.

19 The figure of the Italian concertina player was a familiar one at both Blackpool and the English sea-side in general – see Critchlow, p. 29 and Stokes, p. 104. This particular concertina players claims to be Vittorio Pozzo, the famous Italian football coach *(1886–1968)*, but is not.

20 See Simon Martin, *Football and Fascism* (Oxford: Berg, 2004), pp. 196–207

21 See John Foot, *Calcio. A History of Italian Football* (London: Fourth Estate, 2006), pp. 87–8.

22 Mr Slide's words here are based on Beckett's 'The Capital of Ruins,' as quoted in O'Brien, p. 335.

23 These are Vittorio's very own words – see Foot, p. 34.

24 See W.J. Sollas, 'The Chancelade Skull,' *Man* 25 (1925): 157–161.

25 See *Waiting for Godot*, p. 64.

26 See http://www.bl.uk/projects/theatrearchive/cairoli.html

27 See *The Montreal Gazette*, 4th October 1937.

28 See *Waiting for Godot*, p. 46.

29 This was Peter Bull's experience, the actor who really played Pozzo in Blackpool – see *To Sea in a Sieve* (London: Corgi Books, 1956), p. 156. Anthony Quayle was an eminent British actor (1913–1989).

30 Mr Slide's words here are based on those of Beckett as quoted in Knowlson, p. 346.

31 Mr Slide's words here are based on those of Beckett as quoted in O'Brien, p. 335 .

32 Mr Slide's words here are based on Beckett's letter to Jocelyn Herbert as quoted in Knowlson, p. 671.

33 See Cross, p. 110.

34 Professor Luce was indeed Samuel Beckett's moral tutor at Trinity College, but the beggar man in the wheel chair is *not*, of course, Luce, he merely quotes him. The Blackpool citizen draws throughout on J.V. Luce's Introduction to A.A. Luce, *Fishing and Thinking* (Wykey: Swan Hill Press, 1990), p. vii.

35 George Berkeley, *George Berkeley, A Treatise Concerning the Principles of Human Knowledge*, ed. J. Dancy (Oxford: Oxford University Press, 1998), p. 104.

36 See John Walton, *Blackpool* (Edinburgh: Edinburgh University Press, 1998), p. 140

37 See *Waiting for Godot*, p. 22

38 A. A. Luce, *Sense Without Matter* (London: Nelson, 1954), p. viii.

39 See Cross, p. 110 and Ted Lightbown, *Blackpool: A Pictorial History* (Chichester: Phillimore, 1994), p. 56.

40 Luce, p. 1.

41 Mr Slide's words here are based on those of Beckett as quoted in Dougald McMillan and James Knowlson (eds), *The Theatrical Notebooks of Samuel Beckett, Waiting for Godot* (London: Faber and Faber, 1993), p. 133.

42 Luce, p. vii.

43 See *Waiting for Godot*, p. 89.

44 See David Yallop, *To Encourage The Others* (London: Corgi, 1990).

45 The italicised words from here on are based on Iris Bentley, *Let Him Have Justice* (London: Sidgwick and Jackson, 1995), pp. 172–3.

46 Mr Slide's words here are based on Beckett's letter to Arland Ussher as quoted in Knowlson, p. 296.

47 See Blackpool Louis Toussaud's 1954 Catalogue, The Critchlow Archive, Blackpool Public Library.

48 See *Waiting for Godot*, p. 92.

from *Dunsinane*

Ewan Fernie and Simon Palfrey

Dunsinane is a complete novel, an extract from which is featured here. It is a novel which takes up its story where *Macbeth* ends, but it aims to be not so much a sequel as a *reliving*. Like Shakespeare's play, this is historical tragedy with a difference. For *Macbeth* has the most curious relationship to the past. It doesn't really speak from Shakespeare's time, or eleventh century Scotland, but rather from a nerve-raddled apprehension – or memory – that is always about to come true. This makes it uncannily present, and yet always ahead of any moment in which it is experienced. *Dunsinane* seeks the same effect.

It is not, then, historical retrieval, or postmodern hyper-text, or a spot-the-allusion academic game. It is a head-on encounter with a raw, bleeding, intimate work, its texture thickened by echoes not only of *Macbeth* but also of earlier and later works from the medieval period to Dostoevsky, Wagner and Yeats. This results in a fictional world whose permeability to influences from the past and future redoubles the uncanniness of the original play. *Macbeth*'s secrets are our own, its time our own. Macbeth's story is coming true even now.

Macbeth stands at the heart of our culture – perhaps the most studied, performed, known story of all. But what is at stake in this familiarity? What is forgotten because of it? Rather than merely write about the play, or after it, we wanted to do justice to the *experience* of it, to the way those who love it really live in it, for better or worse. Shakespeare's play is full of gaps or omissions that beg further explication. We imagine these gaps as wounds of possibility, begging to be entered and given life.

Our story starts where the curtain falls. The tyrant is dead and the time is free.

But is this quite true? Is there something wrong? It doesn't feel quite right, it doesn't feel really *finished*. And yet, surely there can't be any more horror?

We meet Macduff cleaning up after battle. He wants to get away from Dunsinane as fast as he can. The castle is cursed, he can feel it; to remain will be to suffer a fatal infection. But first there is one last task to complete.

He has rescued a lovely 12-year-old girl called Gru, who in the horrors of war has just lost her baby. Macduff packs her off to a nunnery. She joins the sisterhood and tries to forget her grief and the murderous world of men.

Just as Macduff feared, Dunsinane is not quite dead. A family of survivors remains: Macbeth's faithful old porter (ominously named Duncan), his twin 3-year-olds Fyn and Grim – and Gru's lost baby, who is discovered by the porter, miraculously alive. The porter finds one other thing – the severed head of Macbeth, which he takes as a blessing and hides for safekeeping. The porter christens the changeling Lulach, and this unlikely little family takes the castle for its home. The porter hopes to protect his boys from history. But boys grow, and Fyn leaves home, leaving his father bereft and anxious. Lu cooks and cares for him while Grim broods, corroding inwardly.

Meanwhile Macduff recoils in disgust from the false dawn of Malcolm's coronation. He escapes to England, and begins his cherished project of political and spiritual renovation: building huge bakeries, feeding the hungry, amassing power. *Malcolm's an irrelevance, Macduff shall be King.* The decisive moment comes when he trains his eye back upon Scotland. And this is where we join the story . . .

* * * * *

From **Dunsinane**

I.

Macduff is coasting the lowlands south of Birnam Wood. He has not come in pomp, but in his solitary car, a private man rather than the fabled Lord Protector. None are with him, not his soldiery, nor his courtiers, nor his holy band of slaves, only his favourite bloodhound and a wordless peasant driver. This is the road home and he must travel it by himself. Not least because he does not quite know what it will mean – quite what it will *be* – to return. All he knows is that he feels strangely opened to feeling. But such susceptibility, he reasons, is acceptable: he must *feel things* like a man. This he has learned.

Yes, he muses as the cart bounces through the gorse, Macduff's is the way of nature: *feed men, and then ask of them virtue!* Was that not the yeast in his idea, the yeast of his success? Morality AND realism. Such, surely, was the Good's only sure foundation. The image of his English bakeries sits flush in his mind, bronzed and beaming like risen bread.

And now the Baker shall rise in the northern land!

But first, a mere detail, he must to Scone to reunite with that idiot Malcolm, the oldest ward in the known world. Over a game of scissors-paper-stone they would arrive at an *understanding*; they would seal it with a giggle and a kiss; and Macduff will be King of Scots in all but name. The theology of succession was always just superstition. The Scots are a rational people and they will bow to reason when it appears in his shape. When it appears in his shape, bearing loaves like the manna of God! And then who cares if he ever sets eyes on the princely Malcolm again? Let him gorge himself to death, the little piggy!

Macduff leans back in his chariot. He is bringing revolution home. All tomorrow's children shall be his.

He looks out of the window and hums as Scotland offers itself in tribute.

O Scotland, Scotland, how I have missed thee!

He washes his face in its sallow light. His heart thrills to be reacquainted with such pale Scottish brightness.

'Gorse and scrub, heather and scrub, scrub scrub scrub!' he sings, rubbing his palms like a miser.

'Heh heh!' he chirrups and his driver, taking it for an instruction, chivvies the horses on harder.

Macduff now rolls fast through the Scottish morning, his cart a richly varnished brown, its glossy red wheels abstracted in their humming blur. With a carefully tended nail, he peels and eats a hazelnut.

Poor land, he admits, yet mine own, *mine own*!

He has been working too long. He must take more time to smell the grass, the flowers, Scottish flowers!

A twitching bunny appears on the plain, a stilled deer, once even a rustic minstrel. Each bulks perfectly in its thingness; and each is silently blessed by the returning father while his mind dances gently as a lamb.

Macduff grins through his grizzled stubble and thinks, yes yes, I am coming home! Why ever did I fear it?

His car is rolling down the gentlest incline, and the nation spreads open to his gaze farther than eye can see.

O Scotland, Scotland, how I have always loved thee!

And indeed Scotland seems an infinite stage for the new day he is bringing. Of course, he must not forget the mountains to the north – untameable, uninhabitable, impregnable even to those bastard thanes in their self-appointed pales. But even at that Macduff laughs again, happy to be caught out, happy even to be rebuked. Yes, remember the mountains; remember you are but *sapien*: let that be a maxim to us all.

His hand rests lightly upon the sleek muscle of his bloodhound's silvery neck. He finds his rhythm slowing to that of the canine's even pulse, and soon enough the great man's head tilts back and his eyes flutter close in the delicious breeze. And like honey from a high jug, sleep descends.

A gorgeous warmth suffuses Macduff's chest and his fingers and his toes. His head nods, as though to heavenly music, and in the fringes of his eyes he sees his pretty chickens pressed tight against his sides, his arms around them like great sheltering wings, and the whole scene quivering with divine laughter. And now he hears a soul, it must be his own, addressing God like an old familiar.

Then I am forgiven?

His soul-voice hangs in the sweet air, soft and lovely like a girl.

And my murdered children still adore me?

God smiles with a face like his own, russet bearded and Scottish.

*And I **deserve** their love?*

The carriage jolts and Macduff cautiously opens an eye; he must not lose this image.

Such is the grace of Grace!

Yes, oh yes, this is a day for loving all, the mouse, the mousing owl, the trees in which they sleep!

'Stop the cart!' he says, suddenly awake and eager for his earth.

Macduff exits clumsily and falls to his old knees by the side of the road. He presses his lips against the ground, holding the kiss for several seconds. Now he lingers where he kneels, scratching at the topsoil with his long hazelnut-peeling nail. Macduff is rubbing his beard in the Scottish earth, fondling it and whispering to it and watering it with tears. Every grain of soil is Macduff's darling, and he will turn each and every one to gold. His red-nosed peasant driver looks away, his peasant eyes full of shame and fear.

Eventually Macduff rises, shakes residual tears from his face like a dog, and deliberately smoothes out his cassock. He signals to the peasant to drive on. He fondles his bloodhound, content to lean back, for this hallowed occasion, into the ease and peace of those who receive. He lets slither a low and delicate fart and resettles in his chair.

Macduff closes his eyes and – O Lord, he can feel it! – his nipples are being stroked by the wing of an angel. He can feel it! What is this *lavishness*? Now he remembers the silken undergarment he had impulsively slipped on beneath his cassock. A day of permissions indeed! His nipples continue to shiver. My God is he open to feeling!

He calms himself by attending to the dog. How he loves dogs! They have long been balsam to him. He looks deep in his hound's dewy-wet eyes and breathes in its doggy scent. He holds the dog's ears and wishes he could just kiss it smack on its soaking mouth.

Good God he needs a woman's touch!

He is gazing in his dog's shining eyes and seeing a black-haired fairy with a wand and a skirt of crystals.

'Hello pretty,' murmurs Macduff, 'don't you love your daddy duff?'

Yes, he thinks, a pretty little ward, that's what the homing man needs – a pretty toy to be girlish with. Look at her, lying deep in his dog's eye. Don't sulk my pretty, put on the crystal skirt and smile for your daddy duff.

And now, with the force of the predestined, the image lurking in the lachrymose eye of his dog resolves into the clearest recollection: that girl, that black haired beauty he deposited in the nunnery on the day he triumphed over Macbeth! The history day, the history man, the history girl!

And instantaneously Macduff knows why his Scotland seems so super-charged, so brimming with the promise of life. He has been skirting Birnam like a courtier, little thinking that his girl, his woman, his marriage! – why not, it is predestined, *why not?* – waits hardly a league away to the north!

She is his Scotland! She will be his crown!

Macduff again leans out of the carriage, his face flapping like a bird, and yells to his driver to alter direction north.

'Faster, faster!' shouts the happy man.

His carriage is careering wildly through copse and bush, risking tree-trunks and crashing low branches as it takes the crow's flight toward the nunnery.

'Faster, faster!' he shouts.

The cart smashes through another copse and the atmosphere suddenly alters. The light is ruinous, the trees twisted and thin. And now from a pile of leaves emerges a human figure, a female. The driver superstitiously stops the cart as she approaches. Macduff is all set to abuse him but then he sees her. His heart is coltish and nervous. Surely it cannot be her, so emaciate, so deathly pale? She drops her head in bashful modesty before him. The head is no more than skull, shaven and scarred to the bone.

'Sister,' he whispers, hardly able to breathe, 'do you know me?'

She shakes her head blankly. Macduff feels himself draw in a great bite of oxygen. *She* was never his crown!

'Sister, where is thy house? Pray, sister, tell me the way.'

He is trying to sound spiritually sincere but he is all serpentine sibilance and haste.

She says nothing, but a sickly twig of an arm turns and points behind her.

'Through there?' says Macduff. 'No, no – it's big, the nunnery, a strong house.'

Her pale lips appear to press out a smile but her head remains lowered.

Macduff finds himself distracted by her naked skull. Is that really the habitation of the spirit? He notes the bone tapering pathetically into neck. Are these the contours of soul?

But still she is pointing through the near trees. She is chewing her free fingers in her teeth and palely smiling at the stranger.

For a moment Macduff feels sickened. He wants to retreat to his dog and find his glitter girl in its eyes. Look at this spectre, her hand but carved bone, her lips paler than snow. She is dead; her age is passed. This is no land for ascetics! Not his bonny Scotland with its bonny dark-haired queen! Why not, he'll string up all the monks and nuns – in the name of reason and love he shall do it! That's it, he thinks, the first age of love and reason, love as reason, reason as love. Why not, him with his sugar queen? A new epoch of happiness for all!

'Goodbye, poor soul', he whispers.

'Wait!' says the female castrate.

Macduff is annoyed as he turns back to face her. Can't she see he is already beyond her?

The creature shufflingly approaches. Her smile breaks open and degrades at once into scattered pegs of darkness. Macduff recoils at the sight of such stumps, like the old barbered Birnam of yore. Now the castrate unsheathes a cross from nowhere and holds it up to his gaze. It is of pale wood, at least a foot high, and covered in pits and tunnels. Lice and worms and roaches are eating it away as she speaks.

'You must live a dying life,' she whispers hoarsely.

Macduff bats the crucifix away and presses on into the clearing. What to do with such imbeciles but raze them?

He steps through a small arch and into the nunnery's grounds.

Before him is a scene of dishevelment. The nunnery's gate is wide open, its walls broken by ivy, its roof all open to the elements. A vestigial rafter falls with a crash. Macduff walks around to the gardens, in his memory well-tended, apple-hanging. He discovers a place of weeds. Women of all ages are perambulating, in various states of undress, alone or in scandalously affectionate pairs. They are weaving gracelessly through weeds that are as high as a man and pushing up to heaven.

Two of the women, one young, one old, stop and smile at him. Their arms are around each other and they gesture for him to join them. Macduff's gorge rises. If he had his men with him he would level this place in seconds. He hunches his cloak around his shoulders and pitches himself like a king in the middle of these perverted creatures. He pulls his knife from his thigh and starts shouting, *shoo, shoo, shoo.* They scatter with barks and shrieks, like rooks might, and Macduff is alone in the nunnery ruins.

For a fallow moment he feels entirely deflated. So this is my pre-possessed future? He snaps a weed and bites its evident poison.

And then it happens, as though by gift of providence: his black-eyed fairy appears, aloft in the garden, flowing though the grass towards him. Macduff drops his weed and his arms go vertical. He puts his knife in its sheath and stares unmanned as the girl nears. She is so much bigger than he had pictured her, fuller and stronger and more real. She stops a yard or two before him. Her eyes are black lightning and not at all dead.

'This is the day,' says Macduff, embarrassed by his folly but somehow sticking fast to its truth.

Her expression glints with spry intelligence.

'– that the Lord has made,' adds Macduff.

Lord knows who he means but the words are speaking through him.

'This is the day that the Lord has made,' he says again.

She is nearly as tall as he is.

'How you've grown . . . ,' he murmurs, and suddenly wonders whether he will pass muster, so many years, he never uses mirrors, what if she sees him as *old* . . .

He stands up straighter.

'You are a woman,' he announces, and holds his hand out for her to take. She does so, and they turn and head around the house to the front gate. She is silent. He does not mind her silence. It pleases; it reminds him of his dogs. Nor does he mind that she has grown. That pleases too; all the better for dressing her up. Abruptly, in precise detail, he imagines lacing her into corsets and pulling on her boots. He feels himself harden; it feels exactly like a smile.

'For Scotland,' he finds himself murmuring quickly, 'for Scotland!'

As effortlessly as a dream, Macduff moves into his cowboy troika and his girl is at his side. She is demure and beautiful and she is speaking not a word. His left hand is on his dog and his right hand is on her shoulder. She does not refuse it. His sleeve is all cunningly gathered at his elbow and his forearm bared to the soft silk fall of her hair.

This is living, thinks Macduff, as he urges his peasant to go quickly.

Macduff is gently jouncing on his leather cushion and shouting at his peasant to drive still faster. Scotland is flying past on either side, the road flying into his bright and happy future, and his soul is revelling within himself. 'Faster, faster!' he keeps calling to his peasant, as if he couldn't get there quickly enough, as though Scotland itself were a high spirited bird-troika that none can overtake. And God is on his side, he feels sure of that, with his girl at one side and his dog at the other. 'Faster, faster!' shouts Macduff, taking vast lungfuls of cold Scottish air.

He turns towards his coal-eyed fairy and heavenly queen.

'Eh, my girl? Eh?'

He laughs at the top of his lungs, clean over the din of his racing chariot. He exults in his resounding laugh and doesn't expect or even much want her answer.

'For Scotland!' he shouts, 'for Scotland . . . !'

2.

The porter is pottering in the castle courtyard in the fading light, sweeping at leaves still coming across the plain of Dunsinane. Each day he sweeps the yard and studies the plain, but nothing lost ever approaches. Young Lu's barley soup hangs untasted over the fire. I won't drink it! thinks the porter. I'd rather drink rain. There's nothing in it, not really, nothing stirring its paws to rise. And yet it's so nearly beer – *live* beer, how he remembers that! Seeds fermenting, the whole world thrumming in the bottom of your glass! Oh, what he wouldn't give for one last one, just a little one: a beer at bedtime; one for the nice old man; one for the road. One before he goes.

If my boy Fyn returns, thinks the porter, we will drink until the dawn-birds cry!

And he smiles and he sweeps and he croons.

'*Autumn, autumn, everything is fallen, Crown my temples with yellow leaf.*'

He plucks one leaf from the dust, then another, and christens them each as he does.

'Ochre – flame – umber – *burnt.*'

Leaf-flecked thumbs crown the porter's brows; he squinnies in a puddle. Quite fetching really.

'*King of shadows, King of rain . . .* '

Now he pulls up the brush by the bristles. He sees a skeletally thin woman, hair stiffened with spunk. Jane Nightwork! In what shallow grave did Malcolm tumble thee? The righteous are always the worst. He fondles the break in her neck, bows, and he is capering with her, serenading her. One last dance! Come on Jane, just for the hell of it, dance out of your grave!

'*We ripen and we drop;*

We drop and so we rot!'

Then he has a thought. Why not; no one around, no sons coming; why not go inside and enjoy a little date! So he takes Jane by the handle, bangs the door shut behind him, and lays her gently down. 'Ah, Jane – ', he sighs, thinking to kiss bristle upon bristle. But as though changing his mind, he now holds the brush to one side, coy at an angle, and begins this address:

'Jane – my Jane – We are brinking a winter without end. Jane – everything is frozen, nothing can take root. We are starving, me and my fine boys. Jane! The very tree of life could die here. I see it, I see it, shrunk to a few brittle whiskers. *Timber!!* I see it fall, squealing and writhing and ssh, here's my little secret, sssh, *no one hears a sound.*'

Knock.

The porter fakes a little shiver and emits a low groan.

Knock, knock.

'O, Jane, my poor mind! Why have I been required so long?'

He risks his tin-whistle falsetto.

> *'This guardian of three*
> *In the wake of eclipse*
> *Tending the tree*
> *For apocalypse!'*

Knock, knock, knock.

The old man drops the broom and straightens. What was that? He hasn't heard that sound in years. He is almost sure he used to be a porter. But surely they don't still *do* knocking, do they? Surely not; it must be a joke!

Suddenly it occurs: Fyn! It can't be! Can it be my Fyn?

'Fyn!' he gasps, kicking the broom from between his feet and starting madly for the door.

Knock, knock, knock, knock.

But just as suddenly the porter stops. My boy would never knock; Fyn would never knock! He would simply enter, bold as the new dawn. It is not my son; there is nothing fresh arising; the new day will surely do me in. And with that the Porter crumples to the floor, heart-stricken. For now he knows, knows with the coldness of what is *done*, exactly who stands at the door knocking.

Knock, knock, knock, knock, knock.

If I just sit here, he thinks, sole as a wintering reed, perhaps this wind will pass on by.

Knock, knock, knock, knock, knock.

Oh, you remorseless ghost!

He always was so bloody remorseless.

It must be him. Who else could it be? The porter has heard the peasant rumours. It is time.

Knock, knock, knock, knock, knock.

It's him, returned from ENGLAND, come to claim what was never his.

Fee fi fo fum . . .

Knock, knock, knock, knock, knock.

It must be him, the wheat chief, the master builder, the man with a pan for a hat.

Knock, knock, knock, knock, knock.
Yes – it is time.
Mac
b–b–blasted
duff.
Open locks, whoever knocks.

3.

But it isn't Macduff.

It is a woman, hair lifting in the wind.

The Porter remembered women; whatever she brings is in her eyes and her mouth. But for some reason he can only see her cheeks. He cannot get past them, the capillaries in bloom, sprung and shooting blood!

Set my life aflame!

His soul is pouring like sunstream to a flower.

Don't speak, he prays; don't spoil it.

How long since he really saw a face! The porter is pouring himself into his look.

No, no, no, don't speak, little sister! Oh please don't bring ____

But she does not speak. Instead she beckons down to the basket she is holding, and slowly unfurls the cloth that covers its top.

He cannot leave her cheeks.

'It is finished,' he says.

'Yes.'

'Finished – must it?'

'Yes, it is finished. And it is beautiful.'

'But O while it lasted . . . !'

'It is finished,' she repeats. 'The first batch, and here is yours.'

She raises her offering. His eyes unclasp from her flush of cheek and move to where her throat must be. He sees a loaf of bread, whiter even than her hands, whiter than he has ever seen.

'Eat,' she says softly.

He is so close he can feel her breath.

'Angel,' he whispers. 'I will.'

4.

The man and woman are sitting at the kitchen table. He is eating and wittering, a delirious song dancing lightly in his mouth,

'O ken ye what Meg o' the mill has gotten,

An' ken ye what Meg o' the mill has gotten . . . '

She is smiling, dabbing at crumbs with a licked finger and then licking the finger clean of the crumb.

'How can it be so soft!' the porter says, yet again, touching the bread. 'There's not a seed or nut left standing. It is so smooth! This is the firstling, bread of the new life. It is the bread of heaven!'

His mouth is full to bursting as he goes on.

'How did you do it? Why me? *Thank you* – but why me?'

'Why you? It is for everyone. That was the decree. Every last subject, without exception, shall receive.'

He stops chewing.

'Decree?' Suddenly he feels sick. 'What decree? Whose?'

Not him, please, not YET; tomorrow, fine, but let him enjoy this day in peace.

'It is the decree of the Lord –

'The Lord?'

'Yes.'

'The Lord?'

The porter's eyes stare and his mouth opens agape; she can see half-chewed bread on a tooth, mushy as wet paper. She gently closes his mouth.

'Not *that* Lord, silly – I mean the Lord Macduff.'

'*Macduff!*'

He remembered how before, before her advent – already it seems so long ago – he had feared and cursed that name.

'Yes – Macduff – decreeing that every last subject – man, and woman, and child – should have on their table this daily bread.'

'For everyone? Not just – not just – '

'All.'

'All of us! A gift. For all!'

'All.'

'Well, praise be: we are chosen – ha! – in NOT being chosen!'

And he rips a chunk from the loaf's white heart, presses it to his lips like a sponge, and acts as if to kiss it.

'Go on – consume,' she says happily.

'Please, yes, I will – I mean, please, thank you – let's –'

Consume my heart away!

He is smiling a smile of infinite benignity, fair crumbs of heaven on his upcurved lips.

She is breaking the bread with her fingers and holding them aloft toward him. How long and expert her digits! How soft and yielding this flesh!

She smiles and her voice is smiling.

'Here you are daddy bear.'

Between the tip of index finger and tip of thumb is a slither of white manna. His mouth opens. She lays the wafer deliberately on his tongue.

'Good dog!'

And they laugh – O how they laugh! Like children!

But abruptly she stops.

She is seeing something. Over his shoulder is the madness of which she's been warned. She gasps.

Two idiots, overgrown idiots wrapped in swaddling cloths.

'Ah – ah – ' – it slips out like an eely scream – 'the brothers Macbeth!'

The boys are staring blankly at the scene: their father, their old father, sitting with a young woman, in a mess of dust and bread, chuckling as he chews.

The porter seems barely to have noticed them. Why would he? All will be so easy in his new life with her. What was it all about before? He can't remember. Why had he fought so hard? He can't remember!

'Father!' says Lu, 'father, it's – it's –

But before he has time to compose his words the second son, Grim, has spat a great glob of phlegm, bright green and streaked with yellow. It flies through the air like some sick globe and falls between father and stranger.

Lu looks down at the ruined bread lingeringly. It is so unlike the good rough stuff that I make, that I would make, if only there were sufficient grain. This white bread is so bland, *so very bland*, all texture and goodness ground out of it. The singularity of each tiny grain as if it had never been!

'It is white bread', he says finally. 'It is *white bread*, father. Don't you *know?*'

His tone seems to allege some horrible religious error.

The woman gathers her basket, covers her head in the cloth, and is gone.

5.

Lu had seen what was happening. Maybe he was the only one who had. The Porter hasn't left the castle in years. Grim spends day and night with tallow-lamp and books, plotting God knows what. Fyn has long gone, and all purpose went with him. Their little farm reflects their sick torpor. Manure and acorns to gather and spread; the odd scrawny pig or duck to sacrifice; the occasional ditch to dig or fence to mend: but nothing whatever to thresh into hope. The crosses Lu erected in the garden are all overgrown with weeds. The Porter and Grim will eventually do as he bids them, in silence or indifference, before speeding back to their respective separations. Ah, and

the times they once had! The games and laughs they once shared! That time
Fyn dressed up as a wizard and commanded them to dance on hands; or
when he sang that song about building a monster from giblets and compost.
And now? Now they wait, for what who can tell? And what does it matter,
now Fyn has gone? You might think they are waiting for death. Or maybe
for that world over yonder finally to creep in and overcome their own.

And it won't be long, thinks Lu, not the way things are heading. For
beyond the river there is another world entire. We the men in sleep, they
the rough-riding night-mare. Lu has seen the vast fields of wheat, their
seeds imported from who knows where. He has seen the women, two cauldrons each, bent double as the water they carry splashes mockingly at their
feet – 'irrigation', he heard them call it. Never such a drought, and the river
lowering by the hour! He has seen wagons, a dozen to each field, stocked to
the brim with wheat before returning at dusk to the Factory. That Factory!
It almost made him believe in Hell.

It is evil, oh he knows it! There has been blight, disease, near famine now
for three seasons. There is more sawdust in their bread than barley; Lu
labours all morning to make the tiniest batch, manically cherishing the
tiniest vestige of anything that might fill a loaf. He seemed to conjure bread
from dust and bone, so little of the threshed barley would he dare to use.
But the outhouse was running low; he was down to the last barrel. They'd
be chewing what's left of the grass soon. Not that the others would care.

But that factory is evil: he *knows* it. It cannot be good to produce such
brightness when all around is such bald, half-patched filth. He had seen the
crumbs spilled by his father; he had stolen to the empty table and touched
them. They weren't just bland, they were like magical snowdrops; they
would vanish to the touch they were so light. You cannot make such – such
spiritual things – and avoid punishment. Spirit is a gift. This cannot be and
it cannot come to good.

Lu recalls the woman; he cannot stop recalling her. He feels something
approaching and it feels like terror.

6.

That evening he heads out, on one of the two aching donkeys that remain
to them. He isn't sure why but he covers himself up in a vast cloak. His
head feels tiny inside the hood. The hood seems to touch him nowhere, but
instead to encircle him, like a rough halo. Let the warm space between hair
and wool be the space of God, protecting him, protecting him: such is his
prayer. He doesn't quite know why but he must not be seen.

He starts to take the long back way around, encircling nearby fields before heading down-slope to the river. He has travelled less than a mile before he knows it is too late. This is not his country! It is like he has slept for thirty years and awoken to the unfoundland; like he has blinked and in that blink a giant ellipse has stretched, a gap when nothing moved but unhallowed birds, blood-billed choughs and pale-eyed jackdaws, who have ravaged all beneath, every last field and tree and hedge.

But the awful thing, the *insulting* thing, is that humanity nevertheless remains. It remains, and in that remainder is the gathering death. For it is not an emptied scene that Lu beholds: not at all. A single kite glides in the dead sky but beneath it is an army of women, hundreds of women moving in slow file, lined across and along fields, indistinguishable in their black coveralls and doing God knows what to the ground they tread. It is too late for harvesting; too early for ploughing. What are they doing? Some sort of superstitious preparation; some service without purpose; some routine of blessing? Lu doesn't understand at all. They are neutered like nuns, but nuns they are not. It is something foreign, an invasion, an interruption, a demonic refusal *not* to work and serve, to serve by working whatever the means. A routine, thinks Lulach, to set Man in the place of God!

Good Lord, give him his brother's idleness any day of the week!

And parked at the side of every field he passes is a train of wagons, each one festooned with the same red and white banner — is it a broken cross? a stag? a lion? a dog? — that Lu had seen fluttering from the roof of the Factory. It is the flag of the future, flouting the sky and fanning our people cold. Lu feels a chill wind up his spine and turns for home.

7.

'I don't know what we can do but we have to do something. They are getting closer and closer. Every farm in the region is his. He is bound to make a progress here soon, bound to! He hasn't visited his Factory yet! And if he goes there do you think he won't come here? For old time's sake? Father! Are you listening? You should know better than anyone. It is unthinkable. It can only be a matter of time. That woman —

Lu stops for a moment; he knows his father's feelings; delicately, delicately.

'That woman who brought the bread is working for the Factory. She must have been — she may well have been sent to butter us up. Do you understand, father?'

'Yes yes yes. But she was a woman in whom I placed an absolute trust.

Absolute! It is lovely to trust another, you know? *Trust* – do you know what it means?'

'Of course, you fool', cuts in Grim, 'it means faith, which is folly, and it means confidence, which is a trick. You bloody fool!'

The porter's face crinkles, alive to tears, moving into a smile.

Now the old man leans gently toward Grim.

'But – you see – her face! Those cheeks. You didn't see her cheeks, my grim boy. They reminded me of – oh, you wouldn't remember. The veins of life! Spring rain! Sun after spring rain, that blush of the renewed! Oh, if that face lies –

Again Grim interrupts.

'Gibberish! Have you studied nothing in all your drivelling years?'

'Grim – no!' pleads Lu.

Lu so wishes Fyn were here; father would listen to Fyn!

But Grim, his face reddening, his brow staring hard at his father, points his index finger, and jabs.

'*There's no art to find the mind's construction in the face.* You read us the text! You! Can you have forgotten? No art, none! *False face must hide what the false heart doth know.* Wake up!'

He clicks his fingers in his father's face.

'You didn't feel her!' says the Porter, rapturously. 'How nimble her fingers, how sweet her breath. Like heaven's breath, oh it smelt wooingly! Oh, what harm can there be in allowing love? She makes our, our mansion *loved* again.'

Grim cannot believe what he is hearing.

'This *loved mansionry*, you old witless man, will see us crumbled into dust. Nothing is safe once we let in the smiling enemy. Nothing! No jutty or frieze in this whole castle but that this *bird* will make her cradle, to breed and haunt, haunt and breed. This maggot-pie gets her claws in and soon we'll be swarming with foreign infidels. Soon enough, mark my words, the things you thought dead and gone will rise up and take us all!'

Grim stops, his words echoing in the silence. Lu looks nervous, but the porter is still smiling. He steps from his stool, kneels before Grim, clasps both hands in his own.

'Grim, Grim, Grim – my Grim – I love you, I will always love you – but you know nothing of love. You cannot *learn* to love, it simply is –

'Love sometimes is trouble.'

'Grim, Grim, still you-

'Which *still* we thank as love. Herein I teach you, *daddy*! The text is old but good. There's no fool like an old fool. "The love that follows us sometime is our trouble." Mark ME, old man!'

And Grim kicks his father away and steps toward the door.

'There is nothing we can do', he says, opening the outer door, his face turned away to the sunset, 'nothing. We are lost.'

8.

Out of the misty darkness comes a figure with two bodies, one upright, the other cropping its shoulders like some malformed twin. Out of the dark it comes, swaying gently like a sea-borne cross.

He has a new and spruce moustache, and fine black boots with golden spurs, and porcelain skin as pure as a babe's. He always was beautiful, and now he has returned!

Fyn!

Father and brothers watch, passive but for a shared tremble, as their long lost loved one hardens into view.

Fyn strolls up with an effortless swing, his face beaming in a smile. He has returned bearing a gift. For across his shoulders he carries a vast pink sow. From its belly comes a deep unavailing groan. As he gets within a few yards, Fyn thrusts the beast above his head. His legs buckle and lock; as if in answer, the sun brinks the heath with sudden airy gaiety. Fyn lets his offering fall. Pig bulk turns in the air, pig trotters beat the ground, pig snout screams. Fyn draws his sword aloft, and with an elegant two-handed stroke beheads it.

A cataract of blood is frothing and rushing from a bore too broad to be called a wound.

Now Fyn deftly toes the still sputtering carcass to expose a belly. It is a woman's belly, convulsed with urgent life.

Fyn picks almost casually at the skin of the sow with his sword's end. He slices its curtain open, falls to his haunches, and laying down the blade drags out a dripping piglet. Fyn drops it to one side, and almost lazily pulls another babe from the burn.

'Would you believe it,' he says quietly, 'brothers!'

He holds the twins high for all to see. His eyes are dancing. The piglets are grotesquely premature. One of them shifts in his grip, and at once Fyn bites deep into its jellied flesh. Instantly it is still. The surviving brother screams a scream higher than human hearing. Fyn drops it from his height and grinds it under boot. Now he sits down heavily in the mess of aborted life; blood smudges his lips like a kiss. He resembles some idol, self-forgotten, lost from his tribe, or some beast of war, readied by sustenance for more.

The spectators stand apart, unsure what to do, unsure whether he is done. *'Meat!'* says Fyn. 'Looks like you need it.'

9.

It is not long before Fyn knows everything – about the woman and Macduff, about the bakery and the dearth, about the porter's boozy frittering – everything. He smiles, drags upon his pipe, and speaks.

'It's easy. EASY.'

They are hanging on his every word.

'Fyn?' urges Lulach, 'come on, tell us. What is easy?'

Fyn takes out his pipe, empties the smouldering weed in his outstretched palm, and whistles harshly across it. Ash and char lift into air and fall at his knees.

'It's easy. We make them a little visit. We show them what we want.'

Lu looks worried.

'What do you mean *what we want?*'

'I mean what we desire, what we lack. Let them know, that is all. That's all we have to do.'

'Right – right then', says Lu, doubtfully. 'We will go and explain.'

'Explain nothing', says Fyn. 'Act. That is all. Show them what we think.'

'Yes, for the good of our family', says Lu.

'For the truth,' says Grim, 'for the truth'.

'Yes, yes,' says Fyn, 'the truth, of course, for your truth, and so on and so forth. Truth is very violent, I find.'

10.

The brothers have arrived at the bakery. Fyn has seen many such things in England but the other two are flabbergasted. Lu's legs are trembling to come so close to what he had but glimpsed and feared. Their castle-grown minds are habituated to stone. But here is something else entirely! Stone arch after stone arch leading nowhere and to nothing: nowhere to sit, nowhere to eat, nowhere to speak. Human breath will vanish instantly into such broad casing air. Even so the brothers enter the belly of the beast and stare into its white-washed silence.

Everything disappears in stainlessness, thinks Lu. He feels his mind scurrying to absorb this enormous blank. It is a denial of life, and of true religion – it is spiritual leprosy – it is the whited sepulchre!

Grim feels in himself a creeping admiration. This, he thinks, is an achievement; here is a true antagonist, one throwing down his gauge for war!

Yet it is Fyn who breaks the silence.

'We have jumped', he says softly, 'the life to come.'

He unbuckles his axe from its scabbard but he does not yet move. He cradles his axe and ponders the scene's strange beauty.

Their eyes adjust. There ARE things to destroy here; things built on the human scale; yet things like they have never beheld. Row upon row of chest high black boxes; long benches between them, immense cauldrons below. Lulach looks and inwardly rages. This is mere replication; it is creation grown diseased and stuttering; it is the Devil's work!

Meanwhile Grim has wandered into the middle of the bakery and is confronting a row of numerous ovens. He means to steal a march on their dreamy leader. He unslings his mallet. A thousand and one ovens contract in his sight into one vast insectile eye. He lifts his mallet and starts to hit. He staves in cell after cell, each dull thud a miracle of destruction. In every one Macduff's brainchild lies rising. Always the same child. Ugh, life disgusts him. Die, die, die!

The pleasure it gives is incredible. It out Herods Herod. He is ruining God's brain and he will leave nothing alive.

Fyn observes his brother whimsically; how he envies him such absorption! How satisfying so to lose the mind in a single action! With an experimental air, he now raises his axe over head, holds it for a moment, and brings it down savagely on a work bench. He drops down on his shanks to attack the legs. The structure collapses; it pleases. But after capsizing three more benches Fyn is bored. He looks at Grim assiduously staving in his ovens and whacks desultorily at an oven himself. Three black feathers spill from it. He lays down his axe and pockets them.

Now Fyn goes outside and discovers a ladder incorporated into a wall. He climbs it. This is a bit more bloody like it! Fyn is dancing on the roof and opening his arms.

'*Swoop!*' he cries, '*I am a swoop!*'

He is a boy again. A single rook's feather escapes from his flap. Lu emerges like a white grub from its cave and looks up anxiously.

'Watch me die!' Fyn laughs.

Now he is killing chimney stacks with the most delicately calibrated force. Find the limit of their resistance, and push just that little bit more! He softly topples another. His smile sets. Let it come down!

Lu turns back towards the cries and grunts and crashes from within. They are amazingly regular and sustained. Oh Grim, Grim, Grim! Hands over ears, this youngest son adventures in the gable end of the bakery. Chained to a table he finds a leather-bound ledger. He opens it and consults its charts. So it is here that the whole region spends its nights. Always in the same boring orgy of productivity, 3000 loaves a time. Here they are, all of them, Angus to Vietch, eternally commemorated in this Book of Death.

He shuts it up and his mouth sets firm.

Nearby he finds a large iron bin, almost as tall as he is. Lu looks over the edge and reels. A million tiny shattered skulls. Squirrels? Infants? Embryos? But why such ritual slaying of small creatures? But he would, wouldn't he? This Macduff just would. He forgets the small and undefended. That is what he does. He has no time for the small things; he has never known that it's small things that count.

Suddenly Lu feels something moving over his head. He looks up and sees a giant blunderbuss pointing at his skull – a blunt iron swaying like a snake before the kill. Lulach pulls out of range and sees it is a vast hammer chained to a wheel. Not a snake at all, but a mad mechanical elephant, poised to do its killing work: to shatter a thousand skulls with its iron trunk, and then a thousand and one more. Lu can make out a little stoup at the bottom of the bin. Instantly he knows what it's all for – oil for greasing the ovens and the doors, oil for greasing this evil elephant. Oh, such oil is the very lubricant of evil!

Lu reaches the oil. A whole vat of it, like a milking trough. How many acorns have been milked for this? He shudders. All those crushed heads.

And with both hands he lifts and upsets the vat of oil. It laves his feet and then spreads slowly, inexorably, until everything all this vast crystal of whiteness – is smudged and yellow and ruined. Ha! A yellow light is dancing in Lu's eyes. Now he strikes his flint and – WOOOSH!!! – a great carpet of flame rushes away from him. He breathes on it like a god and it thrills to his breath. And now he throws back his head and howls.

'Hear me Macduff! Let the holy struggle commence! THE REST IS LABOUR WHICH IS NOT FOR YOU!'

The brothers sit together like children and watch the monster burn.

I I.

The women in the village could see it from miles away. They came out from the ramshackle church, bakers and sisters alike, and immediately smelt the sweetness. They saw that great sweet flame, black and orange. Some of them thought it must be the saving holocaust they had been promised for so long, it smelt so unearthly and sweet. Others looked at the floor, cursed the strumpet Fortune, and looked glumly ahead to the destitution they thought they had at last escaped. The baker-women were chattering like mad, rumours floating like pollen, and resolved as one to return quickly to their homes. The shaven sisters were left alone, and collected into a tight file as commotion came over the crest of the hill. The sisters turned, as though in mesmerised slow motion. They heard wheels and hooves and staccato shouts. A train of carts and horses came straight at them in a cloud of dust, and ahead of the rest raced a ginger-haired man on a white horse.

It is Macduff's adjutant, young and armoured in white steel. He reaches the sisters and raises up his long white sword.

'Silence!' he yells.

His voice is sharp and high.

'The Lord Macduff loves the people. His love is the white loaf he gives daily. You who have baked your own bread must now bake his. Those who will not work he will not love. Bread is the fruit of work. Work makes you free. Scotland will sink if its women do not work. It will sink, I tell thee.'

The adjutant lowers his sword a little and starts pointing it, subject by subject, at the women below him.

'Do you understand? Do you? Do you? Now –

And he pauses a moment, looking up and down the twenty or so women around his horse. The train that followed has stopped a few yards behind. The horses are whinnying and snorting heavily.

'Now', the adjutant repeats. 'Which of you have done this?'

His sword points down the hill to where the bakery stands smoking. None of the women even turn a head. They knew what he meant.

'Which of you, I repeat', the adjutant's voice is even shriller but he enunciates every word, 'have done this?'

The sisters lower their heads, half of them shaven, and are silent.

'So be it', the adjutant snaps. 'The Lord must punish the few to save the many.'

The young man beckons to those waiting behind him. Six more men on horses come forward, unsheath their swords, and slice the sisters across head and back and neck. None of the women move or even scream. In less than a minute all twenty lie dead as stone on the ground.

At this moment another wagon comes rolling quickly up. Four flags deck its corners and a bright purple curtain flaps in the breeze. Before the wagon has stopped the curtain opens and Gruoch jumps out. All of the soldiers turn as she comes hurrying toward them

'You cowards!'

The adjutant in the white armour turns his horse toward her arrival.

'Those who will not work', he says, 'the Lord will not love.'

Gru shook her head.

'Be quiet! I have heard it all!'

'Lady-

'Ha!' interrupts Gru. 'You miserable, stupid, cowards. Is that really the best you can do?'

There is a rustle and a groan and the lean figure of Macduff steps out of the wagon. His silver-beige bloodhound moves beside him like a shade. He holds his arms as if in apology to the soldiers; he shrugs. As one the soldiers bow, the adjutant too from his saddle.

As Macduff moves toward Gru his eyes narrow and a faint smile of court-liness plays on his mouth. He touches her from behind, lightly on the shoulder.

Her face is afire with rage.

'You! You assured me you came in peace. You miserable coward! They were my sisters! You wish me to warm your bed, like a dog, and you will do this?'

Macduff cocks his head to one side.

'Virgin.'

'Do not call me virgin!'

'Sister.'

'Do not speak to me.'

'Do you know to whom you speak?'

'Spare me your threats. You are a fool. Those sisters were innocent. You are a fool, a fool! Look down there, look, look!'

Gruoch points down toward where the bakery smoulders, a half mile away in the valley.

'Can't you see', she continues. 'The Dunsininnies! Look at them, three of them, sitting and admiring their handiwork. Look, fool!'

'Dunsininnies? What are you saying?'

'Them, down there! The Dunsininnies – from Dunsinane!'

'Dunsinane?'

'That's right – them – the brothers Macbeth!'

Macduff's face turns white.

'Dunsinane', he whispers revenantly, and turned to face his bakery. He is cold and white and starts to walk distractedly away.

Macduff's soldiers look at each other, uncertain what to do. Gru moves over to where the sisters lay. A few flies have already gathered over the bodies. She brushes them away and stares intently. A deep gash, usually in shoulder or back, defines each corpse. Remarkably not a single head has been severed. The shaven skulls with their little razor nicks look mockingly ingenuous. Gru licks a finger and tries to clean one of the heads of its blood smudge. But immediately a large fresh wound, like the softest fruit, opens at her touch. A choking rage clutches her throat and for a moment she cannot swallow.

Here it is again, she is thinking, the same old thing. Nothing dies, only life, and then not quickly enough. The girls saw the swords coming, they even had a moment to think about it. What thoughts filled that moment? What words? Gru rocks on her haunches and grimaces. She pushes her hair out of her face and spits. Everything is mockery. There was fault, and punishment, and she had never known the two to meet, not ever ever ever.

Gru looks across at Macduff, muttering to himself, attended by adjutants, beyond the level of her arm. She would save him for some later day. She looks down at the bakery, at the three idiots reclining merrily on the bank. You almost had to laugh; you almost had to love them. But instead, instead –

'I will do it', she says firmly and out loud.

Macduff looks around from his daze.

'I'm sorry?'

He looks spooked and aged and sad.

'I will get them for you. The brothers.'

'You will?'

He sounds pathetically trusting and relieved.

'Leave it to me.'

'You will go there? To Dunsinane? I hoped never to go there again.'

'I will go, on my own, and do it, in my way. Give me one month.'

'A whole month!'

'Yes.'

'And then you will come with me?'

Gruoch smiles brazenly.

'Leave all the rest to me.'

And she starts walking slowly down the hill toward the bakery.

12.

Grim surveys the charred wrack. The mill wheel with its giant spokes pointing at angles like crucified arms. The cauldrons exposed like burnt bone and split with double cracks. The ground bathing in reeking gruel. Now who would have thought his milky brother Lulach . . . He cuts himself short. He cannot be jealous of his younger brother too. To his left he sees Fyn heaving sacks of grain onto the ass's back, singing while he works.

'Ale, ale, nothing but ale,

Drink, drink, all my hearts drink
Hail, hail, all my friends hail
And sink, sink, sink in my drink . . . '

And now from behind he hears soft steps and an unfamiliar hum, a low murmur of preoccupation, more or less peaceful. Perhaps he smells something as well, something rare and herby, maybe lavender. He turns; footsteps cease; humming stops. A fierce shame floods through Grim's body.

It is her.

The woman's face has facets. He doesn't know where to look. Her eyes start dancing over the carnage. An upturned chimney pot by his feet looks absurdly small. Now he sees her looking at his right arm, which hangs up to its elbow in the muck of those pots. He shakes the shit off and sees that long gashes mark his white inner arm, no doubt from when he wrestled with the weight of that grinding stone. Does she know how huge they were? How worthy that struggle? But his gashes now look like the scratches from a frightened hare. Still she glances from there to here, one arm across her chest, the other stroking her neck under the jet peacock's tail of her hair.

He speaks.

'It's not what –'

He pauses, not knowing why he started.

Now her eyes have stopped searching and they rest wryly upon Grim. Again he burns, with electrical force, a blush centred moments to the side of each eye, gathering forcibly into temples. Oh, how he loathes her.

It is with sudden and violent relief that he hears the mule clattering into motion behind him. He turns back to business. Fyn is astride the ass, a whipstick in his right hand, his left gripping the crusty mane. His mouth is clenched over small dark feathers, bunched together like a clutch of arrows. Over the mule's back are slung two huge sacks of grain. The weight of the grain is on each side, bulging like monster's testicles almost down to the ground. A few yards behind Fyn comes Lu, his smaller mule identically dressed. He is grinning widely.

Grim feels fit to burst; he feels like weeping. His brothers, joined to him, bearing with and for him! The brothers Macbeth, so achieved in achievement! This is what it's all about!

Fyn kicks at his mule, whacking its hide once with the whipstick. The animal clumsily accelerates, kicking up clods of mud over Grim as it passes. Grim turns to see the woman move a step back. The ass rattles ahead, and now Fyn dives down to his right and with his whip-arm sweeps the woman up and onto his lap. She doesn't protest; she seems half to have expected it. Fyn extracts a feather from his teeth and, calming her black locks off her face and curling them behind her ear, he threads the soot-black feather through and over her ear-ridge. She touches it, as though to compose it in place. Now she half-smiles, and holds to Fyn's shoulder as he swiftly turns his steed back around to face the others. They have seen this grin before; it is his childlike leader's grin, the one that led a thousand reckless games. He has the woman over his lap, gripping his right arm with her left and looking only at his profile. With his free arm he is holding out the remaining feathers for Grim's inspection. Again, so like the games of yore, when Fyn would reveal the concealed prize, some sparrow or mouse or apple. Grim chooses the smallest; again he doesn't know why.

They are rook feathers; he always loved the ugliness of rooks.

Grim pokes the feather-end through his tunic and wears it at his heart. The others are beaming. Grim sees that Lu is wearing two feathers in his cap, sticking out at a jaunty ramhorn angle.

'Ha ha, a rescue of rooks!' shouts Lu in an idiot's joyful voice, 'a rescue of rooks!'

'Almost brother', says Fyn, 'almost. The rooks have fled. These are crows' feathers – carrion crows. What else?'

'Well what does that make it then?' says Lu, more gleeful and infantile than anyone can remember, 'what shall we call our triumph?'

'Grim my lad', says Fyn, 'you're the scholar – what do we call it?'

But before Grim can speak another voice has entered, generous and sonorous and high, and resounding like all the listening world has somehow hushed at her command.

'A murder', she says, '– we call it a *murder* of crows.'

How the three of them laugh, Fyn and Lu and the woman. They laugh like drains as they turn toward Dunsinane.

But Grim's heart is chilled. He steps aside from his brothers and looks coldly at the woman. She notes his glance and suspends her smile as she does so.

'Witch!' he hisses up at her, beneath the hearing of either brother.

He sees her decline her head slightly toward him; he sees her sustain her blink for a fraction longer than nature requires.

She will steal away it all.

_itic! (by way of an afterword)

Oliver Tearle

In motes of grey dust falling softly, only
between dried leaves of books not opened, barely
one thing will be glimpsed, by someone, glumly:
the critic died a death, they said.

                    Now hear me.

The Editors and Contributors

Susan Bradley Smith began her writing life as a theatre and music journalist in Sydney and later London. Widely published as a theatre historian, she also has research interests in life writing, and sea-change communities. Her most recent publication is *supermodernprayerbook* (Salt, 2010). She lives in Melbourne and teaches in the English Department at La Trobe University.

Steven Connor is Professor of Modern Literature and Theory at Birkbeck College London, where he has taught since 1979, and Academic Director of the London Consortium Graduate Programme in Humanities and Cultural Studies. His most recent books are *Fly* (Reaktion, 2006), *The Matter of Air: Science and Art of the Ethereal* (Reaktion, 2010) and *Paraphernalia: The Curious Lives of Ordinary Things* (Profile, 2011). *A Philosophy of Sport* is forthcoming from Reaktion.

Jonathan Dollimore is currently Honorary Professor at the University of Sussex and Honorary Research Fellow at Royal Holloway College, University of London. Prior to this he was a Professor in the Humanities Research Centre at Sussex, and Professor of English, University of York. His books include *Radical Tragedy* (Chicago UP), *Sexual Dissidence: Augustine to Wilde, Freud to Foucault* (Oxford UP), *Death, Desire and Loss in Western Culture* (Routledge), and *Sex, Literature, and Censorship* (Polity).

Helen Farish has been a Fellow at Hawthornden International Centre for Writers and was the first female Poet in Residence at the Wordsworth Trust (2004–5). She has also been a Visiting Lecturer at Sewanee University, Tennessee, and a Visiting Scholar at the University of New Hampshire. In 2005 *Intimates* (Jonathan Cape) won her the Forward Prize for best first collection and was also short-listed for the T.S. Eliot Prize. She is currently Lecturer in the Department of English and Creative Writing at the University of Lancaster.

Ewan Fernie is Professor of Shakespeare Studies at the Shakespeare Institute, University of Birmingham. He is the author of *Shame in Shakespeare*, editor of *Spiritual Shakespeares* and co-ordinating editor of *Reconceiving the Renaissance*. He has recently completed *Dunsinane*, the

Macbeth novel featured in this volume with Simon Palfrey, with whom he is also General Editor of the 'Shakespeare Now!' series of short, provocative books published by Continuum. He is Principal Investigator of the AHRC / ESRC funded project '*The Faerie Queene* Now: Remaking Religious Poetry for Today's World', for which he has more recently won additional grants from LCACE, the PRS Foundation for New Music and other sources. For this project he has written *Redcrosse: A New Celebration of England and St George* with the poets Andrew Motion, Jo Shapcott and Michael Symmons Roberts, and the theologian Andrew Shanks. *Redcrosse* will be premiered in the Windsor Festival at St George's Chapel and at Manchester Cathedral in 2011.

Mark Ford is Professor of English at University College London. He is author of *A Driftwood Altar: Reviews and Essays* (Waywiser), *Raymond Roussel and the Republic of Dreams* (Faber) and two collections of poetry, *Landlocked* (Chatto & Windus) and *Soft Sift* (Faber). He has edited two collections of the poetry of the New York School, *The New York Poets I* (Carcanet) and *The New York Poets II* (Carcanet), and a volume of essays on twentieth-century Anglo-American poetic relations entitled *Something We Have That They Don't: Anglo-American Poetic Relations Since 1925* (Iowa University Press, 2004).

John Goodby is Senior Lecturer in English at the University of Swansea. He is the author of *Irish Poetry Since 1950: From Stillness Into History* (MUP, 2000), and has edited the *New Casebook Dylan Thomas* (Palgrave, 2001). His poetry is published in *Poetry Introduction 8* (Faber, 1993), *A Birmingham Yank* (Arc, 1998), *uncaged sea* (Waterloo, 2008) and *Illennium* (Shearsman 2010). He was the winner of the Cardiff International poetry competition in 2006 and has translated Heine's *Germany: A Winter's Tale* (Smokestack, 2004) and Soleiman Adel Guemar's *State of Emergency* (Arc, 2007). He is currently organising the Hay Poetry Jamboree, completing a monograph on Dylan Thomas, and translating the poetry of Pasolini and Reverdy.

Kevin Hart is Chairman and Edwin B. Kyle Professor of Christian Studies at the University of Virginia. His most recent books of poems include *Flame Tree: Selected Poems* (Bloodaxe, 2002), *Young Rain* (Bloodaxe, 2008) and *Morning Knowledge* (Notre Dame UP, 2011).

Geoffrey Hartman is Sterling Professor Emeritus & Senior Research Scholar of English and Comparative Literature at Yale University of Yale. His many books include his memoir *A Scholar's Tale* (2007), *The Geoffrey*

Hartman Reader (2004), *Criticism in the Wilderness* (1980), and a volume of poetry called *Akiba's Children* (1978).

Graham Holderness is Professor of English at the University of Hertfordshire, and author or editor of numerous studies in early modern and modern literature and drama. He is also a creative writer whose novel *The Prince of Denmark* was published in 2002, and whose poetry collection *Craeft* (2002) was awarded a Poetry Book Society recommendation. He is General Editor of *Critical Survey*. Graham Holderness is an elected Fellow of the English Association, the Royal Society of Arts and the Royal Society of Medicine.

Duraid Jalili is currently completing an MSc in literature and modernity at the University of Edinburgh, and is also part-time literary commentator for the National Association of British Arabs. Influenced by issues of Arab and Irish diaspora, national identity and socio-cultural conflict, his explorations of the emergent sphere of Arab literature and cinema *in translatio*, of themes of war and systematic conflict within postmodern theory, and of the renewed pan-cultural import of a Joycean socio-political aesthetic, prescribe the necessity of a constant rejection of critical stability, and re-interpretation of predominant modes of literary and socio-cultural thought. He also likes Scottie dogs.

Simon King was born in Cheltenham and educated at Worcester, Sussex, and Loughborough. He enjoys wine, clearly defined regions of ambiguity, and listening to the rubbish men talk in pubs. 'Doctor Simon King' is a fictional character, who may or may not be the author of *Insect Nations: Visions of the Ant World from Kropotkin to Bergson*, and co-author, along with James Holden and Adam Roberts, of *Conceptual Breakthrough: Two Experiments in SF Criticism*, both published by InkerMen Press.

Esther Leslie is Professor in Political Aesthetics at Birkbeck University of London. Her books are *Walter Benjamin: Overpowering Conformism* (Pluto, 2000), *Hollywood Flatlands, Animation, Critical Theory and the Avant Garde* (Verso, 2002), *Synthetic Worlds: Nature, Art and the Chemical Industry* (Reaktion, 2005) and *Walter Benjamin* (Reaktion, 2007). Her translations include Georg Lukacs, *A Defence of 'History and Class Consciousness'* (Verso, 2002) and *Walter Benjamin: The Archives* (Verso, 2007). She is actively involved in editing three journals – *Historical Materialism: Research in Critical Marxist Theory*, *Radical Philosophy* and *Revolutionary History*.

Willy Maley is Professor of Renaissance Studies at the University of Glasgow. He has published widely – some would say wildly – on early modern English literature from Spenser to Milton, and on modern Scottish and Irish writing, from De Valera to Devolution. He is author of *A Spenser Chronology* (1994), *Salvaging Spenser: Colonialism, Culture and Identity* (1997), *Nation, State and Empire in English Renaissance Literature: Shakespeare to Milton* (2003), and *Muriel Spark for Starters* (2008). Willy was founder, with Philip Hobsbaum, of the Creative Writing Masters at Glasgow University. He is a published playwright, poet and short story writer, and former Scotsman Fringe First Winner at the Edinburgh Festival. His plays include *From The Calton to Catalonia* (1990), a dramatized account of his father's experiences as a POW during the Spanish Civil War, co-written with his brother, John. Previous jobs include bank clerk, barman, librarian, writer-in-residence in Barlinnie Special Unit, and columnist for the *Celtic View*, the official fanzine of Celtic Football Club.

Peter Middleton is Professor of English at the University of Southampton. He is author of *The Inward Gaze: Masculinity and Subjectivity in Modern Culture* (Routledge, 1992), *Distant Reading: Performance, Readership and Consumption in Contemporary Poetry* (Alabama University Press, 2005), and (with Tim Woods) *Literatures of Memory: History, Time and Space in Postwar Writing* (Manchester University Press, 2000).

Kevin Mills is Reader in English Literature and Religion at the University of Glamorgan. He is the author of *Justifying Language* (Macmillan, 1995), *Approaching Apocalypse* (Bucknell UP, 2007), *The Prodigal Sign* (Sussex Academic Press, 2009). His first collection of poetry – entitled *Fool* – appeared from Cinnamon Press earlier this year. He is currently working on representations of the religious revival in Wales, 1904–5, and wondering if he should get a tattoo.

Drew Milne is the Judith E Wilson Lecturer in Drama and Poetry at the University of Cambridge, and a Fellow of Trinity Hall. Drew Milne's books of poetry include *Sheet Mettle* (Alfred David Editions, 1994), *Bench Marks* (Alfred David Editions, 1998), *The Damage: New and Selected Poems* (Salt, 2001), *Mars Disarmed* (The Figures, 2002), and most recently *Go Figure* (Salt). His work is featured in numerous collections and anthologies, notably *Conductors of Chaos*, edited by Iain Sinclair (Picador, 1996) and *Anthology of Twentieth-Century British and Irish Poetry*, ed. Keith Tuma (Oxford University Press, 2001). He edits the occasional journal *Parataxis: Modernism and Modern Writing* and the poetry imprint Parataxis Editions.

He co-edited *Marxist Literary Theory: A Reader* (Blackwell, 1996) with Terry Eagleton, and has recently edited the anthology *Modern Critical Thought* (Blackwell, 2003).

Simon Palfrey is a Fellow in English at Brasenose College Oxford. His publications include *Late Shakespeare: A New World of Words* (OUP, 1997), *Doing Shakespeare* (Arden 2004, a TLS International book of the year), and *Shakespeare in Parts* (OUP 2007, with Tiffany Stern), which was awarded the Medieval and Renaissance Drama Society prize for best new book. He is the co-editor (with Ewan Fernie) of Continuum's series of original minigraphs, *Shakespeare Now!*

John Schad is Professor of Modern Literature at the University of Lancaster. He is the author of several books including *Someone Called Derrida: An Oxford Mystery* (2007), a real-life murder mystery centred on Jacques Derrida's secret Oxford life, and a documentary novel called *Nowhere Near London* (2011) which concerns a man on a post-war council estate in Watford who thinks or says he is the late Walter Benjamin. He is currently writing *The Queerest Book in the World*, a telepathic account of the posthumous publication in 1918 of the collected poems of Gerard Manley Hopkins.

Harold Schweizer is John P. Crozer Professor of English at Bucknell University where he teaches courses in literary theory, poetry and the humanities. His new book *On Waiting* came out with Routledge in 2008. He has also published poems, among them a long elegy that appeared in *American Poetry Review*. He is currently completing a volume of poems entitled *The Book of Stones and Angels*.

Tony Sharpe teaches in the Department of English and Creative Writing at the University of Lancaster, which he headed for several years. He is the author of monographs on *T.S. Eliot* (Macmillan), *Vladimir Nabokov* (Edward Arnold), *Wallace Stevens* (Palgrave) and *W.H. Auden* (Routledge). He is currently editing a large volume of essays on *Auden in Context* for Cambridge University Press.

Michael Simmons Roberts, Professor of Poetry at Manchester Metropolitan University, is a Whitbread Award-winning poet and librettist. His poetry collections include *Burning Babylon* (2001), shortlisted for the T. S. Eliot Prize, *The Half-Healed* (2008), and *Corpus* (2004), a collection of poems focused on the body which was shortlisted for the Forward Poetry Prize (Best Poetry Collection of the Year) and the T. S. Eliot Prize.

Jonathan Taylor is Senior Lecturer in Creative Writing at De Montfort University. He is the author of *Take Me Home: Parkinson's, My Father, Myself* (Granta Books, 2007), *Science and Omniscience in Nineteenth-Century Literature* (Sussex Academic Press, 2007), and *Mastery and Slavery in Victorian Writing* (Palgrave Macmillan, 2003).

Oliver Tearle recently completed a doctorate at Loughborough University on the subject of hallucination in late nineteenth- and early twentieth-century fiction, to be published by Sussex Academic Press under the title *The Curtained Room*. He has been published in numerous journals, including *Notes and Queries*, *Critical Sense*, and the *Modern Language Review*, and has also contributed to the online *Literary Encyclopedia*.

Index